STARRING NEW YORK

Starring New York

FILMING THE GRIME AND THE GLAMOUR

OF THE LONG 1970S

Stanley Corkin

OXFORD UNIVERSITY PRESS

Oxford University Press, Inc., publishes works that further
Oxford University's objective of excellence
in research, scholarship, and education.

Oxford   New York
Auckland   Cape Town   Dar es Salaam   Hong Kong   Karachi
Kuala Lumpur   Madrid   Melbourne   Mexico City   Nairobi
New Delhi   Shanghai   Taipei   Toronto

With offices in
Argentina   Austria   Brazil   Chile   Czech Republic   France   Greece
Guatemala   Hungary   Italy   Japan   Poland   Portugal   Singapore
South Korea   Switzerland   Thailand   Turkey   Ukraine   Vietnam

Published by Oxford University Press, Inc.
198 Madison Avenue, New York, NY 10016

www.oup.com

Oxford is a registered trademark of Oxford University Press

Library of Congress Cataloging-in-Publication Data
Corkin, Stanley.
Starring New York : filming the grime and the glamour of the long 1970s / Stanley Corkin.
    p.   cm.
Includes bibliographical references and index.
ISBN 978-0-19-538279-2 (cloth : alk. paper)—ISBN 978-0-19-538280-8 (pbk. : alk. paper)
1. New York (N.Y.)—In motion pictures. I. Title.
PN1995.9.N49C67   2011
974.7—dc22   2010033696

1 3 5 7 9 8 6 4 2

Printed in the United States of America
on acid-free paper

Contents

Acknowledgments

THIS WAS A project that evolved over a number of years, as I developed an understanding of the ways in which the films, history, and representations of space could work and be discussed in fruitful ways. There were many who assisted me in this process along the way. At the University of Cincinnati, I presented various papers in departmental colloquia expertly organized by Jana Braziel, who added to this project in so many other ways. My colleagues—Russel Durst, Jon Kamholz, Lee Person, Maria Romangnoli, Kirk Boyle, Brock Clarke, and Michael Griffith—provided astute comments that helped me on my way. Outside of my department, Maura O'Connor was always enthused about the study and filled with good ideas about the relationships between culture and economics. Colleen McTeague of the Department of Geography was also a great help in helping me to see the role of culture in the definition of space. Gary Weissman was very helpful in providing insights and sources dealing with photography. My friend Dan LaBotz helped me see the possibilities of this material, telling me that the seventies were the vital decade in the process of globalization. He was right!

Outside of Cincinnati, Phyllis Frus helped me to formulate some early chapters with her always astute comments. Neil Smith was a willing and patient discussant for the ABCs of geography. Thanks for the primer! Mark Shiel provided sharp insights based in his own very good study of Los Angeles. Bob Sklar, Dana Polan, and Chuck Maland read portions of the material and helped me to assess my developing manuscript. My old friend Rick Woodward provided helpful comments about the history of photography. Phil Wegner read a later chapter with care and offered helpful suggestions. And Jonathan Auerbach generously offered his time and effort in evaluating the manuscript as a whole.

I also want to thank Shannon McLachlan at Oxford who believed in the project and stood by it to its completion.

STARRING NEW YORK

1

Introduction

THIS STUDY DISCUSSES a significant group of films released between 1969 (*Midnight Cowboy*) and 1981 (*Prince of the City*) that employ New York City as both a location and as part of their central motif. It focuses, ultimately, on the cultural and economic history of this period and develops its method by synthesizing analytical precepts from film studies, cultural geography, and history. I will discuss this approach in greater detail later, but, in brief, my study looks at the ways in which these films provide a refracted view of a moment of significant historical change, as they represent the relative geography of New York, as well as the connection of that space to other locales. It also considers their representation of the built environment, both within the context of their narratives, as well as in a broader historical narrative. Again, these are a complex set of analytical foci and I will return to them later in order to define them and elaborate on their system of relation.

This vision of the various references to geography and history was not what initially attracted me to these films. I first became aware of them as a filmgoer in the era of their release. At that time, I went from being an adolescent, intrigued by *Midnight Cowboy*, to a graduate student of film and a resident of New York City, living not far from the place where Travis Bickle first spies the adolescent Iris walking the streets. I also knew well the various locales of Little Italy (shown in the

Godfather films, in *Mean Streets*, and far more briefly in *The French Connection* and *Prince of the City*), so the fact that these films had representational efficacy was always clear. I also knew that this was a distinctive moment in Hollywood history.

Subsequently, I began to understand that the late 1960s and 1970s were a vital moment of world economic reorganization, the period when a crisis of overproduction triggered a system of commerce that placed certain world cities at the center of a far-flung network of producers.[1] I approach these films with an eye toward understanding the role of popular entertainment, and of popular films in particular, in elaborating this moment; I also question their role in assisting the transformation of previous conceptions of space, urban life, commerce, and culture. I view this vital moment of historical transition through the prism of cultural productions, asking how these objects complexly participated in this shift in belief and practice, while showing how an understanding of a period may be altered through this approach.

The distinctiveness of these New York-based films is almost an article of faith among film critics. For example, in an April 2006 *New York Times* article that focuses on the many contemporary films and television shows shot in New York City, there is a recurring lament for the golden era of productions filmed in that city—the late 1960s and 1970s—by critics and filmmakers alike. This sense of the era indexes the quality and impact of the many successful works by a prominent group of directors that came of age in this decade: for example, Francis Coppola's *Godfather* films (1972 and 1974), Martin Scorsese's *Mean Streets* (1973) and *Taxi Driver* (1976), William Friedkin's *The French Connection* (1971), Sidney Lumet's *Serpico* (1973) and *Dog Day Afternoon* (1975), Woody Allen's *Annie Hall* (1977) and *Manhattan* (1979), all of which I consider in detail. Their view concurs with my own: this period constitutes a distinctive moment in the history of the commercial U.S. cinema ("Hollywood") and in the culture of the United States, a time when powerful and resonant images of New York City captivated audiences. These films, among other factors, provide a means for audiences to reorient their vision of urban life and to reconceive their spatial sense of the organization of cities, as well as the connection of those urban spaces to the world outside of their borders.

The overlap between this intense and successful concentration of films set in New York City and the short-lived but highly distinctive New Hollywood period of film production is one that bears looking into. That this moment of unprecedented decentralization within the industry resulted in a proliferation of films that featured the "other" center of the entertainment industry (New York) speaks to a number of elements that are specifically a matter of film history, as well as a number of factors that are more broadly a matter of the cultural moment. That New York stories were so vital to the industry signals the ultimate end of the first phase of the studio system, and the rise of a generation of young directors influ-enced by the French New Wave and the related auteurist school of film criticism.[2] The relative economic success of some of the early director-driven films, such as *Bonnie and Clyde* (1967), *Easy Rider* (1969), *Midnight Cowboy*, and the *French Connection*, enticed studios to fund other "personal" projects by younger directors, sometimes at their own financial peril.

In his history of the U.S. film industry in the period that overlaps my object of study, David Cook writes that the broad national recession of 1969 to 1971 further drove down film industry profits. Receipts were already on the decline in the period after World War II, as competition from television, as well as suburbanization and the baby boom, significantly changed the marketplace for entertainment. Thus, the major studios substantially shifted their resources toward television production. Further, the end of the studio system changed the structure of Hollywood produc-tions, as now, James Monaco tells us in his *History of American Cinema*,

> Emphasis on free-lance business arrangements in the industry and the rise of the production "deal" for securing the financing and distribution for a par-ticular film, translated into increased leverage, both financially and artisti-cally, for the most sought after stars. . . . The new free-lance system also spawned new kinds of tensions between writers, directors, and stars. No longer simply working on contract for studios, writers could negotiate greater leverage over how their work was brought to the screen and by whom. Direc-tors frequently wanted a new and different kind of identification with a film, which was increasingly autuerist in nature. (20–21)

These structural changes are vital for ushering in the New Hollywood era. As others have noted, the distinguishing characteristic of this period was the role of the independent producer in developing projects that would probably never have received a green light in the studio period. These producers often worked in close collaboration with directors and writers in developing a project. On the shoot, the absence of the studio structure often made the director even more central than he had been during the studio era. This is not, however, to say that directors had absolute autonomy. Many of these films, notably *The Godfather*, had moments when financial backers became impatient with the high cost and slow speed of production, and intervened in the filmmaking process in assertive and disruptive ways. Still, the fact that films could proceed to the point where producers reached a point of panic is further evidence of the relative autonomy of the director.[3]

The list of films above reveals the proliferation of young directors working in Hollywood during the early 1970s. Some of these had come from the emerging film schools (Coppola and Scorsese), some had worked in the theater (Lumet and Ossie Davis), and some came of age in the early days of television (Lumet, Friedkin, Mazursky, and Allen). But because of the suddenly more open structure of the industry, all were able to fashion projects, to a great extent, as a matter of their personal tastes, ranging from the autobiographical films by Woody Allen (*Annie Hall*), and Martin Scorsese (*Mean Streets*), to the auteurist gloss on a large-scale production by Francis Coppola, to the various "small" New York City dramas by Sidney Lumet that were constituted with a kind of thematic unity and focus.

Not surprisingly, there is a distinct autobiographical reason for the New York emphases of these films. Lumet grew up on the Lower East Side, Coppola spent some periods of his childhood in Queens, Scorsese grew up in Little Italy in Manhattan, Allen in Brooklyn. Other figures that are prominent in this study, such as blaxploitation directors Larry Cohen, Gordon Parks Jr., and Ossie Davis also had New York City backgrounds, as did Robert Benton (*Kramer vs. Kramer*) and Paul Mazursky (*An Unmarried Woman*). And although this factor alone would hardly explain this period, since during the studio era many directors and stars also had New York backgrounds and stage experience, it does add an element that, when combined with the emphasis on personal vision, contributes to this phenomenon.

Hollywood's particular interest in New York during the late 1960s and 1970s resulted from other industrial factors, as well. In 1968, the Motion Picture Association of America, under the leadership of Jack Valenti, issued an age-based rating system for films that replaced a practice of censorship with one that advised consumers as to appropriate film content. Valenti, faced with an industry in financial flux, saw the revised code as a means to appeal to those seeking greater "realism" in Hollywood films—and realism became a kind of shorthand for urban textures that often featured scenes of New York City.[4]

In addition, with the rise of a related "film generation" among French directors, these young Americans often became fascinated with the vision of narrative film-as-art that could be created with distinction by directors. Thus, these youthful cineastes often sought to emulate and extend the directorial styles associated with French New Wave filmmakers, including Jean-Luc Godard and Francois Truffaut. Francis Coppola, Martin Scorsese, and Peter Bogdanovich, all students of film history, derived their own methods from these innovators. Beyond their fascination with these French figures, U.S. filmmakers were increasingly influenced by the styles associated with both neorealism and film noir, moving those genres from their post–World War II incarnations to a more immediate vision of (apparent) urban reality in the late 1960s and 1970s. We find ethnic actors who defy Hollywood notions of beauty—such as Dustin Hoffman and Al Pacino; images of milling crowds in public places, and a sense that we are seeing the moral turpitude of an actual city.

But it was not simply matters of aesthetics that drew productions to New York. Technological developments in the 1960s that made cameras and processing equipment lighter and more mobile also encouraged location shoots, and indeed, distinguished many of these films from those on-location productions that had preceded them. Although it is true that films like *The Lost Weekend* (1945), *The Naked City* (1948), *On the Waterfront* (1954), and *West Side Story* (1961), among others, had employed the streets and buildings of New York City and its environs, they had done so in ways that were quite different from these later films. That is, prior to the late 1960s and the 1970s, location production in the United States was constrained by cumbersome equipment and the problems of processing film away from Los Angeles, so that such productions were the large-budget exception. As a result, although other films had been shot in the city, there had never been such a concentration of films over a relatively brief period. These earlier New York films offer fairly limited perspectives on the city, due to the difficulty and expense of moving from setup to setup. As a result, even films that are clearly within a realist-noir tradition like *On the Waterfront*, seem somewhat stage bound, with scenes occurring within clearly constrained spaces. But gradually the means by which the city could be employed, and so the extent to which and way in which it could be used, also changed.

These technical changes took place over almost two decades. In the 1950s, film stock was developed that allowed night images to be exposed with less artificial lighting. In the 1960s, technological changes allowed for smaller tape recorders and cameras. In the early 1970s, the introduction of the decidedly more mobile Panaflex and Arriflex 35 BL marked a large leap forward. In the later 1970s, the Steadicam, which involved a Panaflex and an A-frame mounting device, effectively allowed actors to become part of the crowd, as cameras could capture movement and become part of that movement in less scripted ways that had been possible just ten years before. Indeed, one chronicler of this era argues that the shift in camera technology enabled a golden age of production: "The cameras breathing life into these wonderful motion pictures were as diverse and interesting as the films themselves. Among their number were the ultra-modern Panaflex, the modern Arriflex BL, the transitional Panavision PSR, the French Éclair CM3 and various reflex models of the venerable Mitchell BNC."[5] This overall change in equipment encouraged location shoots, so that the city-as-film-set became a cheaper alternative to shooting on Hollywood backlots, while providing a look that fit with the reigning aesthetic.[6] In comparison to these earlier realist films of the 1950s, a related film, like *Serpico* (1973), offers a far more fluid vision of space, a world where a character's range of motion seems unlimited and in which the camera seems to be out and about in an exploration of city spaces. Rather than discrete parts of the city serving as a soundstage, now the city opened up as one large location.[7]

David Cook, in *Lost Illusions*, his study of the U.S. film industry during the 1970s, defines the period as one of volatility, in which the filmmakers briefly controlled productions, prior to being supplanted by the post–studio system that allowed for small productions but that generally put its money behind presold properties with the potential to be the next blockbuster. He writes;

> In the late 1960s and early 1970s, auteurism became much more to the American cinema than simply a mode of aesthetic discourse. In the unstable environment of the crumbling studio system, the opportunity arose to actually practice one form of it, when the studios' transitional managers briefly turned over the reins to a rising generation of independents and first-time directors whose values seemed to resonate with the newly emerging youth culture market. (156)

But Cook explains that this strategy of ceding creative control was, within the capital structure of the U.S. film industry, unlikely to succeed, as the residual model of Hollywood was ultimately centralized, capital intensive, and risk averse.[8]

The glut of feature films shot in New York, unflattering as their portrayal of the city tended to be, was also furthered by the policies of New York mayor John Lindsay's administration. As a candidate in 1965, Lindsay promised to streamline the cumbersome bureaucratic process of obtaining the permits necessary to shoot films in New York City. In 1966, one of his early acts was to create the Mayor's Office of Film, Theater, and Broadcasting.[9] In 1966, the Lindsay administration created the Mayor's Office of Film, Theater, and Broadcasting, whose purpose was to encourage film production in New York City. Prior to this initiative, arranging location shoots in New York City was forbidding, to say the least. Producers were run through a maze of offices in search of multiple permits, and then were rewarded with required high-price policing costs, the necessity of further expenditure in bribes, and various types of corruption. James Sanders tells us that in 1965 only two features were shot in New York in their entirety. The new office had an almost immediate impact, and soon resulted in New York becoming a center for production. Writes Sanders, "In the eight years of the Lindsay administration 366 films were made; by the second year of the Beame administration, forty-six features were being made in the city" (344). This boom in production also resulted in the refurbishing of the old Astoria studio, which reopened in 1975.[10]

That Mayor Lindsay, the leader of this city facing the continued hemorrhaging of jobs, abetted the production of so many powerful narratives that portrayed his city as dirty, dangerous, and morally suspect is indeed ironic. But perhaps no one recognized New York City's precarious economic condition better than its mayor. Film production provided a clean industry to a city in the process of losing all types of productive enterprise. The city's efforts could be justified as a means to create jobs and revenue. As job loss continued apace in the late 1960s and 1970s, and population declined, New York City increasingly took on the role of film set. As Vincent J. Cannato explains of these productions, "No doubt many of these movies exaggerated New York's problems, but the image of an increasingly dangerous and chaotic city was real enough. . . . With these portrayals, the image of New York City as a place of danger, decay, and division became solidified in the nation's mind."[11] As an effect of this economic decline, the deterioration of the built environment was both a fact and a matter of wide perception, as images of a dirty and dangerous city flooded the national media.[12] The mid-point of my study is 1975, the year in which, in response to a request for federal assistance in order to make payment on outstanding municipal bonds, a famous headline in the *New York Daily News* proclaimed the federal government's unwillingness to assist: *Ford to City: Drop Dead.*[13]

This moment defines a historical nadir for the city's fortunes, as years of decline resulted in the city entering receivership and then undergoing significant financial restructuring. But this point of demise was also the beginning of the city's reemergence as a place that was decidedly different from what it had been prior to World War II. Explains William Tabb, "Urban disinvestment and abandonment are matched by the dynamic growth of corporate Manhattan; planned shrinkage and the decline of social services are matched by gentrification and subsidies to the affluent" (Tabb, 77, 88).[14] And those terms of definition are represented and enabled by these resonant presentations of the city in popular film.

These films are valuable documents for their images of the urban landscape. In the earlier productions of the period of my study, we view streets rife with garbage, abandoned and decaying buildings, and people who are clearly down on their luck. These films also provide further commentary in the terms of their narratives, placing images of New York in contexts that engage their viewers in stories that situate the city as a nexus of commerce, desire, and despair. And beyond this blend of actuality and fiction, the films develop an organizational strategy for depicting relative space. Indeed, as the late 1960s and early 1970s are an historical moment that anticipates the structural changes in the world economy that we define with the spatially loaded term "globalization," we can interrogate various cultural expressions for their role in both representing this incremental change in economic history and for the ways in which they provide us with spatial metaphors that allow us to engage in the process of reconceiving the relative spaces of the world.[15]

These films are clearly not historical in the sense that they employ narratives that access events that are commonly believed to have actually happened. They are, however, powerful expressions of a particular cultural moment. All except for the *Godfather* films are set in the "present" and employ the temporal immediacy that is natural to their medium. That is, film always seems to be taking place right before a viewer's eyes, and it may only seem to represent the past through some textual means of address that explicitly undoes this particular effect. For example, we know that *The Godfather* is initially set in 1945 because it references the war, shows period dress, and is shot with a yellowish tint that signals events are of the past. These other films offer recognizable streets, current dress, late model cars, and appropriate vernacular for the late 1960s and 1970s.

Commercial cinema provides a fruitful expression for considering the ways in which representational works of popular culture provide a means for their audiences to engage in what Fredric Jameson elaborates as "cognitive mapping." Using an apt example, Jameson suggests the ways in which discrete spaces can be reconceived through a representational device (or devices) that have the effect of reorganizing that relative area within a vision of a larger world. Jameson writes in *The Geopolitical Aesthetic,*

> In a classic work, *The Image of the City*, Kevin Lynch taught us that the alienated city is above all a space in which people are unable to map (in their minds) either their own positions or the urban totality in which they find themselves: grids such as those of Jersey City, in which none of the traditional markers (monuments, nodes, natural boundaries, built perspectives) obtain, are the most obvious examples. Disalienation in the traditional city, then, involves the practical reconquest of a sense of place and the construction or reconstruction of an articulated ensemble which can be retained in memory.[16] (51)

Jameson's notion of "reconquest" allows us to see one possible way individuals at moments of cultural disruption and dislocation begin to reorient. In such a situation, the related spatial organization of a number of cultural expressions may gradually help audiences to develop new ways of understanding the connections among the relative spaces of city, nation, and world. The formal strategies of many of the films of the first phase of my study and their particular content situate viewers in a broader tale of anti-urbanism, a story that suggests the need for a broad process of gentrification that would include both the city's physical space and its residents. Films such as these locate New York as a distinctive and largely degraded locale that contains elements of wealth and gentility; but it is largely composed of those on the margins, suggesting, as Travis Bickle would famously assert in *Taxi Driver*, that it "should be flushed down the toilet." And whatever its entertainments, it is a place that can be accessed relatively easily from safer spaces beyond its contours, causing one to ask why a person would choose to live there.

Such a focus on space within a particular historical situation necessarily introduces a specific terminology, one that is more usual to the field of cultural geography than it is to film studies. For example, the terms centripetal and centrifugal as relative depictions of space are important to my overall discussion. These descriptive terms, adapted from the physical sciences, were notably applied to relative space by the French cultural theorist Henri Lefebvre in his *The Production of Space*. Both refer to the way in which relative space is bracketed and given meaning. Centripetal refers to space that inheres, that looks inward and seems isolated from that which is not defined as part of it. Centrifugal refers to space spiraling outward to gesture and affix to the world beyond. Important in my application of Lefebvre's concepts is Edward Dimendberg in his *Film Noir and the Spaces of Modernity* (2004). Dimendberg evocatively shows that film noir defines textual strategies that envision the city in ways that evoke its centripetal and/or centrifugal dimensions.

> Spaces of representation shape subjective experience and imagination, and admit a strong temporal dimension. In the centripetal film noir they include darkness, skylines, and street scenes of the metropolis. . . . A growing permeation of social life by exchange relations . . . yields an increasingly mediated mode of spatiality that alters traditional relations of production and connection to nature. (106)

In my study, I show how this mediation allows for the representational strategies that define space to align with shifts in networks of exchange and mode of production. These changes occur during the long 1970s and define the emerging and increasingly dominant system of globalized commerce.

Correspondingly, I show how these films participate in the related processes of deterritorialization and reterritorialization. These geographic concepts are derived from the discussion of Deleuze and Guatarri, who employ them to discuss the use of language in colonial and postcolonial contexts ("Minor Literature: Kafka," *The Deleuze Reader*, 152–164). My discussion, however, more centrally employs the work of Neil Brenner, who considers these concepts as vital to the conceptual *and* economic rescaling, and in always dialectically interactive. Writes Brenner in his "Global Cities, 'Glocal' States,"

I interpret global city formation and state re-scaling as dialectically intertwined processes of reterritorialization that have radically reconfigured the
scalar organization of capitalism since the global economic crises of the early
1970s. Global city formation is linked both to the globalization of capital and
to the regionalization/localization of state territorial organization. As nodes
of accumulation, global cities are sites of reterritorialization for post-Fordist
forms of global industrialization. As coordinates of state territorial organization, global cities are local-regional levels of governance situated within
larger, reterritorialized matrices of "glocalized" state institutions. (2)

Brenner's model, then, reveals the shifting relationships among political and economic actors, and their implications for geographic formulations. He does so
within the context of the 1970s and the geographic models that developed in con-
cert with globalization. Such a view of space as both material and conceptual provides a productive means of approaching films that are both of the world and
about the world.

These productions offer a frame through which to enter a period of significant
historical change for cities in the United States and beyond. The films picture
selected aspects of the built environment in their *images*. Further, their *narratives*,
which include their visual rhetoric, locate New York City in a state of flux, providing viewers glimpses of specific *processes* of transition. Such a distinction
requires that the film, which is a succession of related images, be viewed both as
the cumulative effect of those images, as well as disaggregated into its component
shots. These elements, then, take on the qualities of photographs. As isolated
images, photographs lend themselves to being employed in narratives but are not
inherently narrative in themselves. Writes Alan Sekula,

> The photograph as it stands alone presents merely the possibility of meaning.
> Only by its embeddedness in a concrete discourse situation can the photo-
> graph yield a clear semantic outcome. Any given photograph is conceivably
> open to appropriation by a set of "texts," each new discourse generating its
> own set of messages.[17]

It is the plasticity of the image's meaning that I am asserting, and this malleability
stems from its distinction from the larger body of linked images that form the
film. Particular scenes of New York, then, visually isolate moments and locales,
and those fragments are subject to reincorporation in historical narratives that are
related to those explicitly suggested by the film text, but which are not the same as
those narratives.[18] These images bear a different relation to the historical "real"

than does the film as a whole, as they create a more direct association between the historical moment, isolated in time and space, and the photographic representation of it. I should emphasize that I am not proposing a naïve realism; rather, as John Tagg argues, only that one may analytically consider such images "the product of a complex process involving the motivated and selective employment of determinate *means of representation*."[19] Indeed, it is my awareness of that complexity of process and attention to the photographic and filmic means of representation that informs my attempts to place these images in a historical context.

These films represent and participate in economic, demographic, and geographic shifts, as they show the ways in which this powerful aspect of popular culture participates in articulating, anticipating, and enabling change. As such, my analysis not only illuminates vital aspects of the period in a manner that provides distinctive insights into the ways in which materiality was altered; it also allows for a broad reconception of the connection between representational works of the imagination and the materiality of history. By viewing these films within the context of such transition, audiences may seize upon distinctive textual elements as significant and resonant. For example, in *Midnight Cowboy* (1969), when we view the demolition of the building abutting Ratso's squat on the Lower East Side (pictured in chapter 2), what emerges is not simply the incipient razing of Rico's own housing; rather, we are able to see the process of gentrification, a point in economic activity when it is in the interest of a developer to devote capital to destruction so that a new and profitable space may result. Similarly, in the first shot of the film, the screen at the drive-in theater in Big Springs, Texas (also pictured in chapter 2) is both iconically of the mythic West and an index of regional depopulation.

Such an analytical frame alters what may appear to be a self-evident narrative device and makes a particular image an important marker in the story of New York City's redevelopment, a story that is part of a larger tale of the city's emergence as a center of an enlarged sphere of global trade. I return to this historical change in the city's fortunes in my various chapters, tracing the relative shift from the nadir of disinvestment and deindustrialization that culminated in the city's default on its bond payments in 1975 to the beginnings of its re-elaboration as a city of gentrified spaces and yuppies. As Manuel Castells and John Hull Mollenkopf explain in *Dual City*,

> Between 1969 and 1975, decay and decline provided the predominant motif, especially in disinvested industrial areas, and poor black and Latino ghettos. During the 1977 to 1987 boom, the white middle and upper middle class professional and managerial strata experienced a considerable growth in income. They fashioned their spaces not only in old upper class areas, but fueled the

creation of new residential and consumption zones in former industrial areas like SoHo and in townhouse areas like the Upper West Side, Chelsea, Brooklyn Heights, and Park Slope. (8–9)

Film images and narratives provide their viewers a dense fabric of spatial relations, and these particular films do no less than remap the spaces of New York City and its connections to outlying areas. One of my recurring points of focus is how these films reconceive space at the moment when the role of New York in a world system of commerce is in the process of being redefined. My interest in New York as a real and imagined spatial entity in this chronology follows that of a number of prominent urban geographers. Neil Brenner (see chapter 4), Saskia Sassen, Neil Smith (see chapter 2), and David Harvey note the 1970s as a moment that resulted in a specific rearticulation of urban spaces and discuss the implications of such reorientation, both material and conceptual.[20]

This approach and object provide connections among this group of films, providing them with a means of cohesion that asks readers/viewers to move beyond the narrative of the industrial history of "Hollywood," or of the artistry of individual filmmakers, so that their contributions can also be seen as aspects of a time when cultural productions often focused on the terms of urban life. This act of reconsideration involves readers of my book and subsequent viewers of these films in acts of cultural reorientation and historical understanding. And although I do not propose that these films be conceived as a unitary genre, I do believe that their intertextual means of address provide them with an aggregated cultural power, a force I elaborate in my study.

FILM AND HISTORY

This is a historical study, one that is intensely interested in the connections between commercial, narrative films, and a broader urban and world economic history. Film history, as I noted above, plays a role in the phenomenon I am discussing, but it is more a component that shapes the fact of production than one that defines the contours of narrative, or the images that comprise such narratives. It also does not sufficiently account for the broader social and cultural resonances of the films. I am most concerned with the ways in which feature films in general and these films in particular respond to, encourage, and redirect existing historical trends and dispositions.

Film as a medium, as I have discussed in other places, is in its core qualities historical. By this I am not claiming, as some of its early practitioners did, that it reproduces an unmediated world; rather, I only point to its qualities that allow it to *apparently* document objective reality. As such, it is a medium that seems to freeze its sequence of found images for posterity. Part of the impulse that catalyzed the technological development of moving pictures in the mid-nineteenth century was the felt need to address the problem of documenting and representing the present as it morphed into the past. In the late nineteenth century, film was conceived as such a device, and early cinema practice frequently expresses this conception. It was a medium that took its place among the various media, such as the phonograph and still photographic camera, that were designed to capture a moment in some form and make it available for later apprehension. Early films tended to document motion, events, and people. Narrative, fictional cinema came after this initial use, and the development of complex narratives through the motion picture medium gradually took shape during the medium's first two decades.[21]

Of course, this earlier and then subsequent documentary use of the medium is not objective in its creation. The images of such productions cry out for analysis. Their codes of perspective are intensely ideological, and the principle of selecting the materials to be photographed is itself a matter of choice. But such a practice reminds us that film does possess the power to inscribe images within its constructed narratives that are of the world, even if not fully objective or "neutral." That is, the images captured and projected can be of places and people that existed materially within a particular historical moment. For the purposes of this study, it is the physical environment that I wish to discuss further, since within fictional films actors tend to play the roles of historical figures, when there is a nonfiction basis for the film—such as in *Serpico*, *The French Connection*, and *Prince of the City*, while the film version of the statue of Columbus at Columbus Circle corresponds to that actual structure. Such images have meaning within the contours of the film narrative in which they occur, where their meaning is reconfigured within the synergistic body of relationships that constitute that text. But as images that mediate between the world and the text, they also have significance within the contours of other historical narratives. In my study I at times look at these moments of expression as distinct from their contextual imbrications in the film itself and reinsert them within a more explicitly material historical narrative. In such instances, the aspects of the film being analyzed offer a relationship between film and history that has largely been ignored in previous discussions.[22] Indeed, too often such discussions have tended to focus on films that fall into the category of historical fiction, and the relationship between film and history is discussed as the role of cinema in producing narratives that are explicitly of historical subjects.[23] Though this is a worthy topic, it narrows what should be a far broader discussion.

In his excellent study, *Change Mummified: Cinema, Historicity, Theory*, Philip Rosen addresses the question of film's historical situation in a manner that is both theoretically perspicacious and astutely applied. In doing so, he opens up the question of the connections between the medium in its various applications and the past itself, as well as narratives about the past. He begins by defining what he elaborates as three key definitions of the relationship between past and the present. "By historiography, I mean the text written by the historian. . . . By history, I mean the object of the text (the real past-ness it seeks to construct and recount in and for the present). . . . By historicity, I mean the particular inter-relations of the mode of historiography and the types of construction of history related to it" (xi). Such precision allows us to see the ways in which definitions of history are often merged, so that stories about the past become accepted as the past itself; or, when they fail to seamlessly replicate "the object of the text," readers, writers, and viewers assume that there is no such object: the impossibility of reproducing the past creates the notion that such a reproduction cannot be imagined. Though not explicitly Rosen's intent, his definitions allow for segmenting the multiple images that comprise a Hollywood feature, as well as provide the analytical precision needed to separate the materiality of the past from stories that reference that materiality within a narrative. Clearly, however, all of these stories that are conveyed in feature films do not have the same relationship to a conceived material past, nor do they intend to.

In his discussion of the theories of Andre Bazin, Rosen talks about this impulse as emblematic of the tensions during the late nineteenth century, the moment of the appearance of cinema, between the concepts of "preservation" and "restoration," a distinction that has relevance both for discussing a text's relationship to the past and for a filmmaker plotting how to represent that relationship. Rosen chooses architecture as his primary explanatory object. He writes, "The dead cannot be brought back to life, but reverence for their remains may keep them alive in memory. Restoration cannot replicate the historical actuality of a building, which is its existence in time, but preservation can provide an encounter with that actuality by refusing to interrupt its passage through time" (56). Rosen goes on to explain this contrast as one that is deeply revealing of the sociocultural temper of Western cultures during that period, "positing the power of temporality and the fundamental value of interrogating pastness" (56). In the two *Godfather* films, for instance, there is an emphasis on restoration, an act that delineates the past as lost but subject to reconstruction in narrative form. In these two films, the historicity of the films may be found only indexically. Such films reproduce a vision of the past through an act of restoration that valorizes the historical but offers it as a mediated discourse.

Broadly, for the purposes of the other films of my study, it is the related ideas of "production" and "reproduction" that I explore.[24] Film cannot restore the remnants of the past and make them a vital, if ersatz, testimony to the qualities of that object and era. It can, however, in a variety of ways—visual, aural, verbal— re-elaborate the memory of that materiality and embed it in a narrative that apparently evokes the fact of the past. Rosen talks of reproduction and preservation as motifs that reveal conceptions of the past. The idea of reproduction locates film narrative's power to express a vision of the past as a sequence of points that can be re-elaborated through a structure that apparently reproduces the past's reason for being, while the idea of preservation constructs the past as an organic entity that perpetually expresses its moment of production, as an entity that reveals the persistence of the now vanished past. In any case, the pairing of these terms reveals two distinct approaches to historicity: are the images and narratives formed *of* the past? Or are they *about* the past?

My approach answers this query with a resounding "yes" to both questions, in regard to certain *images*, and with a clear choice of about in the case of *narratives*. That is, many of these films provide images from the world as it existed at the point of production, so they are both of the past and about the past, merging Rosen's categories of historiographic and historicity. Film tends to work in the domain of reproduction, but I would argue that elements of the films I discuss also work within the domain of preservation. They both preserve and reproduce the specific nodes of the past that are within the scope of the camera lens. Indeed, to borrow terminology from semioticians, films offer signs that are both iconic— referring directly to the thing itself—and indexical—referring less directly and with more nuance to a particular range of meanings associated with those things. Conventionally, images of objects are iconic. A picture of a cow refers to the thing. But the image is also subject to less literal responses, perhaps referring to the pastoral, the bucolic, the metaphorically bovine, and so on.

Narrative film is always a discourse with historicity. It always in some ways refers to its moment of origin and to the world in which that process of conception and fruition takes place. For example, in the book I wrote about Hollywood Westerns and the cold war, I discussed the ways in which these genre films, with no direct references to either the USSR or U.S. foreign policy of the post–World War II era, allegorically and metaphorically considered their contemporary world. This method has been employed by many, and at least implicitly––and often explicitly––recognizes the ways in which Hollywood narratives are of a particular historical moment. Similarly, in this study, the ways in which those productions mediate between the terrain of their narratives and the historical conditions of their productions makes them complexly historical and clearly indexical.

But there are degrees of mediation and levels of reference. Unlike the Westerns I previously considered, the films of this study, though mediated are, for the most part, less so than many narrative films. The propensity for direct chronological reference in this large group of films is in itself notable. There are obvious exceptions to this disposition. As I stated earlier, there are productions such as *The Godfather* and *The Godfather II*, which are both period pieces that include many scenes shot on a soundstage. The rest of the films of this study are contemporary, shot on location, and valuable not only for their narratives about urban life but also for their images of that environment and, though often casually and not as a clear emphasis of the narrative, to other related physical locales.

Further, though others have ventured in this direction and some explicitly, I apply the category of the geographic as a mode of historical analysis, thus offering a refinement to my discussion of the relationship between the film and the past.[25] This seems particularly apt in an era that ushers in that of globalized exchange, a system that is explicitly geographic while also temporal. The transition of New York is explicitly a matter of its role in this emerging system. On the one hand, film offers a temporal set of relationships, delineating a complexity of associations among the moments of conception, production, release, and consumption. But as a visual medium, film also articulates the contours of discrete spaces; further, films develop a spatial logic that asserts the relative connections among a number of regions that they are instrumental in defining. Thus, they work to map relative remoteness and contiguity, revealing the ways in which these relationships are conceptually produced within a given historical epoch.[26]

Below I provide summaries of the remaining chapters. A note on methodology: I have attempted to elaborate a broad trend but to do so through a limited number of objects. I have attempted to keep the number of films discussed in detail down to no more than five per chapter. My reason for limiting the number of films in each chapter was to keep my study sufficiently detailed in its discussion of each film, since I am attempting to provide a fairly precise accounting of not only each film's textual emphasis but also of the way in which it maps its relative geography. I have generally tried to broaden my context by listing other related films. In all, twenty-one films are treated in some detail in the context of this study. I have also developed thematic groupings that are roughly chronologically unified, but the nature of the films produced a somewhat ragged historical line. This asymmetry expresses the ways in which such cultural materials occur and indeed, the way in which history defines itself.

The first chapter of the body of my study is "Sex and the City in Decline: *Midnight Cowboy* (1969) *and Klute* (1971)." I approach these as tales about migration, following the main characters of each film, Joe Buck in *Midnight Cowboy* and John

Klute in *Klute*, though each is immediately or almost immediately involved with a figure who is already settled in New York and who serves as a guide to the city for the relatively innocent newcomer. These films locate the city as a site for sex work in a context that is defined by the decline of its built environment. This type of enterprise stands for the decline of productive employment as well as a means and symbol of a broader urban decline in itself. I employ terms of spatial analysis to show how these films locate New York City, as well as place it in relation to areas beyond, in order to articulate the distinctness and characteristic terms of this urban space. The horizontal framing of Joe Buck's Texas home and John Klute's Pennsylvania exurb gives way, in a transition that effectively reduces the relative space between locations, to lenses and framing strategies that emphasize the horizontally imposing, and therefore physically impinging, city. These films depict the city as a cause of violence and moral decline, even as we are provided images of a different city beginning to emerge. Through their vision of their socially marginal characters, these films provide an intriguing view of the historical process of industrial decline and its moral impact. And as they do so, both films suggest how the process of decline, at its nadir, can become the basis for relative economic rebirth.

The next chapter, "Longing for the Return of Vito Corleone: Race, Place, and the Ethnic City in *The Godfather*, parts I and II (1972 and 1974) and *Mean Streets* (1973)" looks at the city through the prism of the romance and then disenchantment of ethnic life that marks these films. This part of my study dwells on the ways these productions elevate the markers of ethnic "whiteness" as a means of lamenting the decline of the insular spaces and communities that defined the earlier twentieth-century urban experience of Italians, Jews, Poles, Greeks, and other groups that came to the United States in large numbers in the late nineteenth and earlier twentieth centuries. These films focus on the way in which discrete spaces are tied to specific ethnic groups as part of a nostalgic celebration of pre–World War II New York, and how those definitions of space have an embedded dimension of exclusion with implications both for views of commerce and racial separation. They dwell on the idealized space of New York's Little Italy, framing it as a place apart from the broader contours of New York, often reducing its relative relationship by shooting at ground level and across streets, rather than looking at it amid the larger city and shooting down the avenues that traverse the city on a north-south grid. I look at the ways in which these spaces are visualized over time, as well as the terms by which they attempt, but fail, to maintain a local scale of commerce and association. I am particularly concerned with the ways in which these films react to and represent the changing racial composition of the city. With the continued migration of the "white" ethnic populations, who were vestiges of the immigration of the 1880s to the 1920s, to regions at the edge or outside of the city, and the enhancing of immigration by people from the Caribbean, Latin America, and Asia, New York was becoming browner and blacker. These films both represent and contextualize that change through their historical retrospection.

The next chapter complements the preceding one, as it shifts focus to ethnicity's "other," race. Titled "Blaxploitation and Urban Decline: Harlem and the World Beyond, *Cotton Comes to Harlem* (1970), *Shaft* (1971), *Across 110th St.* (1972), *Superfly* (1972), and *Black Caesar* (1974)," this chapter employs these films to look at how they define African American New York by the presence of Harlem, its relative centrality, and its place in a broader geography and narrative of the city. All of these films locate Harlem as a place contiguous to but apart from the racially delineated "white" environs below 110th Street. In virtually every film, Harlem is initially defined anthropologically, located with a crane shot that zooms down to locate a city self-contained, a space that is defined from without, rather than, as in Coppola and Scorsese's Little Italy, one that coheres from within. The films feature white-defined spaces contiguous to Harlem, but, as in the case of *Across 110th Street*, Central Park serves as a border only slightly less forbidding than the walls of the Warsaw ghetto. Indeed, these movies define African American authenticity through the association of and relative comfort of a character within the confines of Harlem; yet, in most of these films, African Americans who succeed move downtown. As such, the productions centrally focus on African-American group identity, its intragroup class system, and the place of African Americans in a city in transition. Key within these films is the portrayal of Harlem's built environment as one in decline and the relatively depressed economic state of its inhabitants. These films participate in a cultural narrative of race and class, showing and asserting a post–Civil Rights picture of a centripetal and enveloping "ghetto" for those who do not succeed and a centrifugal city of possibility for those who do.[27] In contrast to the previous chapter, where I locate the related term "ethnicity" as a marker for a protected-space Lower Manhattan, here I show how the relationships within this depicted "nonwhite" Harlem contrast sharply with sepia-toned images of the world of Coppola's and Scorsese's gangsters. While those films about "ethnic" crime are nostalgic for a kind of localism that cannot be recaptured, these films that feature race reveal a people trapped within a space that is definitional in restrictive ways.

In "Policing the Unsafe City: *The French Connection* (1971), *Serpico* (1973), *Dog Day Afternoon* (1975), *Prince of the City* (1981), and the Rise of Neoliberalism" I look at these narratives of crime and urban corruption. The films recast the city as a sprawling morass largely defined by the scale and lack of distinction of the decaying outer boroughs, replacing the centripetal city of the earlier chapters with a centrifugal one that projects to the neoliberal regime that redefines New York City after it defaults on its bond payments in 1975. These films offer few shots of Manhattan in its vision of a decentered New York, a city with permeable borders that opens itself to French drug smugglers and Spanish-speaking addicts. The unpoliceable city literally sprawls, out of control. It is a region in which threats from within, and without, permeate everyday life, where the most vital economic sector of the city is criminality and perhaps the global drug trade. As a result, corruption penetrates its fabric, including the moral structure of the law. Such films show the limited power of local institutions to constrain international commerce. Arguably, this decentered metropolis, which serves as a nexus for global criminals, is one that anticipates the logic of neoliberalism and the neoliberal regime that articulates the post-1975 New York and the late-1970s and 1980s global order. It is not just the public institution of the police department that is failing. We see frayed systems of transportation, unregulated and unregulatable commerce, and an increasing and bureaucratic federal presence. And in the midst of this decline of the Fordist metropolis, each film offers images of the incipient global city, and the ways in which the market-driven activity of that city thwarts local controls.

Chapter 6, "Vigilance!: *Death Wish* (1974), *Taxi Driver* (1976), and *Marathon Man* (1976)," continues the discussion of the previous one but concerns itself with its complement. Whereas the previous chapter unrolls a narrative logic that shows the world as defined by neoliberal precepts of acquisition and inevitable expressions of unmanageable avarice, this one focuses on the need for controls over those who express that impulse in an antisocial way. This view takes on the contours of the emerging group of neoconservatives, mostly ex-Trotskyites, who were just coalescing in New York City. In a city where public institutions cease to function effectively, how can individuals assure their own safety and that of others? These mid 1970s productions offer neo-noir views of the city to accentuate the extreme breakdown of order and morality, showing how urban blight and angst create the need for self-protection, a stance that they justify as a response to intolerable conditions. All are set substantially in Manhattan, and all reveal the city as the crossroads of history and the world. All provide visions of forces from without, the residue of international conflict and politics, providing a sense of space that makes it unmanageably violent and chaotic. We see the extreme responses to such a view on the level of atavistic and personal narratives of control and revenge. These films offer the centrifugal city as a space of moral disorder but as one that is subject to the extralegal policing and extreme violence of the protagonists of these films. In doing so, they lay the ideological groundwork for the reemergence of a gentrified city with privatized public services and a proactive—public and private—police force.

The final chapter of this study, "Love, Marriage, and Fine City Living: *Annie Hall* (1977), *An Unmarried Woman* (1978), *Manhattan* (1979), and *Kramer vs. Kramer* (1979)," discusses films that explicitly reorient our vision of the built environment of the city and the class makeup of its inhabitants. Its upper-middle-class inhabitants uniformly work without comment in the entertainment and information industries. Their apartments are commodious—even when they are, in the terms of the narrative, not supposed to be—and their friends are like them; all are physically attractive and well dressed. The city has been altered from a place of chaos and tragedy to one of romance and largely resolvable personal problems. Such trials point to a vision of social life that subordinates economic factors, showing viewers the changing dynamics of the urban family but only within a context of relative comfort and safety. They situate their key characters as successful economic actors in a city of possibility. These figures are defined not only by their uniformity of class but also by their common elevation of a notion of the aesthetic. Class is thus redefined as a kind of sensibility, and it is that cultural astuteness that forms the precondition for belonging and succeeding in the gentrified Manhattan. In effecting this make-over for Manhattan and its residents, these films alter the noir references that have marked the earlier films of my study and instead reference drawing-room comedies and melodramas of the 1930s, films that are explicitly escapist in a time of economic depression, and, not coincidentally, another important era for films set in New York City.

2

Sex and the City in Decline

MIDNIGHT COWBOY (1969) AND *KLUTE* (1971)

THE LATE 1960S and 1970s were a time when many cities in the United States—and those in the Northeast and Midwest in particular—were in difficult economic straits, primarily because of factors related to deindustrialization that resulted in the loss of union jobs; further, and related, many had been the sites of riots that had been a regular feature of nightly newscasts in the middle and later years the 1960s. For many, New York City stood as the ultimate example of such chaos, and all types of cultural productions of this era associated New York City with images and narratives of urban decline. Network television regularly featured such scenes in both news and entertainment. Urban crime was a regular feature of both national and local news, particularly the violent and destructives riots in Watts in 1965, and in Detroit and Newark in 1967. Related images of violence and squalor were featured in any number of police dramas, including *McCloud*, *N.Y.P.D.*, *Kojak*, and others. And of course, such conceptions are at the heart of many of the films of the next chapters of this study: *The French Connection* (1971), *Shaft* (1971), *Superfly* (1972), *Across 110th St.* (1972), *Serpico* (1973), *Black Caesar* (1974), *Death Wish* (1974), *Dog Day Afternoon* (1975), and *Taxi Driver* (1976), as well as others.

But in an interesting analogue to the racially charged images of these urban visions, a less present but ultimately no less significant story emerged. In late June of 1969, just a month after the release of *Midnight Cowboy*, the patrons of a

Christopher Street bar frequented by gay men, the Stonewall Inn, resisted the harassment of the police and thus symbolically began the gay rights movement.[1] Images of this incident were immediately featured in the local press, and then in the national press later that year.[2] In a headline that perhaps captures popular—or populist—homophobia, the *New York Daily News* headline of July 6, 1969, read, "Homo Nest Raided, Queen Bees Are Stinging Mad." The article began: "She sat there with her legs crossed, the lashes of her mascara-coated eyes beating like the wings of a hummingbird. She was angry. She was so upset she hadn't bothered to shave. A day old stubble was beginning to push through the pancake makeup. She was a he. A queen of Christopher Street." Such mocking prose reflected broad attitudes, though somewhat more respectful pieces in *Time* and *Newsweek* were published in October. And although for many this was a moment to celebrate, for others, the events on Christopher Street confirmed that New York was a debauched place. Images of the city as a center of rampant sexuality had also been a part of the popular media's reporting on the "hippie" counterculture of the late 1960s, as Greenwich Village, along with Haight-Ashbury, became one of the signature sights of that movement and its associated flouting of sexual morality.[3]

These associations between the New York environs and moral decline helped to define that city in the national imaginary. And while the elaboration of New York City as a place of extreme behavior occurred in all types of media, my particular focus in this chapter is not on this wide range of examples, some of which I will discuss later, but on two widely viewed and influential films, *Midnight Cowboy* (1969), directed by John Schlesinger, and *Klute* (1971), directed by Alan J. Pakula. The films provide resonant examples of the ways in which film narratives of sex, work, and general urban decline can help to elaborate complexly an era of historical transition. These productions simultaneously define New York as a place of limited economic opportunity, as well as a locale where individuals with extreme desires reside.[4] As they help to resituate the city in the national consciousness, we might ask how a revised conception of urban life participates in the momentous economic shifts of the period. Both films show the city as a marginal place that becomes a destination of choice for those who seek to engage in such behavior, becoming part of what Robert Beauregard describes as the discourse of urban decline. Such rhetoric, Beauregard tells us, has the effect of shaping a view of reality. "It [the discourse] legitimates the world as it is. Americans are thereby inclined to be more accepting of the many disruptions and disparities that engulf them, and to acquiesce more readily to society's dominant interests."[5]

Midnight Cowboy and *Klute* in their depictions of urban space and of New York's relative geography in particular offer a vision of cities that shows the physical relationships among geographies that are largely maintained as discrete. That is, both films enact a centripetal view of the city that tends to mark it as distinctive and to affirm its relative moral and physical isolation from other places. In the end, in order to escape its tenacious, compromising grasp, the focal characters of these films plot an escape; because only by removing oneself is redemption possible.

But even as we see the decay and isolation of the New York of these films, through the luxury of a historical frame that allows for hindsight, we can also see certain aspects of these presentations that hint at the class-based vision of redemption that elevates notions of change through gentrification and participation in an incipient globalized economy. Again, these aspects of the films are available, but clearly recessed. In these works of popular entertainment we can see both the resonant terms by which urban areas were judged to be in decay— economic and moral—as well as the less visible means by which they would be "redeemed" by their new roles as world cities in the service of the financial industries.

Indeed, viewed from a certain angle, these films show us the end of an era in American economic and cultural history, a period that began after the Civil War when the burgeoning of industrial production and the mechanization and rationalization of agriculture resulted in a massive migration from rural locales to urban centers. But by the late 1960s, cities in the northeastern and midwestern United States were, by almost all measures, failing.[6] Further, they establish a predominant vision of decay that is economic, physical, *and moral*, a vision that will prove to be resonant and that will recur with varying emphases over the next three chapters.

Such a conception of the city as a place of varied sexual practices was also furthered by the popular liberal sit-com *All in the Family*, a show that debuted between the releases of these two films, in January of 1971. As the show begins, viewers see a house in the decidedly working-class white neighborhood of Glendale, Queens. As the credits roll at the end of the program, the audience is shown images of Astoria, Queens, also pictured as a working-class enclave. In both cases, those watching are called on to imagine the lives of Archie Bunker-like residents who are beleaguered in a city and a world that is changing around them. Archie's urban locale is defined in that initial season as beset by moral, economic, physical, and racial disruptions. Viewers see Archie's fear of being laid off, his efforts to keep the house next door from being sold to African Americans, and his resistance to his daughter and son-in-law's unmarried friends sleeping together at his house. These stories comprise a remarkable selection of historically salient issues. Viewed intertextually, they suggest the ways in which race, class, and sexuality were conjoined in a broader narrative of national decline primarily focused on urban spaces. And though Norman Lear, the show's producer and a well-known political liberal, meant to show the foibles of Archie's entrenched views of the world, no doubt some viewers empathized with this figure's difficulties in facing a rapidly changing environment, even as they may have responded to Lear's political intention.

In episode number five of that first season, in a decidedly post-Stonewall teleplay that aired on February 9, 1971, Archie decides that his son-in-law Michael Stivic's friend Roger—on the basis of his handbag, carriage, and dress—is gay. After some teasing, Archie invites Mike and his friend to accompany him to the local bar to watch football with the "real men." One of those patrons, an ex-football player named Steve, who Archie clearly admires, eventually informs Archie that Roger is straight but that he is not. And while the intended lesson of tolerance is not difficult to ascertain, there is a parallel lesson that suggests that "normalcy" is on the run. That Steve sits in Archie's place of respite, unannounced and undetected, suggests how Archie's insulated space has been breeched.

Within the 1970s are a significant number of New York-based film productions that employ visions of sexuality that flew in the face of assumptive normality as a means of asserting a different view of urban behavior. For example, *The Boys in the Band* (1970), based on the stage play, explores a vision of gay male culture set in Manhattan. Though the film is shot on a soundstage and reveals its stage origins throughout, it was a brave topic for that time and did clearly make the connection between Manhattan and gay sexuality. *Panic in Needle Park* (1971) is primarily about drug use, but prostitution becomes a logical means of earning money with which to buy drugs, and also serves as a form of direct barter. *Dog Day Afternoon*'s (1975) bank robbery and hostage taking, we eventually learn, is to finance Sonny's partner's sex change operation, a detail that also shows the bank robbery as a post-Stonewall assertion of the coalescence of gay politics, as Sonny is cheered by an identifiably gay crowd. *Cruising* (1980) tells of a New York cop's involvement in the world of gay clubs and then gay sexuality, as he investigates a murder. All of these films place unconventional (by their own definitions) sexual behavior as a component of New York City's status as a place where physical and moral disruption is spawned and tolerated.

Midnight Cowboy and *Klute* were significant productions that were complexly involved with these historical events and cultural expressions, though *Midnight Cowboy* was by far the more ground-breaking and notable production. Indeed, its cultural resonance was apparent to critics at its initial point of exhibition. Wrote Roger Ebert, "The basis of *Midnight Cowboy* is one of the essential American myths: The eager youth comes from the country to the city, and his simplicity and freshness are ground up in the urban jungle. Dreiser wrote this story, and Sherwood Anderson, and it is still a good story because it tells what happens every day." Vincent Canby also remarked on its timeliness in the *New York Times*, noting that

"*Midnight Cowboy* often seems to be exploiting its material for sensational or comic effect, but it is ultimately a moving experience that captures the quality of a time and a place."[7] Reviews of *Klute*, while more mixed, also note its urban vision and distinctive use of New York, for, as Roger Greenspan notes in the *Times*, its "structural geometry."[8]

As my previous discussion suggested, these films do not create the association between the city, New York in particular, and scandalous sexual behavior. Beyond the many expressions that are roughly contemporary with them, they also redefine and build on historical associations, asserting New York as a place of iniquity that would, if they remained in it, devour the souls of the films' two protagonists. The innovations of these films are in their explicit picturing of the world of sex, a vision that had only been suggested in earlier productions. They also develop that portrait to include not only prostitution but also male prostitution, and gay male prostitution at that, as they also include other variants of bondage and discipline, and sadomasochism. As such, the urban environment is represented in ways that are distinctive at this time.

And while these films advance and make explicit this equation between New York and unconventional sexual mores, the trend can be traced to the nineteenth century and beyond. The image and reality of the Bowery and its prostitutes and rowdy b'hoys was a staple of an emergent popular culture from the mid to the late nineteenth century, as writers from Walt Whitman to Fanny Fern to Stephen Crane famously documented the rampant sexuality and immorality that proliferated in New York's downtown districts.[9] Christine Stansell tells us in her *City of Women*,

> In a city so concerned with defining both women's proper place and the place of the working class, the alarm over prostitution stemmed in part from general hostilities to the milieu of laboring women from which prostitutes came. "Prostitution" evolved in the nineteenth century as a particular construction, the grouping of a range of sexual experiences which in actual life may be quite disparate. (175)[10]

Such definitions expanded the category of the "fallen woman" and added to the resonance of tales of sexual profligacy that were a staple of the burgeoning newspaper and magazine industries.

When cinema began to attract audiences just before the turn of the century, New York's aura as a place of iniquity became a staple on which the new medium could build, even within the very brief presentations of the new medium. Early films of titillation—from *The May-Irwin Kiss* (1896) to *What Happened on Twenty-Third Street, New York City* (1901) to *The Gay Shoe Clerk* (1903)—all showed New York as a place of relative license. We see the shoe clerk ogling and touching a woman's ankles. In *What Happened on Twenty-Third Street*, a dress is blown up by the wind, exposing a woman's underwear. As films became longer and offered more involved narratives, the tendency to emphasize exotic sexuality and the city in films such as *Romance of a Jewess* (1908), in which a "Hebrew" New Yorker is shown as a object of desire, and *Traffic in Souls* (1913), a film about white women being sold into prostitution. With the emergence of talking films in the late 1920s, New York's connection to sin and sex became a staple of both films about the lower classes and films about the bourgeoisie, including features such as *Little Caesar* (1931) and *Blonde Venus* (1932), both of which associate New York (or its representation) with the urge and willingness to engage in sex out of wedlock. Other such films included *The Divorcee* (1930), Mae West's *I'm No Angel* (1933), and *Libeled Lady* (1936), all of which focus on unconventional desires. And the cycle of films noir that were set in New York, such as *Cat People* (1941), *Scarlet Street* (1945), *Pickup on South Street* (1953), among others, also employed the city as a locale for what the production code termed "low forms of sex relationship"[11] But it is important that the distinction between the graphic terms of these two films and the suggestions of these earlier productions remain distinct. *Midnight Cowboy* and *Klute* graphically depict a world where the squalor of the streets is matched by a luridness that is explicitly depicted. In these films sex is not only variant; it is also dangerous, as in the earlier film we see Joe Buck beating a client bloody, and in the latter, we find that Bree Daniels is under surveillance by a predator.

Midnight Cowboy and *Klute* are distinctly about the sex trade and therefore within the tradition of depicting the city as a place of sin and promiscuity. They build on this vision of the city as a place where that mode of commerce is a vital part of life and in which the rules that define conventional sexual comportment cease to obtain. The films employ New York City as a site of, and a metaphor for, the extremes of urban existence. They advance a contemporary narrative of the marginality of urban spaces and their dwellers within U.S. society, and further define these areas as disruptive of foundational national myths of family and sexuality. Such assertions concurrently become part of the freer expression that is associated with the 1960s, while they allow audiences the moral high ground of standing apart from that expression and making it a function of a type of moral decay not found outside of the city.

Midnight Cowboy tells the story of a young man named Joe Buck (played by Jon Voight), coming to New York from rural Texas in order to become a male prostitute. He believes that he can develop a lucrative business by providing urban women with the sex that overcivilized and less virile city men cannot. He affiliates with a socially marginal character, Rico "Ratso" Rizzo (played by Dustin Hoffman), who offers to teach him the ways of the city and the sex trade. And though success eludes Joe, the film becomes a tale of the evolving relationship between this relative innocent from Texas and a club-footed New York character who embodies the city's trials, as well as his descent into gay hustling in Times Square. The film was nominated for seven academy awards and won three—best picture, best director, and best adapted screenplay. Notably, it was the first X-rated film to win the best picture Oscar and was one of the top grossing films of the year, earning over $44 million on a $3.5 million budget. For its director, British-born John Schlesinger, *Midnight Cowboy* marked a shift from his usual emphasis on the British system of social class, and showed a disposition to interrogate the distinctive terms of New York life.[12]

In *Klute*, a small-town cop, John Klute (Donald Sutherland), comes to New York in search of his friend, a successful corporate executive, Tom Gruneman, who has vanished in the big city. His search is bankrolled by a man named Peter Cable, who is also a corporate executive, and, it turns out, the murderer of Gruneman and several prostitutes. Klute's contact is a young prostitute named Bree Daniels (Jane Fonda), who was one of the last to see Gruneman alive. The film employs many of the conventions of film noir as it chronicles the search for Gruneman and the connection between the cop and the call girl. *Klute* was nominated for two academy awards, best actress and best screenplay, with Jane Fonda winning the Oscar. It grossed $12.5 million, making it a solid financial success. Its director, Alan J. Pakula, who had prior to this film mostly produced, went on to direct a number of political thrillers, including *All the President's Men* (1976) and *The Parallax View* (1974), both of which featured the urban landscape of Washington, D.C.[13]

SPACE, PLACE, AND URBAN ENTRAPMENT

Each film begins in a place that is distinctly *not* New York City, allowing the viewer to apprehend in contrast the images that are, in then end, central to these films. Both films immediately tap into a particular myth of the United States, in order to contrast it with the harsh reality of New York City. Each defines its non-New York settings with shots that are framed to emphasize horizontal space, so that we can see the expanse of land in the West and the closeness of families in the exurbs. This framing is distinct from that which emphasizes the vertical lines of New York City. In each film, the emphasis on the horizontal spaces of Texas and Pennsylvania (in *Klute*) defines a central trope of the world beyond New York. In *Midnight Cowboy*, this space is that of the West, a mythic space that resonates with the cult of the individual—even if incorporation has caused the decay of this tradition. In *Klute*, this horizontal space defines the social closeness of exurban America, a place of families and prosperity—even if that closeness hides transgressive acts and desires. In contrast, the vertical space of New York in both films is dwarfing, socially alienating, and indicative of rigid hierarchy.

The opening shot of *Midnight Cowboy* depicts a blank white frame accompanied by the sound of cowboys and Indians in a movie-battle scene. The camera zooms out to reveal a horizontally expansive desert, as a neon sign, "Big Tex Drive-In," comes to the front of the frame. In this shot, the object that literally cuts the horizontal plane of arid land in half is a movie screen (figure 2.1). This screen becomes a symbol of decay and a symbol of promise. Certainly this arid plain is an uninviting space; but the sounds that accompany this shot tell of a mythic definition of nation, even as the subsequent images show it in the process of being distended. Viewed through the prism of economic history, Big Springs' open plains and relative integration into world systems of communication, including good roads, suggest the prospect of industrial development.[14] If we reconsider the space of the drive-in and project some twenty-five years ahead, we might super-impose an industrial plant down the highway from a Wal-Mart.

But fundamentally, the screen is an image of mediation. Joe has adapted his identity not from the authentic experience of Western living—whatever that

FIGURE 2.1 *Midnight Cowboy*: The drive-in and the Wild West.

might be in the mid-twentieth century—but from the two-dimensional picturing of it at a drive-in. John Wayne is far more real than his absent father, and in the world defined by his mother and grandmother, Western identity has become the stuff of cowboy costumes and frontier-days parades, a matter of kitsch and not of lonely nights on the plains.

Since there was once adequate population to support such local enterprise, the viewer can surmise that the demise of the theater defines a demographic shift away from the region, much as it does in the roughly contemporary film *The Last Picture Show* (1971). As the credits play, we follow Joe in close-up, and the camera zooms out to locate empty store fronts and idle men sitting on the sidewalk in the town of Big Springs, Texas. Joe hops aboard a bus bound for New York City where, in order to compensate for the lack of "real men" there, he intends to provide sex for money.[15] Indeed, Joe's conjoining virility and his self-defined Westernness tell us about the bankruptcy of that myth, a notion that the film further elaborates when Rizzo informs him that his cowboy persona is "strictly faggot stuff."

Klute begins with brief close-ups of two affluent, middle-aged white people and cuts to a wide, horizontally framed shot that emphasizes their closeness with the friends and family that are with them. These people, including John Klute, are seated at a rectangular table in a setting defined by the lushness of a verdant yard in the background, the symbol of the exurban pastoral, denoting comfort, safety, and social coherence (figure 2.2).[16] While *Midnight Cowboy* evokes a romance of the West, *Klute* presents a picture of an America where people wear suits to dinner; in

FIGURE 2.2 *Klute*: A Thanksgiving feast among friends and family.

effect, the world of late-fifties and early-sixties television situation comedies, productions depicting perfect families with minor and faintly comical problems. The
view of this place is slightly ironic, suggesting a social world that exists only in
fiction and with very myopic views of American family life. But such images do
elaborate an ideal vision of America.

As the film proceeds, we find that we are not in the suburbs at all. Gruneman
and Klute reside some ways beyond New York in Tuscarora, Pennsylvania, a factory town, though the company's corporate center is in New York. Tuscarora is
ninety or so miles from Philadelphia and 121 miles from New York City in Schuykill
County, a largely white town in what was once a coal-mining region but which has
been in some measure of economic decline since World War II.[17] That it appears as
a desirable locale in this film suggests how the scenes shot outside of New York are
class bound, picturing not those struggling for work in a depressed region but
captains of industry and those with whom they closely associate.[18]

Both films disrupt their allusions to a better past by elaborating the difficulties
that define the present. In *Klute*, the film jump-cuts from that perfect Thanksgiving scene to one that shows an empty chair in the same room, which is now
darkened. The scene introducing father/husband Tom Gruneman's disappearance
emphasizes the isolation of its participants through a succession of close-ups, and
an occasional cut to a wide shot, which allows us explicitly to contrast this scene
with the preceding one. Family and community coherence in this setting was
defined by the physical proximity of the people pictured, a closeness accentuated
by the horizontal framing of the shots; but now the group has spread apart.

Both films define New York as Manhattan, which is densely populated with both
affluent and less affluent people, and substantially filled with tall buildings. There
is little definition of a middle class, and almost no view of materially productive
employment; no central characters are married, nor are there any children. Arguably, both movies' plots emanate from this definition of place, a historically
current view of New York.[19] Since these films are both about work and the accruing
of capital, they situate New York City in a broader geography of exchange, defining
it as both an area significant for commerce and as a place where goods that may be
traded are no longer produced, thus relatively disengaging it from the regional and
world economy except as a financial center. Within such a vision, sex work becomes
one of its more viable enterprises, as it is defines a commodity whose exchange
value is direct and self-contained. Though it is true that there are suggestions
of other acts of commerce—the entertainment business, other forms of retail
commerce—these are effaced within the narratives of these films.

The only productive manufacturing enterprise we see in *Klute* is a small loft run
by two older Jewish men, a father and son, in which women's clothes are cut and

sewn. The workers are largely Hispanic women. The loft is alternately pictured: by night, when Bree visits the older Mr. Goldfarb, it is a place which recapitulates the terms of Victorian paternalism; by day, it is a place where poor women labor. That productive enterprise is pictured in this manner is significant, romantically situating the past and harshly noting the present, even as both temporal references picture the same physical space.

The Goldfarbs' loft, located on Broadway between 29th and 30th Streets, shows a type of enterprise that still existed in New York in 1970 and that would continue to exist, though the number of New Yorkers working in the apparel industry had dropped significantly, by over 30 percent, between 1950 and 1965. By the 1960s it had become increasingly a low-wage enterprise and, if unionized, governed by contracts that were either ignored by employers or riddled with exceptions that allowed manufacturers to reduce wages and benefits to remain "competitive" with non-union Southern shops.[20] Increasingly, as we move toward the end of the century, such enterprises often employed large numbers of Asian immigrants, both legal and illegal, in dirty and dangerous conditions, often paying below minimum wage.[21]

The paucity of enterprises that might employ characters such as Joe Buck and Bree Daniels and pay them decent wages makes the sex trade all the more attractive. Viewed as a type of work, we can see prostitution as a service enterprise, but one that has little to do with the movement of capital, more like working in a hotel than selling securities. Joe and Bree assume that proximity to the centers of commerce that drive the nation's economy will provide opportunity. However, this view employs a perspective that was far more appropriate in the 1920s than in the late 1960s and 1970s. With the advent of modern systems of communication and transportation, the role of cities had shifted significantly and would continue to shift, from centers of all phases of productive enterprise to nexuses of communication that coordinate the far-flung components of such enterprises. New York in the late 1960s and in the 1970s was in a moment of transition, one caused by the shift from a regional and then national division of labor, to a global means of organization. Explains Diane Perrons of this transition,

While the highly paid control and strategic functions remained in major cities [such as New York, London, and Paris] generally in already industrialized countries, the day to day operations were located near to raw materials, labour supplies or markets . . . and correspondingly widely dispersed across the globe. This pattern tended to perpetuate uneven development, as what are perceived as routine activities provide only low wage employment.[22]

For Joe and Bree, if they cannot or will not service those who manipulate such enterprises, there is no work that will reward them sufficiently.

Dramatically, *Midnight Cowboy* shows us the relative place of marginal workers almost immediately. Many of *Midnight Cowboy's* focal scenes take place not in gentrifying West Greenwich Village, the locale of the Stonewall Inn, but in Times Square, where there is a kind of furtiveness and shame that attaches to the sex acts the film depicts. Indeed, this location will recur in a number of films, asserting its power to define at least an aspect of the city. The role of this location and its resonance as a place of relative urban blight becomes apparent in the first scenes after Joe arrives in New York. As he opens the blinds of his hotel room, our eyes follow his as he looks on the cityscape, which yields a vision of Times Square. What we see is not the glamour of Broadway, or the scale of skyscrapers; we instead see mostly billboards—for Haig and Haig Scotch, Canadian Club, Coca Cola; a low-slung movie marquee; and the chaos of traffic meandering almost without pattern. The color is drab, featuring washed-out pastels.[23]

In this film, Times Square becomes a key visual metaphor of deviance and decline. After this initial scene of Joe in his Times Square hotel, he ventures out walking, seeking the city of his imagination. He finds his way to Fifth Avenue, which is densely populated, but the camera pays particular attention to Joe's eyes assaying the various well-dressed and remote women. Joe ogles these women and at times maneuvers himself into an inappropriate proximity, which, if noted, is ignored (figure 2.3). As Joe continues his hunt, we see a city of opulence. The streets of midtown Manhattan framed by the physical structures of the tall buildings, accentuate Joe's smallness within the cityscape and his excessive closeness to the women he targets.

Eventually he approaches a well-dressed, middle-aged woman crossing Park Avenue with the question, as he leans toward her, "Ma'am, how can I get to the Statue of Liberty?" As he asks this, he and the woman are framed in a mid-range two-shot with Park Avenue in the background, shot in deep focus so that he is diminished within an urban canyon. The woman warily "reads" his innocence and is taken aback by it. Joe's leering, shot in close-up, reveals his intentions, to which she responds, "You ought to be ashamed of yourself," as she walks away. The New York that defines the beginnings of Joe's experience is indeed the one he envisioned when he migrated from Texas: wealthy women and men who lack his overt "masculinity." But in one sense he has over-estimated the cultural distance between New York and Big Springs. Such behavior would be as out of place in rural Texas as it is in Manhattan. But in another sense, he has failed to see how cultural distance is far more a matter of demeanor related to class than it is of proximity, and in this failure of analysis misunderstands how truly inaccessible this woman is, even as she stands beside him.

FIGURE 2.3 *Midnight Cowboy*: Joe cruises on Fifth Avenue.

Immediately after this Park Avenue encounter, Joe does "seduce" Cass, a woman walking her poodle who does not object to his breaching of the normative physical distance between them; but, as we see later in their interaction, it is she who is hustling him. When Joe asks her for money, she asks him if he thinks "she's some old slut on Forty-Second Street?" Cass's question not only results in Joe paying her; it also highlights what becomes obvious as the film goes on: people in this more prosperous region of New York are attractive, well dressed, and self-assured; the city is clean, the buildings are impressive. But Joe finds that he has no place in such environs and is consigned to be relatively close to these spaces, but in a distinct region, Times Square. And while Times Square in a previous era signaled the glamour and possibilities of the city, it is that implied contrast between then and now which animates the film's representation of decay.

The Times Square of *Midnight Cowboy* delineates a central feature of the city Joe Buck and Rico Rizzo inhabit, a different city from the one defined by shots of Fifth and Park Avenues. In the first scenes in Times Square we see Joe walk by the male prostitutes dressed like cowboys, while the street itself appears in a state of decay. The crowd, though less dense than that of Fifth Avenue, is also more racially mixed, and not as well dressed, with people apparently too young or too old to participate in the prosperity of the city. Though we see Times Square in any number of films from this era—*Taxi Driver*, *Mean Streets*, *Shaft*, *Fame*—in none is it pictured in quite this way, where its general seediness is so distinctly connected to its role as a marketplace for male and female prostitutes. Indeed, in *Fame* (1980) we see high school students traversing this area as it is in the process of being sanitized.

Soon, when he is locked out of his room, economic necessity drives Joe to become one of the "cowboys" he has seen in the movie arcades. It is after his initial assignation with an adolescent boy, one that nets him no money, that a long shot finds him pacing the middle of Forty-Second Street, dwarfed and entrapped by the street and its buildings, with the movie marquee advertising *The Twisted Sex* in the foreground (figure 2.4). As the films goes on, Joe's increasing comfort within the world defined by Forty-Second Street defines his "urbanization."[24]

Times Square becomes a synecdoche for New York at large and for cities in general, expressing urban decadence and physical decay. By 1960, Times Square's status as a center for runaways and hustlers was a matter of concern to many. Forty-Second Street had long been a gay cruising spot, but its tendency toward commerce and violence was a change. In 1966, with the Supreme Court's decision protecting pornographic expression, the Square saw its legitimate businesses give

FIGURE 2.4 *Midnight Cowboy*: Joe seeks tricks in Times Square.

way to pornographic bookstores, peep shows, and massage parlors. Again, these enterprises were a matter of expedience. The new businesses replaced older, less profitable ones.[25] The sex trade flourished as retail and manufacturing businesses fled.[26] Urban sociologist Robert P. McNamara in his study of the Times Square sex trade provides an evocative description of the place in the years just after Joe's time: "The 1970s and 1980s offered the area no relief from the deterioration and Times Square became a chaotic scene of drugs, sex, and crime. The Deuce and 8th Avenue became a no-man's land of the crack trade. Amid the denizens of porn palaces, con men, hookers, drug dealers, and muggers, Times Square's fall into disrepute reached its nadir."[27]

As the film goes on, Times Square becomes the city's center of commerce—not Wall Street or Fifth Avenue. In this film about the distinctions among contiguous spaces, and the redefinition of the concept of proximity itself, to be physically close to these more significant centers of trade may be relatively meaningless; to be linked by other more compelling means to those who live, work, and shop there—class, knowledge base, business interest—may be far more meaningful.

Joe's relative proximity to potential clients in New York emphasizes the distinctness of this urban locale, not only for its built features but also for the ways in which its interpersonal space is socially configured. This becomes all the more notable in the context of the film's composition, as these early scenes of New York quickly follow its opening in Texas. Whereas these New York shots emphasize vertically bound space that literally pushes strangers toward one another, the non-New York scenes emphasize the vast horizontal spaces of the Texas prairie, spaces in which a relative paucity of population both constrains and enables possibility. As we see Joe tormented by the social conformity of small-town life, we also encounter a place that potentially allows physical room for development, both personal and economic.

This view of New York is related to that which we find in other films that emphasize New York's suitability for unconventional and exceedingly casual sexual practices. Both *Panic in Needle Park* and *Taxi Driver* emphasize the claustrophobic contours of Manhattan. But their means of doing so is distinct. Both make the spaces of the city confining, but offer a view that does not emphasize the verticality of the city's landscape. Rather, both take place primarily in parts of the city with fewer large buildings than Joe Buck's Times Square or Bree's mid-town Manhattan. Perhaps this reduction in vertical scale is a result of *Panic* and *Taxi* taking place solely in Manhattan, offering little opportunity for contrasting the city's space and function with other places, and little opportunity for the redemption of their protagonists—though in *Taxi Driver*, Iris returns to her family in Pittsburgh.

Unlike these films, *Midnight Cowboy* and *Klute* highlight the distinction between rural and "urban" space, providing a visual means of emphasizing the city as a decaying environment. While the West evokes nostalgia, the economically retrenching city has no comparable allure. These films view the city in terms that contrast with their opening scenes. New York appears as declining and, conceivably for the working classes, a place without a future.

In his 1984 study *Uneven Development* and then later in *The New Urban Frontier* (1996), the geographer Neil Smith articulates the manner in which capitalist enterprise relies on and creates radically distinct geographies in order to sustain its dynamism. He finds that these geographies are a matter of the way in which the relative landscape of development is configured and reconfigured by powerful social and economic forces, a process that redefines the value of a given space, and thus its use; and then through its use, its subsequent revaluation. He explains that urban areas in the northeastern and midwestern United States in the 1960s and 1970s had become less interesting to investors because of their relatively high ground rent, a fact that made the possible increase of such rent unlikely. This inescapable cost also made production in such areas uncompetitive in a world where capital and goods were becoming increasingly fluid. Capital sought more dynamic spaces, such as the suburbs and exurbs, and later migrated to regions where costs were a fraction of those in developed regions. But consequently, as New York, and Manhattan in particular, became a deindustrialized area, it also opened up its environs for types of use and development that resituated it as a financial center with a far-flung system of production.

Smith shows how the use value of space is not a matter of its natural geography; rather, he explains that all space is relational and therefore its relative value a matter of human volition based on rational assumptions of how it may be configured to yield profit. Technology has altered both the meaning of space and the meaning of distance, creating new equations for the profitable production and movement of goods. And indeed, both films play with representations of time and space in order to destabilize these categories and show the power of humans to redefine such concepts. Such re-elaborations of the time-space relationship have always been a part of motion pictures, as they are indeed part of the shifting meaning of each term in a Fordist world. Indeed, the moving image symbolizes the relative human mastery of time and space, as they offer images of other places and other times that that seem immediate to the viewer. Film technology, like the technology that regularizes time, has the power to show how humans can order time into consistent and regular intervals. But these later twentieth-century films alter that emphasis to some degree, as they suggest how the human manipulation of time and space may define those entities variably, and that such definitions may be further indexes of the ways in which a post-Fordist system of production renders some individuals extraneous. Thus for Joe and for Bree, space is often far greater and time more languid that it is for those engaged in the dynamism of defining and managing the emerging post-Fordist economy.

Joe rides on the bus to New York through a range of distinct physical spaces; initially these are rural, and then more populated. We see Joe sitting behind the driver as an arid Southwestern landscape appears out of the bus's window; then the world changes at an irregular rhythm. He arrives in Dallas relatively slowly, and then he is soon amid neon lights and heavy industry, and then within reach of New York radio. These irregular connections between time and space reveal his relative social place. What is for him a few days on the bus, for an executive is a few hours on a plane, or split seconds on the phone. Since Joe is outside of the vanguard of his economic moment, he has no vocabulary for seeing how technology has altered the relative relationship between New York and Big Springs, so assumes that his Westernness will be a scarce and viable commodity in the New York sex market. Joe's constant "partner" on his bus ride is his transistor radio, which could provide him with a more contemporary view of relative time and space, as well as modern commerce. It could perhaps tell him of the homogenization of the nation and the death of regionalism. Perhaps Joe would have been more successful if he saw sex as a feeling rather than an act. Then he would have perhaps imagined himself into the developing information industries, writing ads for mass media that "sell sex." But such an analytical frame would elevate him into the vanguard class of the postindustrial world, a perch that he is not destined to inhabit. Thus the radio and subsequently the television remain only sources of entertainment, and Joe remains a bodily worker.[28]

In *Klute*, Tuscarora's connection to New York is greater than that of Big Springs because of proximity, a fact well represented in the films. In John Klute's case, New York is easily reached and part of the world of the Tuscarorans. New York is where Cable and Gruneman go for work, in order to engage in the business activities of the city; but they also engage New York as a place where one's transgressive self may partake of the various opportunities available. In their world of higher echelon executives, New York is a physical center of both information exchange and of vice. The conjoining of these activities is very much a matter of the city in transition, as both activities burgeoned as industrial production subsided. And while New York may seem quite close to Gruneman and Cable, who can travel by helicopter or corporate jet, this proximity is further asserted by Klute's nontrip to New York. He simply knocks on Bree's door, with no representation of his having traversed any distance ever appearing on screen.[29]

The class implications of such a model of trade also extend to a range of social interactions; for example, in the matter of housing this issue of relative proximity and closeness becomes a matter of class rather than of geography: a resident of Manhattan may live only a mile or so from an East Harlem housing project and possess a town house with a value of several million dollars. But that individual may have more contact with an estate owner from New Jersey or Westchester County than a person living in those housing projects. Each of these films pictures a neighborhood on the verge of substantial gentrification, poised between desolation and the rebuilding and habitation of those areas by a largely white, substantially middle-class group of "urban pioneers," individuals who represent the vanguard of the emerging new economy of the late 1980s and 1990s.[30] Indeed, the same type of neighborhoods are featured in *Taxi Driver* (Second Avenue and 12th Street) and in *Panic in Needle Park* (the Upper West Side).[31] For gentrifiers, proximity *does* matter, as it brings their residences into an orbit of other property owners with whom they share elements of upbringing, class, and race, even if they are not quite in their league in matters of wealth.

In *Midnight Cowboy*, Joe and Rico Rizzo squat in a condemned tenement on the Lower East Side. As the building next door undergoes demolition, Joe and Rizzo walk by an ever-growing pile of rubble to enter their squat. This debris suggests that Rico's own residence will soon be facing the same fate, further providing a sense of urgency to his desire to move to Florida (figure 2.5). In broader terms, such demolition signifies the beginnings of redevelopment, as the expense of razing one structure is only justifiable when there is some hope that the land on which that derelict structure stood has some substantial worth as a site for redevelopment. Demolition illustrates the point at which values have hit bottom and investors see the prospect of a market for new construction; in effect, in the near future Joe and Rizzo would be displaced by the forces of gentrification. Indeed, such a process was well at work to the west of their hovel, as West Greenwich Village was beginning to make the transition, a change that would take place over the next decade or so, from counterculture center to a district of increasing affluence.[32]

Not incidentally, this glimpse of a gentrifying city also provides one of its culminating scenes. Joe and Rico, while sitting in a coffee shop, are given a flyer by two "characters," as Rico calls them, inviting them to a party. The area of the city where this event takes place is still in the rudiments of redevelopment, but the fact that middle-class artists have discovered the under-utilized spaces of the city represents an early phase on gentrification. This gathering of "freaks" signifies an alternative space for Joe and Rico to ply their wares, a market that is neither Times Square nor Park Avenue. A woman, who, despite her association with these artists has a corporate veneer, buys Joe's services. Though Joe experiences an initial

FIGURE 2.5 *Midnight Cowboy*: Ratso's squat faces demolition.

inability to perform, he seems to have found his market and is possibly on the road
to success in his chosen profession. The party and this client represent the emergence of urban "pioneers," revealing that the bohemian bourgeoisie is finding its
way to the margins of Manhattan. Paradoxically, however, though this migration
may be good for commerce, it seems possible that soon Joe and Rico will have no
place to live. Explains Neil Smith in his discussion of the role of the art industry in
the gentrification of the Lower East Side during the 1980s, "For the real estate
industry, art tames the neighborhood, refracting back a mock pretense of exotic
but benign danger. It depicted the East Village as rising from low life to highbrow.
Art donates a salable neighborhood 'personality,' packaged the area as a real estate
commodity and established demand."[33] Joe benefits from his lack of sophistica-
tion, becoming part of the novelty of the gentrifying city. However, as development burgeons, it is likely that he will himself become increasingly marginalized.

Bree Daniels and John Klute live in somewhat better circumstances, and their
danger is not so much a matter of location as the fact that Bree is being stalked.
Nevertheless, her Hell's Kitchen apartment (441 W. 43rd St.) consists of one large
room and is often shot through a dingy skylight. The streets are dirty, as is the entryway and stairway to her building. Klute sleeps in the basement of this structure, in

a cell-like room that has no window and no furniture but a cot. Such relative squalor situates the declining city in a way that brings attention to the historical fact that by the late 1960s and early 1970s, there had been broad disinvestment in the city's housing stock, an economic condition that is also connected to the decline of the middle class as a presence in Manhattan. Unlike the Lower East Side, which was about to become highly desirable as a site for gentrification, this location's proximity to the decay of Times Square—including the proliferation of the sex trade in that area—would depress the demand for housing in this neighborhood. It would also not attract speculators in the way that the Lower East Side did for at least the next few decades.[34]

The geographic focus of each of these films locates the protagonists' places of residence contiguous to a region that was historically defined by its ethnic and/or sexual characteristics. Chad Heap, in his insightful study *Slumming: Sexual and Racial Encounters in American Nightlife, 1885–1940*, tells of the reorganization of the city in the late nineteenth and early twentieth centuries into districts largely defined by class and to some degree by ethnicity. Such a pattern allowed for the practice of "slumming," when those of greater means would venture into a district that was defined by its exoticism and partake of its cultural delights. Often, according to Heap, such ventures would be of a sexual nature. In New York, Greenwich Village, the region directly west of Ratso's flop, would be a site for gay men and women to explore. Other areas of sexual assignation in the early twentieth century included not only Times Square but also the area to the south and west, called the Tenderloin district, the area directly to the south of Bree's apartment. It is indeed intriguing that these films show the historical impact of this earlier districting, revealing how slums are often defined by their explicit displays of sexual commerce, and that in an economically beleaguered city, those districts may spread. They also suggest how such commerce may become increasingly invisible through urban renewal, increased policing, and the push for housing at the urban core created by the forces of gentrification.[35]

While there were any number of local policies—the ineffectiveness and corruption of the police, tax policies, and so on—that exacerbated New York's decline and the sense of its decline, a broader view situates it within a changing world system of exchange.[36] The chronology represented in the films is one defined by economic historians as the time of transition between the postwar economic system elaborated from 1944 to 1946 and the less encumbered routing of capital that marked the 1990s, the period in which multinational corporations dominated a far-flung global economy. The postwar system was defined by the Bretton Woods treaty, which pegged international exchange rates, and established the International Monetary Fund and the World Bank. By the late 1960s, with the United

States no longer the clear center of world economic activity, the desirable effects (from the United States' view) of the Bretton Woods system were in the process of waning. Domestic spending as a result of the ongoing war in Vietnam and the Great Society programs, and competition from Japan and Germany in particular, created deficits that were draining the United States of its gold reserves and driving the economy into recession.[37] The Bretton Woods era and the later globalized system are related but marked as distinct by the U.S. government's renunciation of the gold standard in 1971, which soon resulted in national currencies being allowed to float on the international market, creating fluidity in capital circulation and, as a result, in investment and production.[38]

The role of the United States in the production of manufactured goods shifted gradually and eventually became a national phenomenon. But its first symptoms occurred in the cities of the Northeast, both large and small—New York, Boston, Philadelphia; Springfield, Mass.; Hartford, Buffalo, and Newark, as these urban locations found their manufacturing base eroding during the 1940s and 1950s. It next became apparent in the centers of heavy industry in the Midwest: Detroit, Cleveland, and Pittsburgh, as the production of steel and automobiles declined precipitously in the 1960s and 1970s. The process we see in motion is that of capital seeking out new venues for cheap production, leaving behind the unions of an earlier era, as well as a range of other infrastructural costs.[39]

In the late 1960s, New York City was undergoing substantial capital flight. In these films we see the impact of such flight in the deterioration of the built environment and the paucity of available work. Though each of these characters experiences different financial results from the sex business, both recognize that the prospects for reasonable gain outside of that trade are limited and are in the area of service or entertainment. In a moment of despair and with his money running out, Joe momentarily considers the prospect of working as a dishwasher, a job he had in Big Springs, but chooses not to. Bree, on the other hand, actively seeks to work as an actress but is never hired. Both films locate the alternative to the sex trade outside New York, where one may assume a different position in the world of social and economic relations.[40] In more concrete terms, both of these films concern themselves with how individuals who are on the lower end of the economic scale make a living. For those in this class, New York becomes an ensnaring location, limiting the prospects of leaving.

Housing patterns show that any number of residents, primarily those of the waning middle class, were moving to non-New York environs. Not surprisingly, many of those leaving had formerly been employed in relatively lucrative industrial-sector, primarily union jobs. As the U.S. economy, and particularly its urban economy, in the early 1970s and 1980s, shifted away from such activities, cities in the Northeast gradually remade themselves, with varying results, as centers of a new economy. In New York, this change was dramatic. John Mollenkopf and Manuel Castells tell us, "The shift toward corporate, nonprofit, and public services produced important changes in the city's labor market at a time when racial succession and immigration were simultaneously reshaping the city's population and labor force." The decline of good-paying work in the production sector accelerated a trend that saw white ethnic families leave the city in large numbers during the late 1950s and 1960s, to be replaced by new immigrants, female-headed households, and, eventually white male professionals. Mollenkopf and Castells go on to elaborate,

> New York has thus been transformed from a relatively well-off, white and blue-collar city into a more economically divided multiracial white-collar city. These transformations had a strong impact on space and place. The magnificence of the Manhattan central business and shopping district and the resurgence of luxury residential areas may be juxtaposed with the massive decay of the city's public facilities and poor neighborhoods.[41]

These films define the beginning of this process in their visual terms, dwelling on the decline of public space, showing clear distinctions between regions of the city, and defining who belongs to which sector.

In *Klute*, Bree guides Klute through a subterranean city defined by the sex trade. Such a tour further confirms the definition of New York as sexually corrupt. This world updates images of various films noir from the late 1940s and 1950s, as this enterprise largely defines the city, much as nefarious deeds in politics and business defined the city in Robert Rossen's *Body and Soul* (1947), Abraham Polonsky's *Force of Evil* (1948), and Jules Dassin's *Naked City* (1948).[42] These noir conventions include a voice-over narrator, severe high- and low-angle shots, and high-key lighting. Bree introduces Klute to her amoral former pimp, a madam who tells of a man from Grosse Point who likes to scrub her bathtub (Mr. Clean), and a storefront porn theater filled with businessmen on their lunch break. But all of these encounters take place in only private or quasi-public space—the pimp's over-decorated apartment, the madam's rooftop patio, and a badly lighted storefront. We never see sex workers on the street, nor are there many street scenes at all. Where Joe inhabits the afflicted city, the various characters of low morality that define *Klute* afflict the city, so that interior space becomes a place for deviance. Though Klute comes to New York because of his regard for the missing person, his attachment to Bree draws him into the ever-present world of drugs and prostitution. This world of immorality is the shadow of a more conventional life that we cannot quite see. And, as Bree points out, that conventionality merely hides a deeper perversion.

Klute's vision of New York's interiors reveals an afflicted city, virtually the opposite of the vibrant urban community Jane Jacobs had lauded in 1961.[43] Where Jacobs saw the commercial life of the street as the key to urban vitality and safety, *Klute* depicts a city where vice has moved indoors because the life that exists on the street is too squalid and violent. The exterior shots of New York feature almost no glamour; the film primarily depicts New York as a place where voyeurs strain to see the sordid acts that take place beyond its doors and windows, an emphasis that is an explicit formal strategy. It is no accident that streetwalkers, the lower rung of prostitutes, are those who are murdered.

And though Bree does consort with some element of prosperous New Yorkers, she only fleetingly encounters such people. As in *Midnight Cowboy*, *Klute*'s city is a place where those who do not prosper are all but shut out of the world of the successful. Such a vision signals something of a departure. Historically U.S. cities had been, since the onset of industrialization in the nineteenth century, and particularly with its acceleration after the Civil War, both the symbol and the engine of prosperity. This is not to say that there was not a tradition of anti-urbanism within U.S. culture. But coexisting with that tradition was the fact of the city's economic dynamism. This fact resulted in the demographic shift of an overwhelming majority of the U.S. population to cities. By 1970, approximately 74 percent of the nation's population was living in urban areas.[44] Cities, partially as a result of the pressures that a rising population put on real estate, became places where people of various classes lived in relative proximity to one another.[45] In the 1970s and 1980s, with New York, and Manhattan in particular, becoming increasingly a two-tiered economic system, this was less true. Adrienne Winghoff-Heritier notes the middle-class flight in the period around 1980:

> For most households with an annual income around $40,000 life in Manhattan had become too expensive. And for social and racial reasons, it no longer seems acceptable in many parts of Brooklyn and the Bronx. As a result, many middle-class New Yorkers withdrew to the suburbs. . . .
> While the white and (to some extent the black middle class) can escape expensive or deteriorated living conditions in the inner City, the poor are the prisoners of the city, unable to leave it behind for a more pleasant life in the suburbs.[46]

These films of Manhattan depict this increasing segregation by class.[47] And as a result of the visual styles of the era and the ways in which films were more technologically able to traverse the city spaces, New York is not merely a backdrop to this sordidness but is also an active participant.

Such segregation, viewed within the context of world trade, shows that by the late 1960s the postwar system of economic organization among the United States and its allies was under duress. Various economic historians place the center of this disruption between 1965 and 1973—a time, as Robert Brenner notes, when formerly omnipotent U.S. producers were experiencing reduced rates of return on investment, with profit falling by a rate of 43.5 percent.[48]

In such an economic environment, relatively unskilled younger workers like Bree and Joe Buck had few legitimate employment opportunities that would promise significant economic return. They resituate sex as a commodity that speaks to that condition. In such a view, the commodification of sex becomes a symptom of the catastrophic success of consumer capitalism in having turned all human activity into a transaction of goods. *Midnight Cowboy* and *Klute* help to define a moment of transition, a time between the decline of the city that burgeoned with industrialization in the late nineteenth and early twentieth centuries and a certain type of gentrified rebirth. Fittingly, they show the sex business as primarily a buyer's market. Sex work becomes like any other kind of unskilled labor—devalued by its oversupply.

The New York of these films, in effect, mirrors the economic situation found in developing countries where traditional units of economic self-sufficiency—families, clans, and villages—are being eroded by market systems of exchange. In such a condition, a significant number of women who migrate to the city work as prostitutes who serve relatively prosperous males of their own nationalities, and at times foreign visitors—some of whom travel to that locale primarily to partake in the sex trade.[49] Like these women, Joe migrates from an underdeveloped locale in order to partake of a relatively marginal existence within a more developed place; and Bree's clients, like those of some number of those women in developing locales, tend to be visiting businessmen. As the city situates our protagonists as workers in a rapidly changing economy, one that is beginning to become involved in far-flung systems of trade, we can project that the sex trade itself is about to become an increasingly global industry in the 1990s, providing the motivation for international migration, as women move, or are forcibly moved, to cities in nations with higher standards of living.[50] What they often find is a system of virtual or actual slavery and a permanent place on the social margins.[51] And despite the vicissitudes of such work, it is possible that in the later part of the century both Joe and Bree would find themselves under further economic duress as sex workers from outside the United States find their way to New York.

Finally, these films show us the degree to which economic success is a matter of adapting to the ethos of the postmodern city. New York is too unpredictable for Bree to remain safe and too limited in opportunity for her, or Joe, to find sufficiently remunerative work. The cautionary tale of her life spills over as a lesson for Joe: the sex trade is no way to make a living.

THE ESCAPE FROM NEW YORK

Neither film resolves its plot in New York: each ends with its couple leaving New York in search of a better life. In both films this out-migration suggests to us that life in New York can never be anything but arduous and perverse. The world beyond is depicted elliptically, but the viewer is led to believe that it is a land of the possible. In *Midnight Cowboy*, Florida, Joe and Rico's destination, is potentially the anti-New York; and in *Klute*, the joining of Klute and Bree as a conventional couple can only take place in the somewhere beyond the city, as New York becomes the geographic barrier to "normal" American life.

Midnight Cowboy offers the more explicit resolution. Joe and Rizzo take the bus to Florida, a locale that Rico repeatedly asserts will deliver him from his physical infirmities and the squalor of his life. In his final days in New York, Rico seems literally to succumb to his environment, as he becomes more disheveled and obviously febrile. Says Rizzo in close-up so that we can see the fear on his face: "I can't walk. Do you know what they do to people who can't walk?" Such a sentiment grows from a vision of urban life as pitiless, and both men resolve to leave as quickly as possible.

Their need to leave the city sends Joe back to Forty-Second Street. As Joe sees the necessity of removing Rico from New York, he becomes a far more effective economic being, changing from a benign hustler to a cold-blooded thief and assailant, entrapping a middle-aged man whom he beats and robs. Joe has apparently learned how to make money as a hustler, casually allowing himself to be picked up at an arcade. The camera shows us his craftiness through two-shots of him and his john, named Townie, as they proceed to Townie's hotel.

Once they enter the room, the two men are shot in a sequence of close-ups. When they enter the same frame, Joe has become a menacing presence looming over his victim. In response to Townie's offer of ten dollars for him to leave, Joe informs him that "it's not enough," empties his wallet and beats him bloody. The close-ups of Joe striking Townie with a telephone capture his face contorted by rage; low-angle shots show his presence enlarged. This act of attaining money defines him as having mastered the ways of the city, but it has transformed him. It is through this culminating act of urban desperation that Joe recognizes not only the necessity of taking Rico away, but also of getting away himself. This transformation of Joe confirms the economic lesson: in a world defined by the absence of amenities, one must get money at any cost—or migrate to a different world.

As the bus traverses the interstate, the skies brighten and the world becomes greener. Upon leaving they take on new personas, as Ratso asserts that he should be referred to only as Rico, since that was the reason to leave, to start anew. When they reach the Florida border, Joe casts off his cowboy clothes and declares his wish, in a close-up, to "get some sort of job. Cause hell, I ain't no kind of hustler. There must be an easier way to make a living than that." As he declares his intention to get outdoor work, the camera cuts to a two-shot of Rizzo and Joe, revealing that Rizzo has died. The film ends as the bus pulls into Miami and Joe, wearing his pastel shirt and chinos, blends into a milling crowd. Though it is difficult to picture Joe as a success story, it is clear from the moment the bus crosses into Florida— where he is greeted by the freckled and friendly young waitress at the coffee counter, who wishes him well—that he has entered a less hostile world.

Klute offers a slightly more ambiguous judgment of the New York effect. Bree sees her tormenter killed, as Klute saves her by knocking Cable through a window. While this resolves the question of who is stalking Bree and what has happened to Gruneman, it does not resolve the problem that is Bree's life. The scene cuts to a two-shot before the fireplace in Bree's apartment, with Bree on the floor and Klute in a chair, her head in his hands, asserting both domesticity and submission (figure 2.6). We then see her apartment, emptied of furniture, with Klute distant in a long shot and off-center, as the Bree's voice-over tells her therapist, "Whatever is in store for me, it's not going to be setting up housekeeping in Tuscarora." Bree enters the scene and, as she leaves, Klute follows her, both with suitcases in their

FIGURE 2.6 *Klute*: Klute and Bree prepare to leave New York.

hands as the voice-over tells the therapist, "I have no idea what's going to happen. I just can't stay in the city."

The United States that exists outside of the boundaries of New York offers at least hope. As our protagonists reach out to the world of another America, their actions suggest a cultural resolution to the film's economic problems. Both films leave us to assume that the problems of making a living may be resolved in the world beyond New York; that Joe in his "Average Joe" clothes might live gainfully and productively in south Florida; that Bree, with her straight-John husband will leave New York, and perhaps her neuroses, behind and set up housekeeping in Pennsylvania. Such a perspective blends well with the anti-urban rhetoric of the day, where structural problems of the national economy were cast politically as moral problems of urban behavior. Such anti-urban rhetoric only exacerbated existing economic trends. Capital and population flight were a matter of the general movement toward an increasingly globalized economy, but one that was made more palatable by the general sense that cities like New York, as depicted in these films and elsewhere, were not only in a state of chaos but that they were in, but not really of, America.

3

Longing for the Return of Vito Corleone

RACE, PLACE, AND THE ETHNIC CITY IN *THE GODFATHER*,

PARTS I AND II (1972 AND 1974), AND *MEAN STREETS* (1973)

This chapter focuses on a group of films from the early part of the 1970s that are concerned explicitly with issues of ethnicity and, more implicitly, with race: *The Godfather*, parts I and II (1972 and 1974), and *Mean Streets* (1973). Arguably, these director-driven productions were possible because of the shift in Hollywood's mode of production during the late 1960s, a shift that fostered a new aesthetic, one that typically highlighted a realist disposition featuring location shoots, non-heroic characters, and ethnic actors who seemed to fit their urban environs. Through these films, all important examples of the "New Hollywood" period of U.S. film production, we are afforded a perspective on how definitions of "race" and "ethnicity" changed in intriguing ways during the late 1960s and 1970s, and how those definitions are enlarged and rearticulated in Hollywood films that explore their resonance within the contours of a specific urban space.

   In these films Francis Coppola and Martin Scorsese, Italian American grandsons of immigrants who were raised in New York City and its suburbs, articulate the key cultural terms "race" and "ethnicity," words that have significant implications for the historical redefinition of New York City and of cities in general, as they enable a nostalgic view of the city of the past and a complementary view of contemporary urban decay.[1] By asserting the "whiteness" of Italian Americans and associating that group with the cultural and economic benefits that accompany such a definition, these films rearticulate broad assumptions of New York's good old days, the days prior to a racialized vision of decline. In dwelling on this particular "national" group and its symbolic New York "homeland," these films participate in the burgeoning discourse of "ethnicity" as it develops in the 1970s, a discourse with significant implications for national conceptions of urban environments and, ultimately, of international trade and migration.[2]

Symptomatic of the contemporary romance of ethnicity and preceding the release of these three films, Mario Puzo's novel *The Godfather*, published in March of 1969, became an event in itself, as it eventually sold over 12 million copies worldwide. Puzo's novel focuses on the community basis of organized crime, showing the relative humanity of Vito Corleone, a Sicilian immigrant who becomes a success in the United States. The film rights to the novel were soon sold for over $400,000 dollars, at that time a record amount, and both *Godfather* movies were popular and critical successes. By finding visual terms that captured the novel's conception of a world that had passed, *The Godfather* and its sequel not only built on a pre-sold title: they also distilled its focus and aligned it with important cultural trends. Similarly, *Mean Streets*, a much smaller film, eventually received wide recognition and praise, while garnering some smaller awards.[3]

By the mid-1960s, the definition of "ethnicity" was in the process of changing, as national groups that had formed the core of immigrants coming to the United States from 1880 to 1924 were in the process of reaching a level of social mobility that altered residential patterns, as well as cultural behaviors and identifications. Historian of U.S. ethnic groups Richard Alba shows that by the late 1960s the conditions of life for Italians, Jews, Greeks, and others who had largely come to the United States around the turn of the century had changed dramatically, with the biggest shift occurring in the period after World War II, the moment that Francis Coppola employs as the beginning of the first *Godfather* film. During the two decades after the war, these groups gradually achieved relative social parity with native-born whites of all national backgrounds in income and education; further, statistics show that after 1945, these "white ethnics" were likely to marry outside of their discrete group and to live among those who did not share their national background.[4] Such social mobility and assimilation would seem to conform to the views of the important group of sociologists and historians prior to the 1960s, such as Robert Park, Oscar Handlin, Will Herberg, and later, Arthur Schlesinger and Stephen Thernstrom, who wrote of "ethnic" affiliations becoming less significant for immigrant groups over time, as all such groups eventually enter "American" society.[5] But the actual picture is far more complex. Explains Alba,

Whatever the cause, the celebration of ethnicity and the perception of the stubbornness of ethnic difference have come to occupy a place of honor. . . . Accompanying these surface changes is a belief among scholars and the lay public, that ethnic differences form a possibly permanent substructure, if not the ultimate bedrock of American society. During the 1960s and 70s this belief took on an increasingly strong form. (2)

Alba goes on to summarize his findings that among those of European ancestry (non-Hispanic whites), ethnicity became an important cultural marker just at the moment when it ceased to organize social life to the degree it had earlier in the century. He defines that role as one of self-identification and voluntary practice, activities that may become definitional for the individual and a cohort of the like-minded, what he calls "the subjective orientation toward ethnic origins" (20). Indeed, this subjective orientation included the fetishization of the notion of ethnicity, a cultural concept with little historical salience and only a very brief history at that.[6]

Matthew Jacobson calls the "ethnic revival of the 1970s . . . a complex affair combining ideological strands of anti-modernism, anti-elitism, cultural conservatism and articulated class-based grievances."[7] Jacobson goes on to trace the ways in which this vision of ethnicity borrowed aspects of the rhetoric of the 1960s Civil Rights movement, even as such views often included racist elements and easily morphed in the "politics of resentment" in the 1970s and the coalescing of white ethnic "Reagan Democrats" in the 1980s. It is at least arguable that the concept of ethnicity originated around the end of World War II and took hold of the U.S. cultural imagination only in the years around the publication of Puzo's novel and the production of these films.

Certainly the concept of ethnicity gained traction as a means of separating those "whites" from more stigmatized people of African descent. Such distinctions have their basis in the legalisms of the eighteenth and nineteenth centuries that defined racial categories as a means of determining to whom racially restrictive statutes applied. Indeed, as early as 1790 the laws of naturalization were articulated as pertaining to "free, white persons." But the vexing question of who could be racially excluded by any number of statutes, from Jim Crow laws that segregated public places and conveyances to laws determining who could vote in the pre-Civil War north, has been a matter of tortured judicial reasoning for virtually the entire history of the United States. With the immigration of darker-skinned Jews and Southern Europeans, the courts in the 1920s were faced with the task of once again defining the applicability of the 1790 act. Eventually, with much tormented logic, statutory law settled for the time being on the equation between "European-ness" and whiteness, thus including the groups of these new immigrants, and excluding those from Asia and Africa.[8] This distinction would have significant conceptual and economic impact over the next decades and certainly forms an aspect of the backdrop for the ethnic nostalgia movement of the 1960s, 1970s, and beyond.

And while the concept of ethnicity gained currency in the years around the end of World War II, it further became a means of not only identifying certain groups but also of defining them.[9] Indeed, the particular "groups" who form the core of a typical ethnic subdivision of population had little coherence prior to their immigration to places outside of Europe. In the United States, Jews became classified as such, though in Europe they were a dispersed population that practiced significant variations of worship, spoke an amalgam of languages, ate different foods, and followed all variations of social custom. In the United States they became Jewish Americans, a somewhat coherent entity, a view that elided the distinctions among those from the rural lands of the upper Baltic and those who came from Venice or Budapest. Similarly, Sicilians, Neapolitans, Milanese, all became Italians, even though Italian nationalism in the late nineteenth century was a concept very much in the making, and language, custom, food, and so on, varied widely. As such, the efficacy of these terms largely emanates from the immigrant experience. Yet U.S. practice and affiliation at least since the 1960s has allowed for the reification of those origins, making them the apparent basis for group identity, for culture.

These films explicitly operate in the register of "ethnic nostalgia"; that is, they replicate the longing for a lost community that never quite existed. And that longing may become powerful enough to trigger actions that actually produce group identity at the moment when the imaginary terms of that identity are clearly altered.[10] In that desire for a condition that is at once unattainable and historically unavailable, this sentiment is projected onto a place, a transference that has the power of providing this longing with the status of the material, the concrete, since such an association provides geographic definition and thus apparent solidity to this notion of cultural coherence. In this projection of longing onto a specific space, this feeling entraps that location in a perpetual moment; in effect, these films offer ethnic nostalgia as a means of reifying a particular time by elevating a distinctive vision of a certain space.

These films project the stopping of time onto their bracketing of space. As many critics have pointed out, *The Godfather* films are expressly about business—a word that is used with notable frequency in both films—and its role in creating discontent. The recurring lament of the films distinguishes between the violence that must be done in the interest of profit, and the personal feelings that make such action regrettable. An example of this is when Tessio, one of the Godfather's chief lieutenants, sends a message to Michael Corleone, the heir to the family throne, when the under-boss recognizes that he will be executed. In a very tight two-shot with Tom Hagen, expressing affiliation as their faces register regret, he laments: "Tell Mike it was business. I always liked him." This is followed by his request in close up, "Tom, can you get me off the hook, for old time's sake." To which Tom replies in another tightly composed two-shot: "Can't do it Sallie," again with regret and the affection that the use of the more intimate form of his name implies.

But such a critique should not be considered a broader critique of capitalism.[11] Rather, it more properly constitutes a criticism of a certain *phase* of capitalism and the valorization of another. And even as these films fondly recall a space and a mode of production, they show the inevitable march of more and more dynamic and extensive systems of exchange. In effect, they suggest that the future impact of the exponential growth of capital will be to shrink of the world and diminish the discrete neighborhood. As they look back fondly on a previous moment of community coalescence and of a related scale of commerce, they also acknowledge, through their nostalgia, the impossibility of return and the inevitability of a more impersonal, and ultimately global, system of trade.

Where immigration historians and sociologists of the 1950s and early 1960s surmised that groups over time would become less visible entities within the U.S. landscape, the Civil Rights movement had the secondary impact of producing a kind of ethnocentrism that defined the protobiological terms of group identity constitutive of an individual's connection to a "culture." And although none of these films asserts in any significant way an argument for the distinctness of Italian blood, they do offer a vision of culture that makes assimilation all but impossible, and therefore foolish as a group aspiration. In idealizing the bonds of immigrant community life, these films also elevate the pattern of residential housing that enabled such cohesion: the ethnically segregated urban neighborhood. In some ways Puzo's novel and Coppola's film stand as elegies to a passed era of Italian American distinctness as a community, as they look back on an earlier period of group cultural and geographic coherence; but these elegies are quite contemporary and even forward looking in their capitulation of ethnicity. By the 1970s, Italian American suburbanization was a notable phenomenon.[12]

For Italian Americans, and indeed for all of the major immigrant groups from the turn-of-the-century migration—Jews, Greeks, Poles, and so on—the 1960s and 1970s marked the end of an era, a terminus characterized by the shifting of urban populations. Where cities from the turn of the century to the 1950s and early 1960s had been home to ethnic whites, by the end of that decade and beyond, cities became predominantly African American, Hispanic, and Asian. In U.S. cities, the new immigrants and African Americans had replaced the older groups. There are any numbers of reasons for this shift: local, regional, and global. Locally, the ongoing decline of a significant number of jobs that allowed a middle-class life style made living in New York a less compelling priority than it had been in earlier decades. Further, the development of a federal highway system and relatively inexpensive home loans through the FHA or the VA provided a subsidy for suburbanization during the postwar period. And as the white ethnic middle class vacated New York City, the property they left behind declined relatively in value—at least for the short term—and often became the residences of those who were moving to the United States from the Caribbean, Central and South America, or Asia, an immigration that was enabled by the passing of the Hart-Celler Immigration Act of 1965, which shifted the basis of immigration from national origins to occupational status, as well as creating initiatives for reuniting families. In New York, this change in policy had a dramatic impact. After immigration was restricted by the Johnson-Reed Act of 1924, the number of foreign-born New Yorkers declined until 1970. In the 1920s, about one-third of New York's residents were from outside of the United States. By 1970 that number stood at 18 percent. In the 1970s and 1980s, close to 2 million foreign-born people came to reside in New York. By the 1990s, a third of New York's residents were foreign born.[13] Needless to say, this change in population dramatically altered the city over time, and it is no accident that ethnic nostalgia for the "other" New York becomes visible in the late 1960s and 1970s.

As a number of demographers have pointed out, by the 1970s the larger cities of the Midwest and Northeast had dramatically changed their racial makeup as a result of migration from within the United States. This movement of African Americans had occurred in phases after the Civil War, but accelerated in the period from the end of World War II to the 1960s. By the early 1960s, African Americans were more urbanized than whites. The settlement patterns of African Americans were constrained, however, by historical blocks to residential dispersal and access to capital to buy homes. As a result, African Americans found themselves stuck in the decaying inner cities with little promise of developing the economic means of transforming those locales. Further, the rapid decline of urban manufacturing from the 1960s on effectively reduced African American access to jobs that might have led to a rise in socioeconomic status. Thus, the shift of industrial production from cities to suburbs to exurbs to underdeveloped locations abroad resulted in an entrenched African American presence in the declining U.S. inner cities.[14]

The three films focus on Italian Americans, and were all released between 1972 and 1974. In important ways these films employ New York as a central location and a key metaphor for the changing nature of U.S. cities, associating their decline to the numerical decline of "white" residents. And indeed, it is the very "whiteness" of these Italian Americans that enables their upward mobility and dispersal, a historical fact that has significant implications for both the future of New York and for the future of those who are left in the city.

These films are far from isolated as popular expressions of ethnic distinctiveness focusing on both older immigrant groups and a kind of nostalgia. They constitute just one element—but a vital definitional one—of a cycle of films from the 1970s that focus lovingly on Jewish and Italian communities in New York City. Their emphasis typically dwells on the past to show it as a superior moment in group and city life; or, they are set in the present to show how the erosion of community has created a cultural loss for the group and the broader environment. Indeed, the far less popular but significant *Hester Street* (1975) and *The Prisoner of Second Avenue* (1975) focus on the Jewish experience of New York, with one film set in the past and one set in the present. Fittingly, *The Prisoner* is a comedic treatment of contemporary decline and the demise of neighborhoods defined by ethnic communities. The *Lords of Flatbush* (1974) and *Saturday Night Fever* (1977) provide yet another take on Italian American ethnic communities of the present, but focused on Brooklyn. And the markers of Jewish ethnicity, while not featured, are important textual elements in any of the films by Woody Allen, as is Italianness in the films of Martin Scorsese, even when such films are not specifically about community, such as *Annie Hall* as well as *New York, New York*, and others. Such a concentration on the terms of white ethnic life with a particular focus on its now changing terms suggests that feature films were responsive to the popular phenomenon of ethnic longing.

These three films of Italian Americans show the ways in which that ethnic group defines New York. Fittingly, one is set in the past (*The Godfather*); one is set in the present (*Mean Streets*); and one is set in both the more distant past and the less contemporary present (*The Godfather Part II*). Not incidentally, all three focus on crime and criminality, but certain types of crime, particularly those that can be defined as having deep community roots—illegal gambling, the usurious loaning of money, prostitution—and as relatively benign. They are contrasted with the more nefarious activity of drug importing and sales, a practice associated with, as one Don puts it in *The Godfather*, "the darker peoples, the colored." Such a distinction further divides the old city and the contemporary one in racial terms, between good ethnics and those who are marked by race. Crime of a type becomes a business like most others, and the crime practiced by Don Corleone and Giovanni in *Mean Streets* is defined as morally superior to any number of noncriminal activities. These men are depicted as community leaders and protectors of the weak. Indeed, *The Godfather* makes explicit connections between the world of the Mafiosi and that of national politicians, with the latter asserted to be perhaps more corrupt than those in organized crime.

THE NEIGHBORHOOD

All of these films focus on the contours of a self-contained Italian American community, Little Italy in Lower Manhattan. In a sense, this neighborhood becomes the homeland in a way that Italy never was. Explains Zlatko Skrbis, "Homelands are spatial representations that are influenced by political and cultural actors, rather than a simple fact of geography. It is important to view the homeland as a constructed and imagined *topos*, rather than a clearly definable entity."[15] This neighborhood offers the coherence of the village with the amenities and prospects of economic mobility that the small and impoverished hamlets of Sicily and Naples could never provide. It becomes the metaphoric device for characterizing an idealized vision of Italian American life in the United States, as well as a certain vision of the city. Even when it is absent, as it is in many scenes of both *Godfather* films, it serves as a marker of what community cohesion should be. This vision of community is asserted as a perpetually desirable state but takes as its defining feature a pre-1945 moment.

Each of these three films pictures that piece of New York in a distinct era: *The Godfather* is set in the late 1940s and the early 1950s, *Mean Streets* takes place in the late 1960s and early 1970s; but only *The Godfather Part II* shows the formation of the ideal moment that articulates the center of all three narratives: its New York scenes are in the 1910s and 1920s, while its scenes from the later 1950s are all set elsewhere. In all, these films depict the time when immigrants from southern Italy came to cities in the United States and then left those places.

There are explicit narrative elements, which I will subsequently discuss, that mark these films as racially exclusive, but at this point it should be noted that none of these films has a significant African American, Spanish-speaking, or Asian character. This is not to say that there are no references to these increasingly present, in historical terms, ethnic groups or that they are completely absent from these films. It is, however, notable, particularly in *Mean Streets*, how little screen time includes a face that is not white, since we know that by 1970 New York had a substantial component of Asians, Hispanics, and African Americans, and that Little Italy was being subsumed by the Hispanic Lower East Side and by Chinatown from the south. Indeed, to provide historical perspective, Vincent Cannato in an essay in the *New Republic* from Feburary of 1998, elaborates on the degree of change.

Between 1982 and 1994, 132,000 legal Chinese immigrants settled in New York City, in contrast to just 7,500 Italians. Roughly one-third of the Chinese immigrants settled in lower Manhattan, while others headed for the city's

newer Chinatowns in Flushing, Queens, and Sunset Park, Brooklyn. Gentrification is also taking a toll. Eighty years ago, the tenements lining Elizabeth,
one block east of Mott, housed the teeming masses of the Italian ghetto.
Today, the street is home not only to the occasional Italian butcher shop,
with its ancient scales and cases, but to antique stores, an art supply store, a
trendy bar like the M&R, even a computer store. . . . Only a few Italians,
mostly elderly, still live in the tenements. Most local business owners live
in the outer boroughs or the suburbs. (http://www.getny.com/littleitaly.
shtml)[16]

The world of these films has largely eroded and was eroding even in the period
depicted.

In all three films idealizing ethnic enclaves involves a particular spatial reorientation, since they view their community as self-defining and largely self-sufficient.
The community does not appear to be connected to the nearby financial centers of
lower Manhattan, nor does it seem to have much to do with the entertainment
district of Broadway, the Jewish (and then increasingly Hispanic) Lower East Side,
or Harlem. References to these places and the people and activities that define
them are all but nonexistent. *Mean Streets* does have one scene shot in the decaying Times Square of the early 1970s, and in *The Godfather* Michael and Kay go to
Radio City Music Hall for the Christmas Show, and shop on Fifth Avenue during
the Christmas season of 1945. But this takes place when Michael is clearly outside
of the family fold and his geographic movement back to the Corleone compound
reconnects him with his compatriots. Such a geographically restricted sense of
place derives from visual strategies that literally shrink the city to redefine its scale
and ethnic character at a moment when anti-urban rhetoric was focused on the
predominance of cities in which whites were or were soon to be a minority.[17] These
films make the New York of the past into an urban village defined by its relative
intimacy.

When viewed chronologically by date of release, the first glimpse we get of Manhattan is in *The Godfather*, about one-quarter of the way through the film.[18] The
scene of the horse head in the movie mogul's bed dissolves into a close up of Vito
Corleone in a small parlor in which he, Sonny, and Tom discuss the details of a
projected meeting with Sollozzo, the Turk, who seeks the backing of the Corleones
for his drug trafficking business. The closeness of the room and the intimacy of the
conversation all emphasize the bonds among the three men, suggesting that their
association is personal first and professional second. As they discuss Sollozzo's
profile and business interest that concerns the Corleones, the shot cuts to a street
scene featuring the exterior of the Genco Olive Oil Company. For those who have

read the novel or have seen second film in *The Godfather* sequence, we know that this storefront is the site of the business that Vito began in the 1930s with his partner, Genco Abbandando, a neighborhood establishment in all senses of the word (figure 3.1). The shooting script defines it as: "An unimposing little building in New York City on Mott Street."

The sense of viewing the better past is defined by the yellow tint of the frame. Further, in marked contrast to the images of the decaying New York we find in most other films of this period, such as in *Midnight Cowboy* and *Klute*, the street is immaculate and the shot takes place at ground level, so that the Genco building becomes only its storefront, with the fruit cart in the foreground. Included in the shot is a car, a short man wearing the type of cap we associate with Italian immigrants at the turn of the century, and three boys who are around ten years old. The sum of these images provides us with a view of Manhattan that is fairly idyllic. By placing the camera at ground level, Coppola provides a sense of enclosed space and intimacy, elements that are recapitulated by the frame composition. As Sollozzo walks up the stairs to the parlor, we see a clean but dimly lighted stairwell as Tom and Sonny lay out the case for accepting Sollozzo's offer. Sollozzo soon enters the parlor, which by now is populated by all of the Corleone sons but Michael, as well as by the Don's two lieutenants, Tessio and Clemenza.

This scene defines the "problem" of the film, one that poses the Corleone family empire between its previous role as a community organization devoted to serving its immigrant clientele, including ministering to the desire for "harmless vices,"

FIGURE 3.1 *The Godfather*: The idealized world of the past, as Sollozzo arrives.

and its role in exacting justice in intragroup disputes. To engage in narcotics trafficking, reasons the Don, would be to involve the family in an enterprise that he
judges as far more destructive and one that is reasonably prohibited by law.

The offer, on the face of it, seems only to extend an existing crime empire, and
that is the view of the most in the room, including Tessio, Tom, and Sonny. But
such a business would involve the Corleones in a system of trade that is truly far
flung and international. As Vito refuses this offer, we can see him at odds with his
sons and associates, and that the terms of this disagreement are philosophical,
based on the degree of criminality he is willing to undertake and the scope of his
family business. The Don seeks not to enter the global marketplace in a way that is
distinct from his business of importing cheese and olive oil from Sicily. But he also
refuses to bring the destructive power of heroin into the community that he both
exploits and protects. This gesture of refusal can be understood as an attempt to
define a neat "before and after the fall" division of New York, Italian American,
and global capitalist history. In such a reduced formulation, the past becomes a
condition that can be worshiped but never recovered. Through the medium of film,
however, it appears to been preserved as an ideologically loaded image.

In various writings, Fredric Jameson has discussed the turn to the nostalgic in
Hollywood film as an explicit means of substituting a gloss on the past for a more
material view of history. He bemoans the impossible beauty and style of such
images, as he considers their historical content. Writes Jameson of the reifying
tendencies of periodization, and the broad "realities" they tend to produce: "It
seems possible that the deeper realities of the period—read, for example against
the very different scale, say, of diachronic and secular economic rhythms, or of
synchronic and systemic global interrelationships—have little to do with our cultural stereotypes of years thus labeled and defined in terms of generational
decades." It is precisely these deeper realties that the invoking of nostalgia works
to repress.[19] Move note 19 to c, above. The film asserts a time, place, and people in
images that seem explicitly referential but that suggest a lament of the present
cast upon a narrative of the past. And that lament is specifically about the loss of
an imagined community. At the center of this community lies the district defined
as "Little Italy" in Manhattan.

It is strategic that the first scenes of this film are dated in 1945. We see Michael
in his uniform, having just returned from the war in Europe, in one of the early
shots of the film, at Connie's wedding. Historically, the war and immediate postwar period define a moment of tension, as this ethnic group is poised between its
distinctiveness as an immigrant group and its assimilation into life in the United
States.[20] And indeed, World War II does serve as something of a marker for this
transition: it is an indication of the time of residence in the United States, and one

of the nation's adversaries had been Mussolini's Italy. Some Italians on the West Coast were interned, and some were placed under travel restrictions, but unlike the Japanese, whose non-European racial status and legally defined marginality in U.S. society allowed their massive rounding up and internment, there was no parallel action against the Italians.[21] In New York, after Pearl Harbor, Italian Americans rallied to the allied cause, while Italian language newspapers that had previously supported Mussolini now denounced him[22] In the Corleone family, Michael's enlistment had been a matter of controversy, a fact that is dramatized in the last scene of *The Godfather Part II*, in an outtake from the earlier film in which Michael tells of his enlistment. This scene becomes a coda for a time that has gone, since the more contemporary aspect of *The Godfather Part II* devotes itself to the utter dissolution of the Corleone family in the years after Vito's death, with Michael being responsible for the murder of two of his chief lieutenants—both of whom had been close to his father—his brother-in-law, and his brother. He has also ostracized his sister, refusing to be in proximity to any space she occupies.

In this final retrospective scene, it is clear that Vito and Sonny are antiwar, though whether this is a matter of their sympathies for Mussolini or cynicism regarding acts of U.S. nationalism is unclear. But Michael's reemergence as a war hero in this opening scene and his father's acceptance of him in uniform apparently signals something of a transition: where Italians had formerly been a nation within a nation, World War II symbolically results in their being interwoven into the fabric of the United States; but whether this rite of assimilation is complete or ultimately telling remains to be seen. Within the logic of these films, and also within the logic of *Mean Streets*, such a vision of assimilation is at least problematic if not destructive to the terms of group identity.

The visual strategy of *The Godfather* films explicitly resituates the view of the city that defines it in pre-1970s and, indeed, prewar terms by providing camera placements that emphasize the local, even as they draw a boundary that cannot be sustained, and thus they explicitly traffic in a nostalgia that includes dress, cars, and group definition. Indeed, it offers the very act that Philip Rosen defined as restoration, a means of time travel that allows for an encounter with a vision of the past. But this nostalgia also extends to visual style, as the golden light of memory bathes most external shots of Manhattan and of Little Italy. The camera placements that typically define these shots re-elaborate a kind of localism through an idealized prism. The film posits Michael as the figure of the first generation born in the United States who, will attempt to define the transition from Italian American to that of American of Italian descent. But rather than a romance of assimilation, *The Godfather* films become a family tragedy, and by implication, a community tragedy of the results of such broader worldly aspiration. And this dissolution is revisited in *Mean Streets*, and arguably, in any number of films by Martin Scorsese, including *Raging Bull*, *Goodfellas*, and *Casino*.

In *Mean Streets*, the film's opening credits include a shot of the main character, Charlie Cappa, shaking hands with a priest on the steps of the old St. Patrick's cathedral on Mott Street, and as the credits end we find ourselves in the midst of the San Gennaro festival, which runs through Mott Street in Little Italy (figure 3.2). This church symbolizes the formerly central place that Lower Manhattan held for New York's early nineteenth-century Catholic population. That population was predominantly Irish. The cathedral became a parish church in 1879, when the new St. Patrick's was built uptown on Fifth Avenue. Today its liturgies are given in English, Spanish, and Chinese. St. Patrick's stands as both a symbol of community, and of community dispersed, a state that defines the tensions of this film. Similarly, despite the fact that there are virtually no Italians currently living in Little Italy, festivals have remained an important staple of commerce, and indeed, there are currently more "Italian" festivals in the 2000s than there were in the 1970s. Such festivals serve as markers of ethnicity in commodified terms that become associative. Italianness is food, neighborhood, and certain religious medals. Such thin definitions allow for celebrations of ethnicity but in reified terms. Scorsese's establishing shot

FIGURE 3.2 *Mean Streets*: Charlie on the steps of the old St. Patrick's.

of the extremely crowded street defines the exterior of his neighborhood as both exotic and celebratory, even as we are immediately taken inside to an image of a man shooting drugs in the dingy bathroom of a local bar. As the owner of this establishment, Tony Devenziano, finds this drug user, he roughly throws him out the door, saying, "What's the matter with you? Not in here," a statement reiterating the sanctity of place that we found in *The Godfather*.[23]

It is indeed ironic that this opening scene begins where the first New York scenes of *The Godfather* left off. We are in precisely the same locale some twenty-five years later, and the drugs that Vito attempted to keep from his neighborhood are very much a feature of that location. We once again see that neighborhood in virtually the next exterior shot in the film, as Charlie emerges into the streets still crowded as a result of the festival. Unlike in *The Godfather*, the camera is mobile and follows Charlie closely, providing a sense of the intimate scale of the neighborhood and its geographic configurations. We see Charlie amid the crowd and then navigating into the café/grocery store where he is to meet his uncle. As he meanders, the camera at times cuts away for a close-up of an older and nontheatrical Italian face. The grocery itself is captured in its small scale and "ethnic" details: its pictures of Italy, its jukebox, its antiquated meat slicer. Such views exoticize the mundane, as they define the terms of ethnic distinction by the "ordinary" objects. A similar assertion takes place in *The Godfather* as Clemenza teaches Michael how to make tomato sauce with sausage. Again, the mundane details of ethnic life are asserted as both distinctive and definitional. All provide a sense of place and a social continuity with the generation of Italian immigrants that settled in this neighborhood around the turn of the century. Again, we can see the association of ethnicity with commodities allows for a postmodern rewriting of the term, and thus makes ethnicity a thing with which to identify.

As in *The Godfather*, *Mean Streets* also functions as a paean to an earlier vision of ethnicity and community, but rather than being set in the more glorious recent past, it is set in the fraught present, as figures like Charlie and his uncle attempt to define continuity by remaining community leaders even as the community ceases to exist. The "problem" of the film is whether Charlie, who is a low-level mob figure, can protect his cousin Johnny-Boy from the violence of a loan shark, while maintaining his stature with his Uncle Giovanni, a higher-level crime figure. Charlie, in a close-up, even exclaims with impatience that the problem of the neighborhood is that its inhabitants lack concern for one another. The means by which Johnny may be spared are the bonds of community—if Charlie can use his local influence to mitigate the terms of this financial relationship. Again, as in *The Godfather* films, the shots that define the central location of the film are tightly framed, but the mobility of the camera suggests both the isolation of community and the kinetic nature of 1960s life. This more dialectic visual style marks this film as defining a moment of transition. It asks about the role of continuity in a world marked by the dynamism of change. That drugs cannot be cordoned from this neighborhood makes perfect sense within the logic of the film, just as the further dissolution of community seems inevitable, despite the efforts of Charlie.

The visual strategies of these films seem almost intentionally to counter the views of the city defined by Michel de Certeau in *The Practice of Everyday Life*. De Certeau employs the image of Manhattan as viewed from the top of the World Trade Center as a means of locating the essence of the contemporary city. In de Certeau's perspective, the distanced and dehumanized gaze actualizes the late twentieth-century metropolis. By considering this image we can see precisely the strategy of these films, as they militantly adopt visual schemes that contradict this vision, resisting the imperial in image and narrative. In de Certeau's view, the scale of the city reduces individuals, as it does all objects that fail the test of mass; its proportions in all regards—height, commerce, population, ethnic variety— explode to create an aura of unmanageability. But the vigilance with which physical space is constrained in these films of the early 1970s suggests that the de Certeau perspective has already been assimilated, and that the narratives of these films are either about the desirability of living in the past or the need to turn back the clock of urban dynamism. While the *Godfather* films resist the present with their classical style, their long takes and stable cameras, *Mean Streets* employs a kinetic style as means of capturing the uncertainties of the present and thus of defining the undesirability of such anxiety-inducing motion.[24]

In *The Godfather Part II* we again reference the historical definition of this immigrant community, but the reference in this chronology extends back to the moment of leaving Sicily and the arrival into New York harbor, passing the Statue of Liberty, and seeing the young Vito being processed for immigration at Ellis Island. Vito is quarantined and he sits in his cell, not having yet reached Manhattan. The film cuts to Michael's son's communion party in Lake Tahoe, a garish and impersonal affair marked by the band's inability to play a Sicilian tarantella. It is several long scenes before the film returns to New York, with the title marking "New York City, 1917." As in *The Godfather*, these images are also sepia-tinted; unlike that film, they are even more grainy and washed of color, giving a sense of a more distant past and the greater tug of nostalgia. Our first scenes of the city streets occur in this section, but only after we see the twenty-three-year-old Vito with his wife and son in his apartment, and then Vito and Genco Abbandado at the Italian-language theater where they encounter Don Fanucci of the Black Hand, the first of the immigrant-organized crime syndicates, the precursor to La Cosa Nostra. The scene shifts to the same streets we have viewed in these two earlier films, but some three decades before *The Godfather* begins. The camera again shoots them from ground level, and though they are now shot from north to south, looking down the length of Manhattan Island, as opposed to the contained streets running east to west, the lined-up produce carts cut the view of the street, which are crowded with (presumably) Italian shoppers and a few cars attempting to make their way through the narrow passageway at the center of the street (figure 3.3). Such crowding, the slow movement of the foot traffic, and the intimate connections between the merchants and their customers define this as a distinctly premodern place, an area of and for Italian immigrants.

THE GROCERIA AND THE WORLD

As we see the cars on Mott Street attempting to wend their way through the throngs of foot traffic in *The Godfather Part II*, we are viewing the beginning of the end of an era. Although the streets of lower Manhattan look inhospitable to the encroaching automobiles of 1917, the fact of those machines will profoundly disrupt neighborhoods such as the one pictured, and have significant implications not only for the settlement patterns of Italians but also for their relations to newer immigrant populations. The coming of the automobile will also have implications for commerce of all types. Indeed, as we look at those same streets in 1945, the fruit cart in the foreground is the only one, and the street's throng has been replaced by a smattering of pedestrians. We see the continuation of this

FIGURE 3.3 *The Godfather Part II*: A car intrudes on the streets of Little Italy.

process in the opening scenes of *Mean Streets*. Although the festival dominates those narrow byways, it is a fleeting activity. At its conclusion, those streets will revert to being throughways for autos. And indeed, the role of the automobile within the history of New York and of urban spaces in general tells us that it served as a harbinger and cause of significant change. As the car becomes a predominant form of movement by the 1930s, the local economies of neighborhoods like Little Italy begin to decline. The fruit cart had to be removed from the street so that cars and trucks could traverse it; by the 1950s the small neighborhood specialty store was being supplanted by car-friendly supermarkets on the edge of urban zones, spaces that allowed for massive development and configurations that included parking lots.

The car, then, is both a specific historical marker and a synecdochal device. It is both a cause, in the way it creates the possibility of an entirely different urban scale and organization of space, as well as an effect, in that the dream of greater individual mobility is linked to a desire to make the traversing of relatively larger spaces more possible. Beyond the impact of automobiles on work and residential patterns, the effect of trucking on systems of commerce was monumental. As Douglas Rae tells us, the shift from fixed path shipping—railroads and waterways—to variable path was an important factor in the disruption of neighborhoods much as Lower Manhattan.[25] Fixed path shipping organizes population and productive means at a centralized point. As roads became an important means of conveyance, that centralization of population and productive capacity was no longer necessary. A factory could relocate to the wide-open spaces of Long Island, or a worker could find cheaper and more capacious housing in New Jersey, and then drive his or her car to work in some other area of the region, and on everimproving roads. And as the population of Little Italy dispersed, so did the fruit carts and eventually the small Italian markets that served geographic niches within the community. This shift in scale had important social implications for relatively insular ethnic groups, as well as for commerce in general, as it became another factor eroding local and then regional markets.

Though in the years immediately following the war, Italian Americans, among all white ethnic groups, tended to stay with the five boroughs of New York in greater proportion than, say, Jewish or Irish Americans, they increasingly dispersed from lower Manhattan into the Bronx and, after the mid-1960s, to Staten Island. Indeed, the process of "Americanization," the film suggests, is something of a metaphor for suburbanization. Don Corleone himself has performed a relatively early act of out-migration, as his compound is set in Long Beach in Nassau County, and we see him and his workers constantly commuting from that locale to Manhattan and Brooklyn. And the compound itself shows us spacious housing, ample yards, and a means of limiting access to the compound from the outside that would indeed be difficult in a higher density residential setting.

Since the need to preserve the contours of community is a vital assertion of this film, the compound serves as something of a transitional space. We can see the enclosure of the Don's Long Beach enclave and the proximity of friends and family as a quasi community. But such a community is an artifice, something made and only thinly articulated. It has none of the features of propinquity that define immigrant urban communities: shopping, socializing by chance, and economic reinvestment. The Corleones have placed this group in their current situation. It did not arise through a sense of group affiliation, nor are there businesses in which they work or stores that they patronize in the immediate proximity. The absence of such elements of social and economic life defines the artifice of the compound. And it is in the act of commuting that violence occurs. Within the two films the compound functions as a symbol of the distending of community, and in the process of the community's dispersal, the affiliations that maintain it weaken, inviting treachery and violence.

The commuter Don cannot operate in the way that the residential Don did, and thus the nostalgia for community becomes a textual feature of both films, and lower Manhattan in particular becomes a place touched by fond memory, a place out of time. Indeed, we can see a fundamental shift of conception occurring in these three films. In an early example of the Godfather's community role, in *The Godfather Part II*, he intervenes when Signora Colombo is about to be evicted by her landlord for keeping a dog in her apartment. Vito's approach to Don Roberto, the landlord, takes place on the street and is a casual encounter, enabled by community proximity and familiarity. Initially the landlord rebuffs him, but then learns of Vito's reputation and makes amends. Again, it is Vito's place *among* the community that is the basis of his power.

While the two *Godfather* films define the neighborhood as a place that keeps people together, in *Mean Streets* it serves as a place to keep others from entering. In *The Godfather*, when the various crime bosses agree to traffic in heroin, the vow "not in our communities" reveals the sanctity of such space and the way in which they envision it as a magical zone that is insulated from the horrors around it, as laid out by Don Zaluchi in the opening quote. Such a vision of community maps whiteness as the zone of desirable urban locales and defines a dichotomy of black and Italian spaces. Such a formulation assures the equation of whiteness and Italianness.[26]

Though in *The Godfather Part II* Michael's business has burgeoned into a national and international empire, including outposts in Lake Tahoe, where he lives, and Las Vegas, Miami, and Havana, he still seeks to exercise control over the now dispersing Italian community in New York. This effort to maintain his former empire as he creates a new one is best expressed by his relationship with Frank Pentangeli, a figure with all the attributes of ethnic authenticity, from face to voice to Toscano cigar (figure 3.4). And as Pentangeli begs Michael for the authority to vanquish his competitors, the Rosato brothers, an authority Michael refuses to give, the worst slur for the Rosatos that Pentangeli can summon is: "They recruit spics. They recruit niggers. They do violence in their grandmothers' neighborhoods." He also notes with disparagement that they are in the business of dope. Says Michael, "There are things that I have planned with Hyman Roth. I don't want them disturbed." Pentangeli replies, "You give your loyalty to a Jew over your own blood." Such an exchange reveals the values that pervade the two films as well as their erosion by matters of business of a certain scale. Pentangeli's passionate disavowal of those who possess other than Italian "blood" reelaborates what was "good" about the old regime and defines a wish for the condition of insularity, even as he coarsely defines his own racism.

In *Mean Streets*, the neighborhood becomes a place that the protagonists of the film attempt to maintain by enforcement and exclusion. The desire for such exclusivity is a matter of its visual portrayal, and indeed, such a view has the contours of this space eventually devolving to the bar owned by Tony. This is a place that defines the male bonds among the film's key characters, a place to which various others are brought. We see the heroin addict, who is thrown out; the Jewish girls who Johnny meets in the more cosmopolitan Greenwich village, who are defined

FIGURE 3.4 *Godfather part II*: Fredo and Frankie Pentangeli in Tahoe.

as outside the community and objectified; an African American dancer, who Charlie lusts after but breaks a date with because of her blackness.

The bar also serves as the recurring meeting place among the principals in the film's motivating problem: Michael, who has loaned the money; Johnny-Boy, who owes Michael; and Charlie, who tries to broker an amicable arrangement between the other two. The film shows the inability of Charlie to adjudicate his friend's debts, a result that ends in violence. This is in marked contrast to the power of Vito, as noted above. Such a failure has been foreshadowed by a shooting that takes place in Tony's bar, which is later explained as a youth's attempt to avenge an insult of a crime boss, but the boss, named Mario, disavows the act and the actor, suggesting a relative lack of control over the elements of this terrain. And though the violence is anarchic, and the boy who performs it marked by his long hair and casual dress—clearly not one of the aspiring young mobsters—that it takes place within the orbit of business and social relations in Little Italy marks it as the failure of community leaders to maintain order within this circumscribed area. Such disorder points to the end of an era.

In a revealing scene that suggests the erosion of the film's nostalgic vision of ethnicity, we see Charlie and Johnny enter the courtyard at the old St. Patrick's Cathedral on Mulberry Street. As they spread their handkerchiefs to sit, respect-fully, on the tombstones, and talk about Johnny's debt, we see the space between them open up. Johnny eventually reclines on the tomb, leaving him at a skewed angle from Charlie as he attempts to get his friend to intervene with his uncle to get his debts forgiven. It is clear at this point that the younger man has affiliated with Charlie and sees him as a potential conduit to a more powerful crime figure who can perhaps deliver him from his pressing obligations. As the split between the two becomes apparent, we hear Latin music, sung in Spanish, gradually growing louder and excited voices speaking Spanish (figure 3.5). Charlie gets up from his sitting place and looks toward the window to see the party. He watches with curiosity and shakes his head slightly from side to side, and then returns his vision to John lying on the tomb. As they leave the courtyard, the shot cuts to a high-angle view of the courtyard, reducing their size within the frame. As they move toward the exit, the music still plays, becoming still more significant as the human figures diminish, leaving us with an impression of Italian graves overseen by Puerto Rican tenants and their enveloping sound.[27]

Mean Streets is a film that enhances its emphases through the use of aural affects. The cadence and accents in which the central characters speak assert an authenticity that is definitional within the movie. This rhythm is accentuated by Scorsese's use of popular music, which runs from The Ronettes' "Be My Baby," a 1963 New York City girl group at the beginning of the film, to his use of more

FIGURE 3.5 *Mean Streets*: Johnny and Charlie party in the graveyard.

contemporary rock and roll by the Rolling Stones and Eric Clapton. But perhaps most significant is his integration of Italian-language popular music by Jimmy Roselli, Renato Carasarone, and Giuseppe Di Stefano into his pop soundtrack, a gesture that integrates the music of an earlier generation with the urban do-wop sounds of the 1950s and early 1960s. Since the mood and the cultural reach of the film is importantly defined by the soundtrack, then the sound of the Puerto Rican bandleader Ray Barretto becomes more than an incidental detail within this scene and within the film.

In the rare moments when the film ventures outside of its immediate neighborhood, the shots become more open, the environs more vital, the city looks more like how we might imagine a city to look, and it is precisely this city—dynamic, crowded, multiracial—that the film attempts to keep out. In a letter, Scorsese refers to the neighborhood as "a sub-culture, like a medieval fortress eight or ten blocks square" (Scorsese Papers, Box 7). When our protagonists leave their immediate neighborhood, they are utterly disoriented, as Tony says, "I don't know my way around the Village," a distance of only a few blocks, certainly less than a mile. Indeed, in this scene, their journey is necessitated by the failure of a local thug to pay his gambling debt to Johnny; the screenplay shows that the quasi-tribal distinction of group is transformed into a geographic one. The original screenplay has

Charlie saying, "Next time don't bet with Napolitans (*sic*)." The amended and produced version has him saying, "Don't bet outside the neighborhood" (Scorsese
Papers, Box 6). But even within the film, the effort to maintain a world defined by
the scale of the neighborhood and populated by Italians of a certain type ultimately cannot succeed, and the outside of such a world is shown to be dangerous
and alienating.

This quest for insularity to some degree coalesces around the desire to restrict
community and to restrict space. And while the vision of ethnic nostalgia that suffuses
all three films is explicitly about neighborhood and community, it is also very
much about scales of commerce. Prior to 1945, the Godfather presided over a kingdom
of petty vice. With the introduction of Sollozzo and his proposition that the Don
enter the world of international drug trafficking, we can see that the scale of enterprise will become far more expansive and complex. Heroin trafficking necessarily
involves an expansive international network that includes politics, agricultural
production, international shipping, and various tiers of industrial refining that will
involve the Don in regions and processes that are largely impersonal and beyond
his control. Although it is true that the Genco business was also in the business of
importing, the scale of the olive oil business is distinct from that of heroin in
almost every way, and that scale is an explicit matter of both *Godfather* films.
Indeed, though the business is technically one of international trade, of products
from Sicily being imported to and sold in New York, the proportion of the enterprise is not only smaller in terms of capital investment and circulation; it is also a
trade that is conducted on a largely personal level between individuals who are
associated with one another in relatively intimate ways. It is a matter of a Sicilian
immigrating to the United States but maintaining his contacts and affiliations, and
employing those relationships as a basis for bringing products that are desired by
his fellow immigrants from their region of origin. The Don's importing enterprise,
while a cover for his illicit enterprises, is similar to those activities not in its relation to the law but in its relationship to the community. All of his enterprises serve
the Italian American community both civically and materially, as they enrich the
providers of those services. In *The Godfather Part II* we see the Don and his family
return to Corleone, Sicily. As he and his family leave the train, they are greeted with
embraces, while the sepia-tinged images emphasize proximity between the Don's
family and that of his hosts. A romantic version of *The Godfather* theme plays in the
background as Vito and his family tour the small wine-making facility on the villa.
Again, this is far from an industrial operation; rather, it is run by a family, a craft
product made in relatively small quantities for a distinct market.

Similarly, the violence that is an important element of this part of the film is
also personal. After his feast with his friend/supplier, Vito is taken by car to Don

Ciccio's villa, where he is introduced to the aging Mafioso. The shots of their inter-action highlight their proximity, and when Vito bends over to tell the hard-of-hearing older man his family name, he is literally within a fraction of an inch of him. It is at the moment he states his name that Vito slices Ciccio across the mid-section. Vito kills the elderly Don to avenge the killing of his father, the originating event of this film and the reason that Vito flees Sicily. We have no way of comprehending this act of violence except as personal. Vito gains nothing material as a result of it. If we contrast the death of Ciccio to the death of Luca Brazzi, the enforcer who works for the Corleone family in New York, who is killed by Sollozzo after the Don refuses to join his heroin business, we see that there are no connections between Brazzi and these men except business, though the type of killing is equally violent and intimate.

COMMODIFYING ETHNICITY: MICHAEL CORLEONE AND LATE CAPITALISM

The failure of both Charlie in *Mean Streets* and Michael Corleone in *The Godfather Part II* is that they cannot produce community coherence, or, for that matter, even family coherence. This failure lies at the center of each film and marks each, in its own textual terms, as a personal and community tragedy. But the very terms of these communities, both of which are in some ways defined by "blood," are so suf-fused with nostalgia that their revival seems beyond possibility. All three films are marked by a sense that more dynamic and extensive systems of trade are inevi-table, and thereby they implicitly question the prospect of any alternative to the kind of nostalgic ethnic exclusion that they dwell on. As these films focus on resis-tance to change and localism, they articulate the need to adapt to the reality of the present, as they define a before-and-after moment in the history of New York City—before decay, the ethnic white city; after decay, the racialized one.

Most telling is the role of ethnic festivals in both *The Godfather Part II* and in *Mean Streets*. By dwelling on these events as a set-piece in the chronological extremes of these three films—the earliest depicted moment and the latest—we can see the idealization of these "community" events in the earlier chronology and the decay of that event in the later. In Coppola's film, we encounter the festival of San Gennaro as the backdrop to Vito's confrontation with Don Fanucci, an encoun-ter that begins with Corleone offering him less than one-third of what the Don has requested as his share of the proceeds of a robbery, and which ends with Vito killing him on the stairway of his apartment building. The festival offers a back-drop for a more legitimate and humane community authority to ascend. The cutting of the scenes juxtaposes conflicting notions of tribute, as we see dollars publicly pinned to the statue of Christ, and then clandestinely shoved under a hat in café as Vito pays Fanucci. We see, later in the film, that it is Don Corleone's regard for his constituents that separates him from a purely avaricious figure like Fanucci. The use of the festival as a set-piece in this film allows for an explicit contrast with Martin Scorsese's presentation of the same festival in the early 1970s, as the "ethnic" celebration had become a means of generating tourism dollars and its meaning had substantially shifted to a marker of commodified ethnicity—ethnicity as a thing to be traded in the postmodern market place. Johnny-Boy tells us that he hates the feast and its crowds "with a vengeance," a statement of his general disaffiliation with any romance of neighborhood and ritual. The throngs we see in *Mean Streets* walking along these same environs and celebrating the same festival some fifty years later show us a more contemporary view of the event, a perspective that now allows us to see the event in contradictory ways—as a symbol of continuity, and as a symbol of a culture reduced to kitsch.

These images provide a commentary on the erosion of community and the degrading of its public space. But even within the texts of these three films, such a diminishing was always there and built into a model of capital acquisition that goes unchallenged, if lamented, in all three films. In the first of these films, *The Godfather*, the "hero" of these films and the prototype of a more humane model of business, celebrates his daughter's wedding with a few hundred of his closest friends at his manse in Long Island. The very scale of his lands and of his party should suggest to us that his model of capital formation extends beyond the local, and indeed, in the first scenes away from his compound we find Tom Hagen attempting to use the Don's powers in Hollywood. That the Corleone family can affect film production through its infiltration of Hollywood unions suggests that, despite explicit statements and representations, Don Corleone is not simply a man of local import. Says the producer Jack Woltz after having rebuffed Hagen's initial entreaty, "You should have told me your boss was Corleone, Tom, I had to check you out." As in New York, some measure of the Don's power is defined by his reputation, an index of his degree of influence. And if he has influence in these unions, might we also surmise that there are other such entities that he has infiltrated?

Prior to this scene we see Tom Hagen *flying* from New York to Los Angeles. This flight reveals that we are witnessing a world where the business concept of "the local" is being, or has been eclipsed. That fact is further brought home by our finding out, though retrospectively, that the Don has been involved in the creation of Las Vegas, as we see Fredo shipped out to that city when New York becomes too dangerous. Again, the family's stake in legalized gambling in the West shows us that the house of Corleone is no longer just concerned with the doings on Mott and Mulberry streets. Its scope has expanded significantly. When Vito tells

Michael, and then Michael tells Kay, that the Corleone business seeks to be "completely legitimate" in the near future, it is an aspiration to a higher level of capital formation.

In *Mean Streets*, this expansion of influence is defined by the conversation between the two Mafiosi, Giovanni and Mario, discussing world affairs. Says Giovanni in response to the televised news,

> Our life has honor. We have no show to put on because we do what we have to do. They know where to come when they need us. I realize this during the war, World War II. Vito Genovese during World War II, he worked with the government, taking care of the docks. . . . What did he do? He was there, that's what he did.[28]

Again, this reference to shipping during World War II and the dockworkers union shows us how the terrain of the mafia was already involved in global exchange, even as its romance is of far more constrained spaces.

But it is *The Godfather Part II*—clearly the most contemporary of these films despite its explicit and implicit lamentations for the past—that lays out its vision of economic success in ways that anticipate the era of global capitalism. It is Michael who leaves New York for Lake Tahoe, exponentially increasing the family's distance from its seat of power: Vito moved from Manhattan to western Long Island, Michael has moved from Long Island to Nevada. The reason this is possible is a matter of the increased scope of the family business. Even as the film's shots of New York in its earlier chronology define the sanctity and insularity of place, it juxtaposes that vision with establishing shots of the Lake Tahoe estate that focus on the sweep of the lake and the majesty of the mountains in the background. Where Connie's wedding was within a walled compound, Michael's party for his son Anthony's first communion opens out to the vistas of the West.

Tom Hagen's flight to Los Angeles foreshadowed the Corleone family business, as truly a hemispheric enterprise, with interethnic associations. We see that Michael is the model of the traveling businessman in the age of globalization, the father who is never home. And while the problem of the first *Godfather* film was the question of expansion, the problem of this film is the results of such expansion. We see Michael's involvement in domestic politics through his association with Senator Geary and his testimony before the Senate committee. Indeed, the central plot event of this film is the intrigue around a virtual takeover of Cuba. Says Roth in close-up, "In short, we're in full partnership with the Cuban government." And even as Castro comes to power to disrupt these plans, and the intrigue among the criminals places them at odds with one another, Michael shows no sign of economic dislocation. He is able to ruthlessly extract profit from his various businesses, legal and illegal, and to extract vengeance on those who cross him, as shown by his inducing the suicide of Frankie Pentangeli even as he is guarded by federal agents, and of Hyman Roth, even as he is shielded by the INS and FBI. Though Michael has failed to become a partner with Battista in Cuba, his reach defines him as the very model of the global capitalist: one who is beyond the influence and control of national governments. He has become a cosmopolitan, in this case a term that articulates his interest in the multinational circulation of capital and the social and political power that this far-flung circulation affords him.

That his movements have become geographically expansive does not, however, result in his articulating a more embracing and open-ended view of self and community. Such an expansion of domain is focused on a narrow view of trade and his functioning on a businessman's means-ends logic. He is dislodged from regional and national spaces, and indeed, dislodged from any human relation that might impinge on the logic of his economic decisions. As the scene cuts to the scene of some nineteen years before, to Pearl Harbor day, we can see that the life pictured and the spaces associated with that life are clearly a matter of the past, and that to some degree the logic of his father's dream—to be a worldly and American success—has been fulfilled; even if the realization of this ideal is ultimately isolating. And it is the element of regret that this scene induces that leaves us pining for the symbols and feelings of ethnic nostalgia.

4

Blaxploitation and Urban Decline

HARLEM AND THE WORLD BEYOND, *COTTON COMES TO HARLEM* (1970), *SHAFT* (1971), *ACROSS 110TH STREET* (1972), *SUPERFLY* (1972), AND *BLACK CAESAR* (1973)

WHILE THE FILMS of the previous chapter focus on the terms of "ethnicity" and imply or express explicitly the disregard and condescension of their white characters for African Americans, here we see the focus of the films turn to race, but race as viewed, for the most part, through a normatively white lens. In this chapter I look at five significant expressions of the "blaxploitation" genre: *Cotton Comes to Harlem* (1970), *Shaft* (1971), *Across 110th Street* (1972), *Superfly* (1972), and *Black Caesar* (1973), all popular and some well reviewed.[1] My concern is with Harlem as a presence in these films, how it is defined as a discrete space and how it occurs in relation to other distinctive portions of the city and region. The films make Harlem a specific marker for racial identification and legitimacy, if not authenticity, for the films' protagonists. They afford an intriguing opportunity to see how aspects of mass culture map the idea of race within a particular historical context—that of the culmination of the city's economic crisis and then rebirth, a moment poised between an older regional system of production and distribution, and the emerging fluidity of far-flung systems in the 1980s, 1990s, and beyond. The engine behind the phase of gentrification that began in the late 1970s, and that has continued with some irregularity to today, has been New York's reemergence as a global financial center and as a place for services derived from that economic activity. As such, Harlem, which has long had an identity that distinguishes it from the center of Manhattan, has been far slower to prosper and, as it has begun to prosper, it is becoming increasingly less African American.[2] In these presentations we can see that the ramifications of this economic emphasis on international commerce were and are profound.

Like many of the genres and subgenres of the early 1970s, blaxploitation films owed their existence to a combination of factors, some a matter of the changes in the mode of production for commercial film in the United States, some a matter of the cultural politics of the era. When small and independently produced films like *Cotton Comes to Harlem* (1970), a film adapted from a noir crime novel by Chester Himes but decidedly different in tone, starring Godfrey Cambridge and directed by Ossie Davis, and Melvin Van Peebles's *Sweet Sweetback's Baadasss Song* (1971), a film written, directed, produced by and starring Van Peebles, achieved unexpected commercial success, more mainstream producers and distributors increasingly drawn to projects with a significant emphasis on race.[3] *Shaft* (1971), with its notable commercial success—based on a screenplay by the white writer Ernest Tydyman, and packaged by MGM, starring Richard Roundtree, and directed by the estimable Gordon Parks—marked a turning point for this type of film, and spawned a number of sequels and knock-offs.[4] These films represent, respectively, a film for a relatively small audience directed by an important African American actor, Ossie Davis (*Cotton*); a fully independent production (*Sweet Sweetback*); and a relatively low-budget but clearly mainstream film (*Shaft*). And though *Sweet Sweetback* was an extremely influential film for defining the genre, its ultimate impact was some-what less than films like *Shaft* and *Superfly*. This was a matter both of the degree to which it was a work of a singular filmmaker and its more specific means of address to audiences.[5]

The broader industry strategy that allowed for such productions was not so different from that which motivated the production and distribution of other niche projects of the era, such as *Easy Rider* (1969), *Bonnie and Clyde* (1967), and any number of surprise hits.[6] But blaxploitation films from *Shaft* onward were largely defined by a relatively greater degree of corporate control and a relatively lesser degree of autonomy on the part of the filmmaker. Like those more clearly director-driven films of the era, however, these productions sought to appeal to niche audiences, but in this case that market is to some extent defined by a racial demographic rather than one of age. These films seek to appeal to a black urban audience, along with contiguous white youths. Writes Ed Guerrero, in his largely critical account of *Shaft* and its impact, in *Framing Blackness*: "Although the film was carried to smash-hit status by black audiences, it was able to play well with whites also" (92). Mark Reid defines this cross-racial appeal with precision and differentiates it from the more specific black audience of the Van Peebles film, citing its ability to draw "a black popular, or unpoliticized audience," as a well as to a "white male viewer [who] might enjoy the sex and violence" (83). Perhaps the white audience was also drawn in by the unthreatening racial politics of these films.

As cultural events, the appeal of these films is fostered by the emphasis on definitions of race and ethnicity that became a part of mass culture in the 1960s. With the rise of the Civil Rights movement through the preceding decade and a burgeoning rhetoric of race pride, audiences were drawn to and intrigued by scenarios and themes that they could see as reflecting on or typifying definitions of race. And indeed, all of these films feature Hollywood versions of black vernacular speech, dress that can be associated with urban styles of the day, plots that have significant racial components, and a range of black characters.[7] Further, these blaxploitation films are marked by their setting in an identifiably black community.

For reasons of chronology, genre, and Hollywood's disposition to repackage the last big thing, the shadow of *The Godfather*, both the novel and the film, seems to loom over these films in any number of ways, providing models for characters, plots, and visual styles. Even *Shaft*, which was released almost a year before Coppola's film, draws on that very popular novel, including Mario Puzo's vision of white ethnic solidarity and Italian-American gangsters. In an obvious homage, *Black Caesar* was released in England as *The Godfather of Harlem*. While there are almost no African Americans in the mob films, there are virtually no blaxploitation films without Italian mobsters and cops. Such a contrast suggests the uneven ground defined by the terms "race" and "ethnicity" in the early 1970s, as well as the different ways in which white and black criminality and community were conceived and represented. While a certain atavism pervades all of these films in their enactment of criminal violence and retribution, the very terms of criminality and its relationship to the discrete communities represented is quite different in black exploitation films, as crime further disrupts a community that is already in disarray.

These five films depict New York City in a time when the industrial basis of the city's economy was on the verge of substantial change. It is therefore not surprising that all of these films are about enterprise of some kind, and about specific enterprise within a specific geography. But none of these films emphasizes work that exists outside of crime and policing. In both *Godfather* films and in *Mean Streets*, as well as productions such as *The Brotherhood* (1968), *The Gang That Couldn't Shoot Straight* (1971), and *The Valachi Papers* (1972), not to mention films about Jews as an ethnic group ensconced in a discrete location, *Hester Street* (1975), *Next Stop Greenwich Village* (1976), or the later *Ragtime* (1981), part of the texture of these films is defined from the outset by the existence of bakers, café owners, restaurateurs, funeral-home owners, and florists who define the ambiance of place and the bonds of community. As *The Godfather* films have at their center a vision of local capitalism morphing into a more global and "rational" system, so these films have a racialized vision of economic relations that takes root in Harlem, but the scale of that commerce is strictly local. The films define an ethos of African American economic uplift and dramatize actions that reveal black criminals attempting to take control of the turf of their own people. Such efforts, in a some-what perverse way, suggest an awareness of the economic scheme put forth by the federal government to promote black enterprise.

So it is not just the presence of James Brown, a figure who prided himself on his up-from-poverty economic success, on the soundtrack of *Black Caesar* that sug-gests the power of a vision of African American business development.[8] One his-torical marker that captures the climate in which these films participated is Richard Nixon's signing of Executive Order I 11458, in March 1969. This order directed the Secretary of Commerce, Maurice Stans, of later Watergate fame, "to coordinate federal government programs and policies, which may affect or may contribute to the establishment, preservation and strengthening of minority busi-ness enterprise." And beyond the governmental elaboration of race as a distinctive category for the purposes of business development, this act of recognition was part of a developing and a complementary focus on racialized space, as specific development zones were introduced; this concept would grow in importance as a conservative catch-phrase and find its fuller geographic expression in Reagan-era enterprise zones in the South Bronx and Harlem. For our criminal protagonists in all of these films, Harlem is already an enterprise zone, but one of criminal activity that produces little if any trickle-down effect.

Correspondingly, all suggest the limits of such a strategy of racial uplift, including its negative consequences for communities. African American–owned businesses generated less than $500 million of revenue in 1971––a figure that is less than one-tenth of the figure achieved by the hundred largest black-owned businesses in the year 2000––creating an impression that the general rhetoric of Black Enterprise seems a further instance of the federal government's general lack of interest in the inner city's economic condition. Given the represented state of urban housing and the historical condition of Harlem and neighborhoods like it, the result of successful entrepreneurship would be, and was, to vacate historically African American locales.

Despite their genesis as elements of a cultural moment that features affirmative acts of ethnic identification and assertion, as well as celebrations of race, these films offer a vision of "cultural" blackness that redefines its codes in a manner that reconciles them to the vicissitudes of deindustrialization, since the rhetoric of uplift minimizes macro-economic causes as a reason for the lack of opportunities for individuals. As these films, not unusually for commercial productions, focus intensively on a small group of distinctive characters, blackness is asserted in various ways; but to some degree, it is defined by an individual's relationship to the restricted spaces of Harlem. Our protagonists' fluid notions of race allow them to traverse Harlem with ease and comfort but also to avoid being *of* that region. And as African Americans who reside in a larger domain, their visions of themselves take on nuance and behavioral variety. On the other hand, beyond our protagonists, for those who form the racial backdrop that creates the blackness of these films, race is not ironic, nor is it relative. There are any number of African American characters in these films who are either unnamed or barely individuated, and for them Harlem is *the* world. It is fundamentally definitional and a matter of their lives existing within the restricted spaces of the ghetto.

But all of these characters, no matter how fluid, are to a degree outside of the dynamism of trade that is in the process of re-elaborating New York's economy. There is clearly a class system at work here, but the classes are the under- and service-classes of restricted scope and attainment. And although it is better to be of the latter than the former, race seems to articulate a space outside of the system of globalization, one that has no complementary emphasis on community solidarity or development. For example, in *Superfly*, Priest is a fairly successful drug dealer but, unlike the Corleones, he involves himself in the global drug trade only as a seller and never as an importer and supplier. Similarly, the numbers trade, a distinctly local enterprise, is also a matter of commerce in *Shaft* and *Across 110th Street*. But such a vision of commerce is distinctly outside of the trends of globalization and increasingly under duress.[9] In these films, African Americans are defined by an articulate system of class, but all classes of African American society are outside of the "action" of global trade.

The dramatization of Harlem and the avenues of African American commerce reveal, and arguably romanticize, a world elaborated by William Julius Wilson in his contemporary study, *The Declining Significance of Race: Blacks and Changing Institutions* (1975). Wilson ably summarizes and assesses the impact of the changes in African American life brought about by blacks' increased political significance in the 1960s and beyond, as well as the complementary economic issues that reduce that significance. With the passage of equal employment legislation and the authorization of affirmative action programs, the government has helped clear the path for more privileged blacks who have the requisite education and training to enter the mainstream of American occupations. However, such government programs do not confront the impersonal barriers confronting members of the black underclass, who have been effectively screened out of the corporate

and government industries. And the very attempts of the government to elimi-
nate traditional racial barriers through such programs as affirmative action have
had the unintentional effect of contributing to the growing economic class divi-
sions within the black community (19). Arguably, then, the social and economic
distance between figures as diverse as Tommy Gibbs in *Black Caesar*, and Gravedigger and Coffin Ed in *Cotton Comes to Harlem*, and the black masses who comprise
the population of Harlem, is largely a matter of relative privilege occurring
within the structure of African American society. The manner through which the
heroes of these New York-based black exploitation films differentiate themselves
is through competence and ambition; but the basis for those drives is shown as
largely a matter of personal qualities rather than life opportunities, a story that
confirms the conservative rhetoric of black uplift.

Embedded in these visions of Harlem is an incipient and emergent process of
globalized commerce. Harlem, as defined at the historical moment of the early
1970s, stands as not a center of black capitalism, but as a place left behind by the
deindustrialization of urban spaces of the United States.[10] Globalized production,
distribution, and exchange has the effect of radically reconfiguring our relative
conception of space; in effect, as Neil Brenner explains, both deterritorializing and
reterritorializing discrete regions. This process, Brenner explains, supplants state-
centered definitions of place and instead reinscribes these points as economic
nexes in the service of global capital's valorizing of just-in-time production, access
to effective modes of communication, and the relative availability of vital components of effective and cheap production. But Brenner cautions against the reification of a particular historical moment, a disposition that is endemic in Hollywood
film and maybe a matter of the materiality of the medium itself. He writes,

> As the role of state territoriality as an organizational framework for social
> relations is decentered, relativized, and transformed, the historical dynamic
> character of social space becomes manifest both in everyday life and in socio-
> logical analysis. The overarching methodological challenge that flows from
> this circumstance is to analyze globalization as an ongoing process in which
> the spatiality of social relations is continually reconfigured and transformed.[11]

Harlem in this formulation is distinct from the Little Italy of the last chapter, in
that it there is no Don with contacts in Hollywood and in Italy. Similarly, it lacks
an economically dynamic character like Sollozzo, who aspires to control a system
of importation and distribution, however illicit. Indeed such a character would be
placed in this setting in the much later *American Gangster* (2007), which focuses on
the actual figure of Frank Lucas, who was importing and distributing heroin at the

time that these movies were made. It is also significant that *American Gangster* provides much less of a sense of place than these earlier movies.

Within the context of 1970s social relations, Harlem stands as a self-contained racialized space in the process of further decline. Such a bracketing of its territory serves to remap its relative location. And this decline is pictured as its apparent, but not actual, remoteness from the financial centers of Manhattan. As we look at its empty and deteriorated spaces, we may also glimpse a historical process of development, a world some thirty-five years later, when a brownstone in central Harlem will be sold to a young worker in the financial sector for a million dollars; that worker will likely be white. The men and women who used to populate the sidewalks and crumbling buildings of Harlem will live elsewhere and probably will remain un- or under-employed.

WORK

Four of these five films provide high-angle shots of Harlem either at their beginning or near their beginning, so that a viewer's first encounter with that region is from a perspective that distances and reduces its streets and inhabitants. Indeed, this view seems sociological in the extreme and separates the black masses, which exist only in aggregate, from our protagonists, who are soon depicted in close-up. Such a view, as de Certeau tells us, is one that is associated with the surveyed city, a space that employs an eye-in-the-sky to take in that which is distant both physically and culturally, but which requires scrutiny in order to be observed and controlled. Such a vision suggests that defined by a guard's eye on a prison tower, or the distillation of that view by a panoptical device. Thus we have the normative viewer—typically white despite the terms of address these films elaborate—engaging Harlem from an angle that is designed to aggregate and objectify African American humans and their associated space. I will return to this convention later, but for the purposes of this section it is important to note the way that such a perspective locates the inhabitants of this region.[12]

All soon narrow their scope as they zoom toward the ground and a more restricted view, and as they do, all feature street-level shots of men milling in small groups, apparently with nothing to do. For example, *Superfly* begins with a crane-shot of a street corner marked by storefronts advertising wigs and cigars, and a relatively empty street. The shot focuses on two men, one somewhat better dressed than the other, who apparently are involved in a nonfocal aspect of the drug trade as users, small-time dealers, and schemers. As they traverse the streets, the ground-level mobile camera finds them passing groups of men on the sidewalk who are, as a mass, not going anywhere Similarly, in *Shaft*, the first shots of Harlem show Shaft addressing a group of men standing on a stoop. The camera zooms out and cuts to a long, high-angle shot of a street strewn with garbage and marked by cars in disrepair parked along the curb. As the film reverts to tighter shots of Shaft walking around Harlem, we again see men on the streets with nothing to do, little business, and as Shaft knocks on doors seeking information, people who are at home in the middle of the day. These crowds of aimless men are also featured in the beginnings of *Across 110th Street* and *Cotton Comes to Harlem*, both of which also employ these establishing high-angle shots (figure 4.1).

All of the films reference the moment of the mid-1960s to the mid-1970s, when the Fordist model of industrial production ebbed and largely vanished, and those who suffered were frequently U.S.-born minorities. As a result, the African American working class that defined Harlem in the 1940s and 1950s increasingly became the African American unemployed in the 1960s and 1970s. Explains Edward Soja, "The black population has probably suffered most from the new urbanization," noting the high rates "of poverty, unemployment, and infant mortality" for "parts of Harlem, Brooklyn, and the Bronx, a cruel reflection of the punitive discipline imposed on the population that most radically threatened the Fordist order of the 1960s."[13] Indeed, following Neil Brenner's discussion of the relationship between the reimagining of urban scale and the process of globalization, the Harlem we see depicted constitutes a place contiguous to the financial centers of international capital; but it also emerges as a vital repository of surplus labor, a source of workers who are readily available to meet the uneven productive

FIGURE 4.1 *Across 110th St.*: Harlem from above.

cycles—defined by both time and space—of flexible work and geographically mobile production.[14]

These films, as products of the early 1970s, devise their rhetoric of individual uplift within the context of a national and regional economy that is stagnating and well along in the process of deindustrialization. The films focus on crime and criminality, and exploring further the nature of those enterprises allows us to see how they address the related conditions of incipient globalization and the decline of work in the African American community. The films form an intriguing counterpoint to the nostalgia for a type of business model that we find in *The Godfather* and *The Godfather Part II*, films that also define the inevitability of a more geographically extensive scale of enterprise. In *The Godfather*, the moment of crisis occurs, as I detailed earlier, when Sollozzo attempts to involve the Corleones in the global heroin trade. The Don declines, as he distinguishes between "harmless" local vices, like gambling and prostitution, and the far more nefarious and far-flung activity of drug importing and dealing. We eventually see that Vito is compelled, with some reluctance and regret, by market forces to enter this business, and that the family, in order to thrive, must engage in a far broader scale of enterprise. In *Part II*, Michael Corleone attempts to define a global empire built from the proceeds of his father's relatively local enterprise.

These films with race at their center all see criminal operations as decidedly local and finite, with the basic plot device—used in *Cotton*, *Across 110th Street*, *Shaft*, *Superfly*, and *Black Caesar*—the wresting of control of Harlem from white gangsters by black gangsters, or from black gangsters by white gangsters. Such a view of commerce reveals the ways in which race becomes a device that, with its secondary meanings and associations with specific spaces, defines constraints of opportunity by assuming the limits of enterprise. In the films focused on the Italian mob, white ethnics are represented as aspiring to far-flung and geometrically expansive business activities, while African Americans—even those who these films define as characterized by a kind of personal dynamism—are stuck in a model of arithmetic growth that sees terrain as finite. Indeed, one expression of this is the centrality of the numbers racket in *Across 110th Street* and *Black Caesar*, a type of criminal enterprise that had existed in Harlem since the 1920s, with relatively local control. That is, African American crime figures profited from the numbers game that thrived in their neighborhoods, though those operations were typically part of larger criminal enterprises.

This enterprise depends upon the definition of discrete communities: it runs as a local racket where a particular criminal group operates an illegal lottery. These groups are largely defined by discrete geography and assume the relative isolation and desperation of their clientele. As states got into the lottery business, these illicit numbers operations declined. New York's lottery began in 1967, suggesting the way in which discrete and multicentered gambling of this type was reconfigured, centralized by the state and organized along geographical lines that supplanted the discrete neighborhood as a unit of organization. The representation of such restricted business activity apparently results from the cramped visions of the criminal protagonists.

Such limits are implicit in the plots of all of these five films, unlike *The Godfather*, where criminality was seen as a community-based activity with some potential benefits to the aggregate—such as Don Corleone exacting justice for the under-taker Bonosera's daughter. Here, the criminals are shown as avaricious and wantonly violent. For example, in *Black Caesar*, based on the film *Little Caesar* (1931), Tommy Gibbs seeks to become the black Godfather. (Edward G. Robinson's shadow is also on the characters Doc Johnson in *Across 110th Street* and Bumpy Jones in *Shaft*.) And though he includes other African Americans in his enterprise, his ruthlessness shows him as other than a community leader.[15] Upon vanquishing his Italian bosses, he forays down 125th Street and draws stares. But Tommy seems to bask in the glare of notoriety and is unable or unwilling to convert his narcissism into acts that do not benefit him directly. He neglects any aspect of community development and promptly moves his residence downtown (figure 4.2). His enterprise presents itself from the beginning as a matter of vengeance and ambition. Indeed, he even fails to improve the lot of his family, shunning his father and offending his mother, as she rejects his effort to uplift her from her job as a maid. Though Tommy stands lamenting the poverty of his youth, his desires are for

FIGURE 4.2 *Black Caesar*: Tommy's new apartment.

personal restitutions and not a more generalized idea of group compensation. And as Bumpy in *Shaft*, and Doc in *Across 110th Street*, restrict their major criminal activities to Harlem, it is difficult to see them as committed to any notion of community cohesion or justice. These films show little work that is not directly a matter of criminality. People sell drugs, gamble, pimp, but few are involved in legitimate and growing business activities.

In *Superfly*, we see an enterprise that is distinctive within the context of these films: the bar/restaurant owned by Priest's patron Scatter, which seems a legitimate and thriving business, patronized by other African Americans and providing a place for performers. The initial scenes shot in this space are intimate, and the crowd appears congenial. When Priest enters the subtly lighted club, a camera at eye level pans the room: we see large groups, mostly African Americans, seated at cafeteria-style tables, with people nodding to and greeting Priest, as we hear the sounds of Curtis Mayfield in the background. The shot cuts to Mayfield singing the film's theme song with animation, then to Priest and Eddie relaxing at a front table and then a close-up of Scatter in a chef's outfit in the back of the room, providing an image of the congenial host.

Soon we see the three men—Scatter, Priest, and Eddie—in the kitchen. In a two-shot of Priest and Scatter, we find that Scatter has been in the dope business and was Priest's means of entry into that enterprise. When the two younger men ask for his assistance in procuring a large enough amount of cocaine to make a quick and sufficient profit in order to retire, Scatter turns hostile, and waves a gun at Eddie, saying with disparagement, "The man picks his own niggers," revealing his relative lack of agency and the connection of this apparently legitimate business to the drug trade.

In a later scene, Scatter, in a panic, seeks out Priest at his white girlfriend's apartment on Park Avenue, to request his help. He asks for money, saying that "The Man, he's trying to kill me. I own that restaurant. . . . Don't do me no good. He owns you." Such a statement is to a degree metaphoric but evocative of a pre-1865 reality, as well as the ways in which African American bodies continue to be inscribed in a system of oppression. In a film about economics and the relative autonomy of the black subject and the black community, a figure that previously seemed a legitimate expression of African American economic power shows the way in which the terms of subjugation infiltrate Harlem and its residents, revealing the many nefarious social forms that dominance takes. Such a statement of insignificance further throws this vision of enterprise into question, as we find that it exists at the pleasure of more powerful white criminals—who turn out to be high-ranking figures in the police department. Soon, Scatter is killed with an overdose of heroin, succumbing to the device that has made him his relative fortune and providing an image of the relative impotence of the black "businessman" and certainly of the limits of legitimate enterprise in Harlem.

Beyond Scatter's bar, it is difficult to find a going and legitimate African American business concern in these five films. While it is true that we see frequent pans of the enterprises on an around 125th Street, those businesses are never connected with individuals nor do we see characters patronizing them. The two most central commercial concerns are Uncle Bud's junk business in *Cotton* and the dry cleaning business in which Julius Harris works in *Across 110th Street*. And while the junk business is clearly an African American owned and operated enterprise, it is also peripheral to our zone of commerce, as it exists on a scow in the Hudson River and has a multiracial clientele. Its proprietor, played by Redd Foxx, is also a largely comedic character and an important element of the film's broad approach to its subject. The dry cleaning shop is not clearly black owned. Such limited visions of entrepreneurial activity do little to present images that pose an alternative to those depictions of Harlem as a place where massive numbers of men spend most of their days idling on corners and stoops.

The limits of work and of capital formation are very much a matter of these films, and an implicit rationale for their depiction of the proliferation of criminal enterprises. The world of the late 1960s and the early 1970s in many ways justifies this representation as part of the realist disposition. Those years marked the appearance of a trend in unemployment among the relatively uneducated and unskilled, a group that included a disproportion of African American men. According to one study, among prime age nonwhite males, the proportion of those who had no job at all in a given year increased from 3 percent to 17 percent from 1970 to 1995.[16] In following the logic of these films that show, in their sum, a massive gap between the everyday denizens of Harlem and the professionalism of their protagonists, we can see again the classed system of social organization that is becoming so much a matter of African American life in the 1970s.

Such a change resulted from the massive number of jobs in the industrial sectors that were moved to other countries. African Americans, and African American males in particular, found themselves particularly hard hit by the decline in production and the enhancement of the service sector of the U.S. economy. Writes William Julius Wilson in *When Work Disappears*,

> Of the changes in the economy that have adversely affected low-skilled African American workers, perhaps the most significant have been those in the manufacturing sector . . . In the 1970s up to half of the huge employment declines for less-educated blacks might be explained by industrial shifts away from manufacturing toward other sectors. The manufacturing losses in some

northern cities have been truly staggering. In the twenty-year period from 1967 to 1987, Philadelphia lost 64 percent of its manufacturing jobs; Chicago lost 60 percent, New York City, 58 percent, Detroit, 51 percent. (29–30)

As a result of the macroeconomic shifts in industrial production, work that paid a living wage in the United States became relatively unavailable for those with limited skills. And in the African American community, the area in which jobs increased was at the low end of the service sector of the economy, primarily for those in the health and social services fields, which meant that women were far more likely than men to seek education and find jobs that allowed them an existence teetering on the edge of the lower middle class. For the neighborhoods where those who suffered from the effects of structural unemployment tended to live, small entrepreneurs felt the impact of their clientele not having sufficient income to buy more than the necessities.

It is no wonder that crime is romanticized in this context. And even in the films where its ravages are a matter of explicit assertion, such as in *Superfly* and in *Across 110th Street*, the characters who seek to leave the life of crime lament bitterly the absence of alternatives. Priest is asked by his girlfriend why he needs to risk his life and livelihood by selling amounts of cocaine far beyond what be has dealt in the past. "Why can't you just get a job?" He replies, "Who's going to hire a man my age who has done time?" In *Across*, Julius, when he and his wife recognize that he is about to be caught and killed for robbing the numbers bank, says almost precisely the same thing. And while it is true that Shaft and the cops in *Cotton* and *Across 110th Street* do have gainful employment, such work requires training and the ability to transcend the ever-declining circumstances of Harlem. And such a possibility, we find, is increasingly improbable with each passing year.

RACE AND THE COLOR OF HARLEM

These films serve as tributes to and arguments for a kind of cultural blackness, a vision of race that these films, to a degree, commodify. An aspect of that cultural blackness is identification with the area north of 110th Street, so that characters navigating the streets of Harlem with comfort is a vital marker of racial authenticity. Such an anchor in a specific geography seems, within the logic of these productions, necessary. The contested term "race" sits at or near their narrative center, as they explore the ways in which the increased social mobility of a class of African Americans redefine inter- and intraracial relationships.

The dramatized bonds of affiliation that broadly define community are increasingly distended as the narratives develop. As the Civil Rights era burgeoned, national terms of racial distinction, on one hand became more rigid, on the other hand more subtle. While legal segregation was dramatically undone by the Federal Civil Rights Act of 1964, insidious forms of restriction remained a part of life in the United States. The end of legal segregation marked the development of an increasingly hierarchical class structure among African Americans. Though the Civil Rights movement benefited and enhanced the black middle class, it also had the effect of further reducing and constraining opportunities for a black underclass. Thus, as we see the protagonists in these films prosper and become accomplished in their work lives, none of those figures, neither cop nor criminal, maintains his residence in Harlem; nor does any figure get deeply involved with a discernable African American community.

This association with place trumps simple definition by color, as we see in any number of films. For example, in *Superfly*, perhaps the film of this group that has the most realistic "feel" to it as a matter of narrative and formal properties, Priest is light-skinned with straight hair, certainly distinctive looking as a figure who is classified as black (figure 4.3). In one scene, he enters an apartment in which a number of African American men are gambling. He stands on the outside of the group and attempts to move his friend and business partner Eddie out of the game to discuss a transaction, an act made more problematic by the fact that Eddie has been winning. Another character aggressively asks him why Eddie has to go, and says, as we look over his shoulder and at Priest's face in tight close-up. "Answer me,

FIGURE 4.3 *Superfly*: Priest takes exception to a questioning of his race.

you white lookin'. . . ." Priest knocks him to the floor, and another close-up reveals Priest's bug-eyed fury. Such questioning brings to the fore a perspective that may well be a matter of audience perception: how black is this character? Yet Priest's response, his general range of associations, and his intermittent recounting of his life's opportunities and trials suggest that such distinctions are specious. The person who challenges Priest's racial identity could easily be seen, by some higher view of genetic purity, as also light skinned and "white looking." Is Priest classified as African American by his looks or by his personal behavior and disposition, factors resulting from his cultural situation and upbringing? He is the one protagonist in this film who actually lives in Harlem, though he often stays downtown with his white girlfriend. Thus, in this film Priest's range of Harlem affiliations and associations mitigates the potential ambiguity of his color.

Priest's goal in the film is to leave drug dealing and leave New York. And were he to leave and go, say, to Mexico, as he states he would like to, the meaning of the character's blackness would be different, because of his relative wealth in that context, as well as the normative meanings of color in that national setting. Blackness, then, we are shown, is not a matter of fine distinctions of appearance. It is a general state of being defined by a combination of factors, including social context and the ability to be recognized by other African Americans as belonging within the category. And, indeed, Priest is black because he associates primarily with other African Americans, dresses "black," and speaks "black."

In other films, such as *Black Caesar*, characters that are assumed to be African American are also light skinned with features that are not necessarily characteristic. And the "black" women who are so much a matter of these films, women who elaborate the sexual prowess of various protagonists, are largely of the straight-haired, light-skinned variety. Yet, audiences seem to have internalized the "one drop" rule that was a matter of the cynicism and nefariousness of slavery in its last decades.[17] Characters who are sufficiently dark skinned and performatively black are all but unquestionably assumed to be in that category. And despite the recurrence of Italian American cops and criminals, individuals belonging to an ethnic group that at an earlier historical moment was not clearly on the white side of the U.S. racial line, there is never any doubt which side of the racial divide these characters belong on, as all function in the domain of white privilege and all are clearly outsiders in Harlem.[18]

In all of these films, then, establishing the "authentic" blackness of characters and showing how those figures are part of a system of mutual recognition and affiliation is vital for their elaboration of the genre; yet the terms of behavior and recognition are various and at times ironic, so that race becomes a social operator that serves a wide range of functions. But such a system reveals its instability at its margins. What if Priest behaved like the dark-skinned Lieutenant Pope of *Across 110th Street*, who is played by Yaphet Kotto? Would he be distinguishable from other ethnic cops in movies who are reformers by training and disposition, such as the title character of *Serpico*, played by the swarthy Al Pacino? But it is indeed telling that this figure who aspires to institutional success in the New York City police department is dark skinned, as are the characters played by Raymond St. Jacques and Godfrey Cambridge in *Cotton Comes to Harlem*; Shaft is also relatively dark skinned but derives his blackness from his role as an ex-cop fighting crime outside of any institutional setting, as a private investigator.

So, on one hand, we can see race as a historical category with all its attendant baggage, while on the other blackness is a relative quality defined by a range of colors and more specific behaviors, depending upon the situation.[19] That is, to be black or to recognize another person as black is a matter of historically conditioned terms of identification and may have to do with proportional judgments of physical and behavioral blackness. And in the social consequences of this definition and the related marked behaviors, blackness becomes a complicated set of negotiations mediated by an understanding of the category on the part of the actor and the audience. When the unsympathetic white cop asks Shaft where he is going, he replies broadly with a smirk, "I'm going to get laid." Such a response both plays to the myth of black sexuality and, by the tone of his response, parodies it. His banter suggests that Shaft knows the limits of "authenticity," a term that takes on increasing gravity as black communities are distended by the out-migration enabled by social mobility, a condition that leads commentators to wonder if one remains authentically black after leaving definitionally black spaces.[20]

The anthropologist John L. Jackson Jr. employs the terms "sincerity" as a means of refuting that less elastic term "authenticity." Writes Jackson,

> To talk exclusively in terms of racial authenticity is to risk ossifying race into a simple subject-object equation, reducing people to little more than objects of racial discourse, characters in racial scripts. . . . Racial sincerity implies something more, what Ralph Ellison might have called the "something else" of race, something subjective, willful, and complexly and compellingly human. . . . With sincerity as a model, one still does not see into the other, one still does not know if one can trust the other's performances . . . ; however, one recognizes that people are not simply racial objects to be verified from without but racial subjects with an interiority that is never completely and unquestionably clear.[21]

And this notion of authenticity becomes even more vexed when it is considered as a motivated assertion, one stemming from any number of sources, including screenwriter, director, actor, and producer. As such, its origin is multiple and not clearly a matter of a specific racialized perspective. Further, the reception of the idea of blackness also becomes various, defined by any number of subject positions, and again, those cannot be fixed to any particular racially defined place of origin. Writes E. Patrick Johnson, "When black Americans have employed the rhetoric of black authenticity, the outcome has often been a political agenda that has excluded more voices than it has included. The multiple ways in which we construct blackness within and outside black American culture is contingent on the historical moment in which we live and our ever-shifting subject positions." Johnson further notes that "whites also construct blackness. Of course, the power relations maintained by white hegemony have different material effects for blacks than for whites."[22] The competing expressions of blackness find their ways to the centers of these films and to a great degree organize themselves around definitional space.

Since there are multiple discourses of blackness within these films, those who are putatively black *and* who are firmly ensconced in Harlem are unironically black. In these films about race and late twentieth-century U.S. culture, the use of African American "extras" to define racialized space is striking. Thus, even at the level of racial performance, we see a tiered system of affiliation represented, and one aspect of that system is the degree to which a character exists outside of Harlem. A character's relative access to wealth depends on his or her ability to navigate normatively white space.

The act of identification and affiliation among African Americans is central to all of these films at their outset. In *Shaft*, *Superfly*, and *Black Caesar*, the principal characters are stylistically racialized: they wear clothes and affect manners that are associated with being black, while those in *Cotton Comes to Harlem* and *Across 110th Street* emphatically are not. These characters wear suits and offer their blackness as an inevitable aspect of who they are. But their demeanor, while representative of a possibility of African American expression, is by no means the only type that occurs in the films. Indeed, the middle-class aspirations of these characters are juxtaposed with the desire for wealth and lack of opportunity that reveal themselves in the actions of African American criminals. Beyond these clearly contrasting groups, there are the denizens of Harlem who are shown as a kind of atmospheric backdrop, many of whom seem to have little to do but congregate on the streets. This range of characterization defines alternative means of comportment and brings the divergent visions of race articulated by these films into high relief. But even this vision of African Americans as a complex social group articulates a kind of hierarchy.

Intriguingly, all of these films have groups of black nationalists, with which the protagonists must consort as a matter of business. But in all of these films such assertions of blackness are denigrated as foolish and self-serving. In *Superfly*, a group of nationalists are told by Priest to "march somewhere else" and dismissed as posers. Revealingly, this scene is initially shot with a tight framing of the three nationalists with Priest and Eddie. The camera is behind and slightly above the one standing nationalist, so that they literally crowd and impinge upon the turf of the drug dealers. But as Priest dismisses them, they literally vanish from the scene: as Priest tells them to go away, we see only him and Eddie sitting alone at a table.

But it is in *Cotton Comes to Harlem* and *Across 110th Street* where this dismissal is most pronounced and comic. *Cotton Comes to Harlem* is most explicitly about race and nationalism, though it adopts a comic, if not ironic tone, and has at its center a back-to-Africa scam. The central African American characters are police officers. Though these figures are constantly afflicted by the institutional racism of the department, they are far from the hip race-men that we see in *Across* and *Superfly*. Gravedigger Jones and Coffin Ed Johnson are their departmental envoys to Harlem, and as such employ their ability to move within African American society and region. When we first meet these characters they are at a rally for a back-to-Africa movement put on by the Reverend Deke O'Malley (figure 4.4). Their distance from and skepticism regarding the plan sets them apart from those at the rally, as does their dress and overall demeanor.

FIGURE 4.4 *Cotton Comes to Harlem*: A rally with nationalists.

Compared to the police officers, however, O'Malley and his hangers-on are more decidedly "black" in their speech, dress, and body language. At points, O'Malley wears a dashiki. In the opening scene of the movies we see him traveling uptown with an entourage, riding in his Rolls-Royce. As he traverses Harlem, moving from the south to the north, shots of the neighborhood are often framed from the car, locating his Rolls-Royce hood ornament amid the petit bourgeois solidity of a thriving 125th Street, and then the relatively empty and boarded-up regions to the north. O'Malley is initially dressed in a flowing black cape, which he eventually removes to show a white linen suit. As he addresses the crowd, he is clearly above them, shot onstage from a low angle that captures his looming above the masses. In this case explicit assertions of blackness are the cause of suspicion.

The film offers the recurring line, a refrain in the opening song, a chant when offered by the Reverend, and an ironic lament when invoked by Coffin Ed and Gravedigger, "Am I black enough for you?" It also provides a symbolic link to African American history in its use of a bale of raw cotton as a symbol and as a McGuffin. Even the performance piece at the Apollo Theater is broad and racial, a song about Cotton coming to Harlem, referring not only to the bale in which the money has been hidden but also to the black migration, when cotton was the commodity to get away from, when it symbolized the worst of the slavocracy in the large plantations of the old Southwest of Georgia, Alabama, Mississippi, and Louisiana. Thus, in this film blackness is that which is explicitly invoked by racist whites and opportunistic African Americans.

The militant group "the Black Berets" is part of Deke's security detail. Their ineffectual posture, connection to petty criminal enterprise, and laughable bush-suits make them absurd, and part of the officers' intended mission to protect black people from black people—from those who are racially insincere. Their dismissal is literally enacted in the film's first scene, as Gravedigger and Ed literally fling a member of that group in the air, showing the group's lack of gravity as well as the protagonist's lack of regard.

All of these films have at their center a desire for African American autonomy over the turf of Harlem, even as more fervent nationalism is dismissed. And all affiliate and differentiate black cops and criminals. That is, the two types are associated by race but divided by ethics and intent. Such a division, of course, further distinguishes our heroes from the masses. In *Across 110th Street*, Yaphet Kotto plays a police lieutenant, named Pope, who is the model of a cop who aspires to institutional mobility. The film is a caper plot that follows a parallel chase between the police and the mafia to find the three African-American men who robbed a numbers bank in Harlem and killed the men who had been counting the money. The bank is run by a local leader, Doc Johnson, who works for the downtown mob.

Pope clearly identifies with (and is identified by) some notion of a black community. But, in a more focal way, he is committed to his own advancement. He is chosen by the department to investigate the murders of the numbers operatives because he is able and black, and because the murders took place in Harlem.

This film offers such aspiring African American professionals as the antidote to the decadence that has set in among white ethnics, who constitute the overwhelming majority of the force. This is also the case in *Cotton*, as an Irish captain is shown to be corrupt. In *Across 110th Street*, the numbers boss has been paying off an Italian cop, played by Anthony Quinn. In a defining scene, just after the first of the three men has been literally crucified by the mob, Vitelli barges in on Johnson and waves his finger in his face, shouting "No more crucifixions." Doc speaks to him with contempt and condescension, as the scene is shot in a series of close-ups, until he gets up from his meal at his desk and approaches Vitelli, showing that, despite the lieutenant's contempt for Johnson, he is within this criminal's grasp. And though Doc, the numbers boss of Harlem, assumes a kind of affiliation with Pope, Pope wants no part of him. He refuses his patronage within the department and his bribe in a succession of close-ups in which Johnson never becomes more proximate, and which culminates in Johnson imploring, "Take the money brother," to which Pope, in the tightest close-up of the scene, in which Pope slightly turns to the side and spits: "Shove it up your ass—brother." Clearly for Pope, racial affiliation is not the primary system elaborating a social network, a fact confirmed by the film's visual language.

As Ed Guerrero notes in *Framing Blackness*, *Shaft* "refined and standardized the conventions of the 'superspade' protagonist, moving the genre squarely into the confines of Hollywood formula" (92–93). Part of this is defining Shaft's blackness in terms that do not rely on his being embedded in a black community. Shaft chooses to live in Greenwich Village and have his office in Times Square. And although Times Square lacks the cohesion of the ethnic neighborhood we encounter in other films of this era, it is a kind of home to Shaft, as the opening scene shows its slightly seedy contours—not nearly as threatening as it appears in *Midnight Cowboy*—and the crane shot zooms in on Shaft walking purposefully amid the relative chaos of picketers, tourists, and hustlers. After the initial shot of the panorama of Times Square, the film largely reverts to close-ups and medium close-ups, showing Shaft as a man with purpose in opposition to the milling crowds.

And rather than Shaft going to Harlem, at the beginning of the film, the characters that are connected to the focal aspects of the Harlem-centered plot come to Times Square. It is these African American representatives of that region who begin to define it (figure 4.5). We see Shaft accosted by two gunmen working for Bumpy Jones. As Shaft buys his newspaper from a stand on the street, he finds in

FIGURE 4.5 *Shaft*: Shaft in Times Square.

a tight shot that two men have been looking for him. "Harlem cats?" asks Shaft. The sense of intraracial connection that marks this scene is notable. What would distinguish these men as "Harlem cats" except for their blackness, and then maybe their shadiness? But this connection, while denoting association, does not define fraternity. When Shaft spies one of the men in his office building, he surprises him and holds him at gunpoint, and then eventually throws him from a window. When Shaft is questioned by the police, the scene is shot in a succession of close-ups which contrast with the two shots that have marked Shaft's conflict with his black assailants. But we learn about relative proximity when Bumpy himself comes to Times Square, and the close-ups define an even wider space, as Shaft shows his disdain for the way in which Bumpy exploits the black community. The end of the scene shows us Shaft in a medium close-up angrily saying, "Fake mother." Yet, even as we see a closer connection between Shaft and Vic, the Italian cop, than we do between Shaft and Bumpy, Shaft's blackness and connection to Harlem is well established in these scenes.

That all of the protagonists in these films are, by whatever devices, socially and economically successful, marks them as emphasizing a degree of black aspiration and success among these more able, if sometimes nefarious, characters. Such an emphasis not only replicates the vision of black enterprise put forth by the

Nixon administration; it also affirms a world where traditional African American communities were distending, as class became a more important marker within the urban African American population than it had been prior to this historical point.

Unlike the figures who define a higher echelon of the African American social system, these "others" are vital to claim the terrain of Harlem as black and thus to make sure that our characters who stretch the codes of racial definition can find a "home." It is indeed intriguing that in a film like *Across 110th Street*, the very dark-skinned criminals who rob the Harlem numbers bank are unironically black and are in and of Harlem. This makes them unique among the central characters of these films. So it is somehow fitting that these black men, unlike Shaft, Priest, or any of the others, are literally unable to get out.

PLACE

The physical space of Harlem in these films is, like Little Italy in *The Godfather* and *Mean Streets*, distinctive; but it is primarily depicted as a region constrained from without, rather than a space that coheres from within. In any number of films the distinctive social terrain of Harlem asserts 110th Street as a barrier, and not simply a boundary. All of these films offer high-angle shots of New York City that zoom down to Harlem. In such a configuration, Harlem appears as an island, cut off from other places by a land barrier (Central Park), an elevated rail line that has the appearance of a wall, a river, and, in the case of *Cotton Come to Harlem*, a highway. It also possesses its own distinctive feel, derived not just from its racial composition but also by its decay and relative emptiness. The juxtaposition that defines Harlem as a relative space also emphasize its lower physical scale, as it possesses no buildings with, for example, the sweep and height of Tommy's apartment building on the East Side, a place that has a balcony that looks out on Harlem, but which is never located *from* that neighborhood.

In a very different type of film, Sidney Lumet's *The Wiz* (1978), the classic *The Wizard of Oz* (1939) is reimagined as a contemporary tale of Harlem. Interestingly, though the production is one of whimsy and fantasy, Oz is marked in central Manhattan by the spire of the Chrysler building and Harlem, through all of the touches of whimsy, looks much like the Harlem of these earlier films and is afflicted by many of the same factors: poverty, drugs, unemployment, and the decline of the built environment. And even Dorothy's journey in its way echoes that of many we see in the blaxploitation films; however, *The Wiz* is distinct in that getting home to the vestiges of middle-class Harlem, a world that is all but invisible in these earlier films, becomes a desirable goal and the intention that drives the narrative.

But in all of these films, including *The Wiz*, Harlem is defined as a place that has historically been outside of the pressures that spawned the physical rescaling of other parts of Manhattan. This view of the region makes its distinctness a fact of geography, as the films have the effect of conjoining that which is man-made and that which is not. In Harlem, crime flourishes in the open spaces created by urban disinvestment and illicit activity, and results in chaos. In *Across 110th Street*, characters are literally snared as they try to leave, making Harlem a ghetto that refers to its historical antecedents in Warsaw in the 1940s.

Each of these films has at least two African Americans at its center and any number at their periphery. As such, they provide an appearance of being about a world that is racialized and posit that at least a subdivision of that world is normatively black. Yet African Americans in all of these films fail to constitute a social world that is self-sufficient in any significant way, a fact that all of these films take pains to point out. As a result, Although there is a white world and a black world, they are not parallel spheres. And some degree of each film's dramatic tension derives from characters attempting to make them so. All of the protagonists live to some degree in the white world: even Priest frequents his white girlfriend's apartment on Park Avenue, and she finds him drug buyers through her social contacts. *Across 110th Street* displays its metaphor in its title: the world defined by Harlem is a self-contained geography; but its social dimension includes white *and* black police officers who don't live there and Italian gangsters who do business there but clearly live somewhere else. Even its residents pine for a return to elsewhere, as in the character Jim Harris (played by Paul Benjamin) seeking to return to Jamaica.

And indeed, the logic of this view of ghetto is asserted earlier in the film as the crime bosses celebrate a family event apparently at the Plaza Hotel, just after the numbers' bank has been robbed in Harlem. As they discuss the implications of the robbery, they look from a relatively high floor out on Central Park and spy Harlem, and the towers of St. John the Divine Cathedral on 110th Street, in the distance. A deep focus shot emphasizes the relationship between these larger-than-life figures of the foreground and the lurking background (figure 4.6). The boss refers to Central Park as "the no-man's land that separates us from the blacks in Harlem," and the shot confirms Harlem as a self-contained community but under control from without, as the boss professes the need not to "lose Harlem."

In contrast with *The Godfather* films and *Mean Streets*, which idealize an ethnic space suffused with nostalgia, these blaxploitation films are of the present and virtually without explicit reference, either visual or verbal, to better days. All provide iconic shots of 125th Street, many of which feature the Apollo Theater. But none explicitly refers to its former function as the center of a glamorous and vital region. For example, in *Black Caesar*, as Tommy asserts Harlem as his domain and

FIGURE 4.6 *Across 110th St.*: View of Harlem from across Central Park.

James Brown chants, "Pay the cost to be the boss," on the soundtrack, we see Tommy strutting down 125th Street amid crowds, and spy the Apollo marquee advertising Wilson Pickett (figure 4.7). A tracking shot shows various storefronts, and though the residual glamour of the name and the spot still obtains, the actual vision of this street is modest, though certainly far more attractive than outlying districts.

And while 125th street is a link with the past, the present is all around and defined by urban despair. In contrast to the commerce on 125th Street, the empty and garbage strewn streets of the outlying areas, places where some people still live, look even worse. We also see interiors of the apartment buildings of Harlem, and they decidedly lack glamour. They show peeling paint, leaking pipes, and broken floors. In *Across 110th Street*, one of our criminals is also a building superintendent, who is badgered by his tenants, in high-angle shots in the stairwell that emphasize the entrapping space of the building, to fix all manner of mechanical systems; until he suggests that the tenants contact the absentee landlord in Mexico, "Where he likes to go this time of year." In contrast, the apartments of those who have moved out of the district—Shaft, Priest, Tommy in *Black Caesar*—all are clean and well appointed in a distinctly 1970s fashion.

In the films that place their protagonists outside of Harlem, the initial forays of their characters into that region, and some subsequent trips, are embellished with a kind of theatricality. This takes the form of Shaft's "uptown, brother" directive to a cab driver, or the momentous music that accompanies Priest as he pilots his Cadillac Eldorado up Park Avenue for several minutes of that film's running time. While the trip uptown is shown as dramatic, there is not a single trip downtown

FIGURE 4.7 *Black Caesar*: Tommy, the king of Harlem in front of the Apollo.

that occurs in these films. The predominant movement of traffic seems to flow only one way: Harlem can be reached from the white city, but the links to the white city from Harlem are far less visible.

As such, the relative isolation and resulting poverty that defines Harlem has the effect of seeming perpetual and inevitable, a consequence of geography rather than racism and disinvestment. And while the visual strategies employed to define Little Italy have the effect of making it into an urban village, as its scale is reduced by ground-level camera placements shooting across the streets of that region but rarely down the avenues, the films of Harlem adopt contrasting visual strategies. As I noted earlier, in almost all of these films the region is located by a high-angle shot that eventually finds Harlem and then zooms down to the ground level. These visual strategies that capture the region lack the intimacy of those in the films of ethnicity, as we see wide-angle shots of streets filled with garbage and, at times, small groups of idle men. Harlem is clearly a ghetto and not a neighborhood, so it cannot be idealized as a space for African American community and families. It looks like a place that one would want to leave, as all of our protagonists do. The avenues are shot from mid-range and ground level, so that we can see down them but never to the region beyond. These films offer a vision of poverty as inhering within racialized urban spaces.

Harlem's centrality in these films suggests much about their emphases. Though these films limit historical reference, even if we open them up as narratives that refer to the past, as is the case in the beginning of *Black Caesar* or, more intriguingly and playfully in *Cotton Comes to Harlem*, that story is not very old.[23] As John L. Jackson Jr. tells us in his thoughtful and intriguing study, *HarlemWorld: Doing*

Race and Class in Contemporary Black America, "Harlem is a place set apart. It functions as a geographical space evoked for clear-cut racial distinction. . . . It is Harlem's well-known and history-laden position as 'the black Mecca,' the 'capital of black America,' and the 'queen of all black belts' that positions it snugly within the quotation-marked-off domain of stereotyped assumptions, both positive and negative" (19). But the association of blackness and the idea and region of New York's Harlem is a relatively recent historical phenomenon. It has its origins in the black migration from the South in the late nineteenth century: some of those migrants came to New York City, but primarily to neighborhoods in central Manhattan, particularly the "tenderloin district" near Times Square. In 1900, African Americans constituted only 2 percent of the city's population. By the end of the twentieth century, that figure was around 30 percent. As African Americans moved to northern cities in the late nineteenth and early twentieth centuries, they found themselves restricted in their housing choices by white property owners and others. Harlem became a destination of choice as a result of its having been overbuilt in the 1890s, leaving speculators with an excess of housing that they made available to the new arrivals. And as African Americans moved in, racist housing practices resulted in this region becoming a primarily—and then almost exclusively—black residential zone.

Its cultural status derived from the rhetoric and prominence of the New Negro movement in the 1910s and 1920s, a period when African American intellectuals sought to align group identity and cultural significance with a particular place. Wrote Alain Locke, "Harlem is neither slum, ghetto, resort nor colony, though it is in part all of them. It is—or promises at least to be—a race capital. . . . Harlem has the same role to play for the New Negro as Dublin has had for the New Ireland or Prague for the New Czechoslovakia."[24] Though the depression took its toll on the economically precarious African American community, Harlem retained its symbolic status, despite being increasingly overcrowded, afflicted by relative poverty and the neglect of absentee landlords. But with the gradual decline of cities in the post–World War II era, Harlem suffered disproportionately. This resulted in general infrastructural decline, a loss of population, and a rise in crime.[25]

None of our African American crime figures (or the groups associated with them) is insulated by his community; rather, they all employ armed guards and hangers-on. These men are far from the group of trusted lieutenants with significant responsibilities that define the Mafiosi clans. African American gangsters are out in the world with little support from friends or family, and all are under duress from competing Italian Americans. As the protagonists of films like *Black Caesar* and *Shaft* become more prosperous, they become relatively less safe, as their residing in predominantly white neighborhoods affords them no cover. Further, they either are encroaching on Italian turf, as in *Shaft*; or, in a film like *Superfly*, the dangerous men of Harlem easily find and accost them within their largely white environs.

Though these changes in place of habitation seem logical within the context of the films and within the historical frame of reference, it does point out the reigning negative conception of the African American enclave uptown, as well as how normative racialized space is definitional for people of color—even if they do not live there. While, for example, it also seems comprehensible that Italian Americans may prosper but choose not to leave lower Manhattan, such a choice seems outside of the logic of these films. This contrast signifies the vision of community specific to each wave of films. As purveyors of regional crime and violence, these gangsters of color wreak havoc on their community. Tellingly, although in all of these films Italian gangs seek entry to the spoils of Harlem, no African American gangster seeks to violate Italian territory.

By the early 1970s, Harlem's descent had passed a point of desperation. The riot of 1964 and the lesser one after the assassination of Martin Luther King in 1968 had exacerbated extant trends toward depopulation and disinvestment, dispositions that were a matter of a broader disinvestment in U.S. cities. Arguably, the decline of African American neighborhoods was accelerated by the Civil Rights movement of the 1960s, which had the effect of opening up other residential possibilities for people of color. Explains one group of urban sociologists, "Up until the mid 1960s, inner-city neighborhoods were best categorized as mixed-income communities. . . . And significant numbers of non-poor blacks relocated to more socioeconomically diverse neighborhoods throughout the 1970s and 1980s, many inner-city communities confronted the growth of two problems, the 'concentration effects' of poverty and joblessness and the erosion of a social buffer that had long played a role in the stability of urban black communities."[26] And although Watts in Los Angeles certainly had a related dynamic, the black exploitation films set in New York reference a region marked by massive disinvestment, unemployment, and the decline of the built environment.

The impact of disinvestment on population density is a matter of the fabric of all five of these films. When in *Across 110th Street* our Italian gangsters exit from the Henry Hudson Parkway onto the streets of Harlem, the relative amount of traffic, number of pedestrians, and even the way in which housing fills a given city block shows us the way Harlem defines a hole that interrupts the fabric of the urban environment, a hole that becomes deeper as the camera moves toward the center of the neighborhood. When, in *Superfly*, Priest pilots his car uptown, we watch the texture of the neighborhood change over the top of his hood ornament, a device that focuses our eye and our scrutiny. When he arrives in Harlem, he is accosted in the entryway of a dilapidated and possibly uninhabited building and eventually chases his assailants into vacant lots and vacant buildings. As he runs, he is framed by a mobile camera that views him from a slightly skewed angle, aestheticizing and exoticizing the urban rubble. This view of Harlem as empty and decayed is key to these narratives, which all focus on issues of crime and exploitation within the black community, showing the tensions between black criminal entrepreneurs and white ones.

Such definitions emerge with no explanation in particular, and thus are naturalized. But with the insights of history and social analysis, we can see that the reason this region is poor and black is that racist housing practices have created a ghetto and that deindustrialization affects those on the margins of the economic system first. Black participation in the New York City labor force declined by around 10 percent between 1960 and 1970, and then declined by another 10 percent between 1970 and 1980.[27] Statistics show that central Harlem was a virtually a completely segregated neighborhood in 1970 and remained so for at least the next twenty years.[28] Demographic studies also show us why it is so easy to get a parking space: from 1970 to 2000, the population density of Central Harlem declined by 32.7 percent while East Harlem declined by 23.8.[29]

Harlem is not only disrupted in both its inside and outside space. These films adopt visual strategies that enlarge its area to make it more encompassing. As an aspect of this vision of dissolution, *Shaft*, *Superfly*, and *Across 110th* street all lump the three portions of Harlem together. Harlem consists of three regions: west, central, and east Harlem. In the west, which includes Columbia University and the largely white neighborhood of Inwood, there are far more whites and far more prosperity. Central Harlem is the historic center of African American life, and East Harlem is largely Hispanic and marked by large, high-rise housing projects that were built in the 1950s. West Harlem includes Riverside Drive, the Henry Hudson Parkway, and the Hudson River, while East Harlem includes the Harlem-Hudson commuter rail line, including raised tracks that cut the region from north to south at Park Avenue. The geography of these films frequently includes the rail cut, the rivers, and the parkway as a means of showing restrictive physical borders that keep people in and out. For example, in *Shaft* and in *Across 110th Street*, the rail-cut that defines the border between Central and East Harlem is a vital visual marker, defining the limits of the neighborhood as well as its insularity. It is there that Shaft finds his informant and corners him.

In order to flesh out the implications of the recurring visual strategies of ghettoization, we can locate these films in relation to Henri Lefebvre's organizing conception of urban space, distinguishing between the centripetal space of older cities with clear centers, and centrifugal cities with far-flung spaces.[30] And while some have argued that the visual device of organizing space centripetally encourages localism and democratic interactions within politics, in these films, centripetal space is the visual rhetoric of ghettoization and an approximation of the ways in which centripetal space is a feature of the map of a colonizer. By centripetal space here, I mean a vision of the world as Harlem, a distinctly Harlem-centered visual map of the region and the world.[31] Though Lefebvre never talks about race in his discussion of urban space, he does provide, as Eugene McCann shows us in his astute discussion of the racialization of urban space in Lexington, Kentucky, that conceptual lines of segregation can easily become reified as an absolute boundary.[32]

These films, then, serve as an intriguing complement to those of the preceding chapter, as they provide a clear contrast between the spaces of race and those of ethnicity. Indeed, their strategies of geographical organization seem to naturalize the racial and hierarchical distinctions between a neighborhood and a ghetto. As such, it is easy to see them, despite their ostensible friendliness to black cultural expression, participating in the culture of racial exclusion that proliferated in a New York City as it moved into its global-city phase of existence. In fact as in these films, Harlem would for a long time remain a discrete and underdeveloped zone, notable for a certain type of commerce. As such, it serves as an index of the uneven flow of capital within a well-articulated system of exchange and of the ways in which proximate space defined as "other" may remain distinct from nearby centers of commerce and culture.

5

Policing the Unsafe City

THE FRENCH CONNECTION (1971), *SERPICO* (1973), *DOG DAY AFTERNOON* (1975), *PRINCE OF THE CITY* (1981), AND THE RISE OF NEOLIBERALISM

IN THIS CHAPTER I further map the transition of New York City's history and representation by focusing on a group of films shot in New York and focused on crime and corruption. The films, released from 1971 to 1981, include *The French Connection* (1971), *Serpico* (1973), *Dog Day Afternoon* (1975), and *Prince of the City* (1981). They mark a moment in New York history, and in urban history more generally, showing the waning of the modernist epoch and announcing the beginnings of the post-modern.[1] Further, this distinction, as many have asserted, is far from simply textual. Indeed, in these representational films we see what Fredric Jameson has described as "the cultural logic of late capitalism," as these expressions elaborate the inevitability of neoliberal politics. Such politics include their own complementary spatial organization, as we see the distended and disorganized polis reach out toward a world system of commerce.[2]

The French Connection tells of two New York City police officers, Popeye Doyle and Cloudy Russo, obsessively seeking a cache of drugs imported from Marseilles, where it has been processed, to New York City. This is very much a chase movie, and as it proceeds, we see Doyle becoming more and more elemental in his single-mindedness. The officers ultimately fail to recover the dope, the money, or to send the smugglers to jail for an appreciable amount to time.

Serpico is the tale of a New York City detective, Frank Serpico, who refuses to participate in the graft that is usual to the job, estranging him from both his fellow officers and his superiors. His desire to seek out and expose departmental corruption gradually consumes him, and also results in his getting shot. This occurs when he is on a drug raid and his partners allow him to get stuck in a doorway, offering no support as he is ultimately shot in the face.

Dog Day Afternoon is the unlikely tale of a Vietnam vet named Sonny Wojcek and his friend, Sal, who hold up a branch bank in Brooklyn, taking hostages, so that Sonny can fund his partner's sex-change operation. The extensive negotiations result in the hostages, Sonny, and Sal all being transported, under federal guard, to JFK airport, where they are supposed to release the hostages and be put on a plane bound for Algeria. At the airport, the guards shoot Sal, and Sonny is taken away into custody.

Prince of the City tells of a detective with the Special Investigations Unit (SIU) of the NYPD, a task force devoted to disrupting the drug trade. The detective, named Danny Ciello, decides to testify about police corruption, but vows his own relative innocence and refuses to implicate his partners. The investigators are initially an arm of the local government, but, as the movie progresses, the investigation grows and ultimately is administered by federal prosecutors. As he testifies, Ciello feels more and more compromised by his revelations and their results. He also finds his own actions and relative innocence being questioned. In the end, we are left to question his initial decision to get involved with the investigators, as well as to question what defines guilt and innocence.

Given their concern with New York as a focal element of narrative, it is no surprise that these four films are directed by esteemed directors whose interest was vital to their productions. Three of these films are directed by Sidney Lumet and one by William Friedkin. Friedkin's *The French Connection* was a multiple academy award winner, including best director, and established him as a major figure in Hollywood. And although Friedkin did direct a number of films that employed urban textures as important elements of the plot—*The Exorcist* (1973, Washington, D.C.), *The Brinks Job* (1978, Boston), *Cruising* (1980, New York)—he did not focus intently on New York, or on urban scenes in particular. Still, his feel for the city and its dynamism energizes the film and makes it a notable production about both time and place.[3]

Lumet, on the other hand, is perhaps, with Scorsese and Woody Allen, the ultimate director of films of New York City. From *12 Angry Men* (1957), a film shot in a studio but which referenced New York, to his recent *Before the Devil Knows You're Dead* (2007), Lumet's extensive and notable career has largely, though not exclusively, situated him in New York. Both *Serpico* and *Dog Day Afternoon* were nominated for multiple awards, including Al Pacino for best actor in both *Serpico* and *Dog Day*. *Serpico* also won Writers Guild and Directors Guild awards, and *Dog*

Day Afternoon's writer, Frank Pierson, won the academy award for best screenplay, while Lumet was nominated for best director. *Prince of the City*, though generally well reviewed, was afflicted by a problematic release.[4] It was finally given general distribution during the Christmas season on 1981, though its New York premiere was in August. Its dark tone and long running time (137 minutes) were not well suited to holiday audiences, and it soon vanished from theaters. And because it was less successful at the box office, it was also less recognized by the various award-granting organizations, though Lumet and his co-writer Jay Presson Allen were nominated for an academy award, and the film did win a New York Film Critics Circle award.

Serpico and *Prince of the City* are generally grouped together as two parts of a trilogy (with *Q and A*, 1990). They are discussed as the more successful films of the three and bear close relationships of plot, theme, and locations. The major distinction, in Lumet's own view, readily apparent in the film, is that *Serpico* is a character study, as is *Dog Day Afternoon*, and *Prince* is far more concerned with the police department as an institution. *Prince* is also far more technically realized, as Lumet develops specific formal strategies within the film to highlight the increasing moral ambiguity of the main character, Detective Danny Ciello. This method involves, primarily, lighting and lenses. Lumet explains:

> For *Prince of the City* I decided to shoot the entire film at an aperture of 2.8 in order to give it a certain visual style. I told Andrez Bartkowiak, my cinematographer, that I did not want any normal lenses. In order to create an atmosphere of deceit, and false appearances, we used only wide angle and zoom lenses. The lighting in the first half was never on the actors but rather on the background. In the middle of the film, the lighting had to alternate between the foreground and the background, and at the end, the lighting was aimed on the foreground only.[5]

Lumet's strategy allows us to see his characters as both part of a system and part of a place, a view that suggests the inevitability of corruption.[6] As the inner lives of the main characters are revealed as more tormented, and actually become so, they stand out against their contexts in more pronounced and garish ways.

Like many of the films discussed in the earlier chapters, these four include markers of race and ethnicity. Often the white-ethnic police are pitted against the racially defined criminals—Hispanics and African Americans—but the emphasis on crime and policing alters the explicit focus, so that group identity is a given, and the central questions of the films are organized around the ability and desire of a law enforcement entity to sustain or create order. Thus, the productions, with the exception of Lumet's *Dog Day Afternoon* (1975), are from the point of view of those who look at crime and seek to control it—though intriguingly, some number of those figures become criminals to apprehend criminals, as is the case of Popeye Doyle in *The French Connection*, and the groups of rogue cops in *Serpico* and *Prince of the City*. The films dramatize a deeply flawed and compromised system of law enforcement. Such a view well fits into the broader vision of the city-in-decline that has marked the films of this era, but the emphasis on policing further points to a city that has ceased to function, and that may never again succeed in being an entity that can be governed from within. Indeed, such judgments of the city's inability to run itself ultimately lead to other strategies of governance, including the privatization of many activities related to law enforcement.

Such a view is a comprehensible historical judgment. As we look at the chronology of these film that mark the last failed days of the Lindsay administration, among the many areas of public dysfunction was the police department. The Knapp Commission hearings into police corruption commenced in October of 1971, uncovering massive and systemic corruption within the system, and concluding that a stunning proportion of all New York City officers took illicit bribes.[7] The police department experienced these revelations as further reason for apathy and loss of morale, which exacerbated rampant feelings of being underappreciated and underpaid by the patrician Mayor Lindsay and his police commissioner, Patrick Murphy.[8] Crime statistics for New York and all of the nation's urban areas spiked in the sixties and seventies; for example, New York's murder rate climbed 137 percent between 1966 and 1973. As the city moved toward fiscal insolvency, police officers became, in some ways, just another group of public employees seeking resources from a city that had few.

More than the films of other chapters, these films assert their representational efficacy in powerful ways. *Serpico*, *The French Connection*, *Dog Day Afternoon*, and *Prince of the City* are all based on actual characters and events, and therefore enhance their documentary authority through their assertion of factuality. This includes the marking of dates, the use of characters and events known to a relatively broad public—such as the Knapp Commission Hearings, the French Connection bust (three of these films reference that drug smuggling operation)—and the use of titles telling of the outcomes of the various characters of the film after the "action" of the film concludes. These methods well coincide with the broader formal strategies of these films: this disposition to document derives from—and results in—a realist perspective. That is, all of these films operate within conventions of representational cinema, emphasizing physical context, naturalist acting, low-key lighting, and apparently ordinary language. The city we see is one that has been left to the criminals, and the role of law enforcement is not to make the streets safe for the ordinary denizens of the city, since we barely see such people. The streets apparently become the site of a moral war between those who stand for good and those who stand for evil. But the distinctions as the films proceed become more and more oblique, and this presents yet another angle of vision that reveals social and physical dissolution. In their focus on the extraordinary difficulty of keeping or making New York City safe, these films expand the terrain of the city and its connection to the world beyond. They open up New York to the world, and as such offer distinctive narratives of world trade and immigration. Further, all significantly expand the horizontal domain of the city while picturing it as less vertically imposing than do, say, *Klute* and *Midnight Cowboy*.

POST-FORDISM ARRIVES

The architectural critic Charles Jencks chronicles the symbolic end of the modernist epoch as occurring at 3:32p.m. on July 15, 1972, the moment when the Pruitt-Igoe Housing Projects in St. Louis were razed.[9] Such a structure symbolized the functionalist modernist aesthetic, as well as a vision of urban life as subject to the administrative power and wisdom of planners and experts. But although symbolic acts such as this have their resonance, the residue of the modern persists in the realm of the postmodern. That day in 1972 points only to gradual shifts in what Fredric Jameson calls the "cultural dominant," though we can easily see the ways in which the transition to postmodern aesthetics and their economic analogues align chronologically. Indeed, the Pruitt-Igoe projects were falling to the ground less than a year after Richard Nixon officially ended the Bretton Woods system of international monetary policy. By early 1972, all major world currencies "floated" in value, which allowed for fluidity in finance and trade that moved toward a multicentered system of world industrial production, as capital was freed to seek out lower-wage regions and global investments of all kinds. Though Jencks's ability to proclaim confidently the moment of transition from one period to another is notable for its certainty, history offers a far more ragged edge.[10] These films, through their emphasis on sprawling space, distended systems, and the illicit acquisition of wealth, effectively show the ideological disposition to rethink many of the core beliefs of modernism and its corollary mode of production, Fordism, and as such reveal to us the rise of the postmodern and its corollary mode of production, post-Fordism or the mode of flexible accumulation.[11] As such, their emphasis on crime and policing within a specific urban setting become more general considerations of issues of commerce and broad conceptions of relative space.

A related and complicating marker is the opening of Number One World Trade Center in January of 1972.[12] The tower's construction and brief status as the world's tallest building point to the city's increasing desperation and its ill-conceived ways of attempting to address its fiscal problems. From its design to its financial impracticality, the World Trade Center was a botch from its conception. Yet, the buildings would become a symbol of New York and the eminence of finance capital in the United States. By 2001, they were home to a number of companies that were significant traders in the regime of globalized capital. It is ironic and historically intriguing that this icon of the dimming modernist moment ultimately served as a symbol of capital in the post-Fordist era of flexible accumulation.

PLANES, TRAINS (SUBWAY), AUTOMOBILES, AND BOATS, TOO

By the 1960s, policing in New York had become substantially an activity done by squad car. Some have argued that this change altered the nature of law enforcement, making it more reactive than proactive, resulting in the elevation of bureaucracy, and disrupting relationships between law enforcement officials and the people they were supposed to protect. Fittingly, these films focus distinctly on matters of transportation, a concern that ultimately relates to matter of scale. Although Europe, Corsica, North Africa, and western Asia—the loci of the drug transactions in *The French Connection* and the destination of choice for Sonny Wojcek in *Dog Day Afternoon*, are indeed remote from the United States, the existence of modern means of shipping and communication, as well as the proliferation of intercontinental plane travel, has the effect of reducing the effective distance.[13] And as remote places seem closer, New York, as defined by an uninviting and inefficient subway system and car traffic that limits movement, presents significant problems of traverse, difficulties that law enforcement officials seek to transcend through their use of cars. Automobiles, as I discussed in earlier chapters, are antithetical to the density and natural social life of cities. Yet, by the 1970s, law enforcement officials have all but eliminated foot patrols and, as a recognition of the nature of urban sprawl, become dependent on cars.[14]

This emphasis on transportation as the key to the city is not just relevant to these films, as we have seen in the films of the first chapter, as well as in the films of the next. This focus may be used to consider the limits and extent of Rico and Joe's Manhattan traverses in *Midnight Cowboy*, the privileged perspective of Travis Bickle in *Taxi Driver*, the role of marathon running in *Marathon Man*, and the fact that Paul Kersey in *Death Wish* chooses the subway as his site for vengeance. In addition, in there are two other films that fit well with this chapter: *The Seven Ups*

(1973) and *The Taking of Pelham One Two Three* (1974). The former well fits with *The French Connection*, which is not surprising, since it shares a producer (Philip D'Antoni), technical advisor (the retired NYPD cop Sonny Grosso, who is the basis for Roy Scheider's character in *The French Connection*), and actors, including Roy Scheider, who is the star. This film is, like *The French Connection* and the others of this chapter, car-focused and also features a focal car chase. *The Taking of Pelham*, featuring a subway hijacking, emphasizes the conjunctions and disjunctions of various modes of transportation, and, as it features the plot device whereby the ransom must be delivered to the hijackers by a certain moment, it dwells on the problem of navigating the city in an expeditious manner, and how that difficulty defines urban life.[15]

This focus on the various means of traversing the city derives from that found in many earlier noirs, such as *Naked City* (1948), *DOA* (1950), *Asphalt Jungle* (1950), and virtually all of the noirs set in Los Angeles, not to mention noirish television shows like *Tightrope* (1959–1960), *Naked City* (1958–1963), and *Highway Patrol* (1955–1959). But unlike these earlier films, the car and the subway now are not symbols of greater ease of traverse, of progress; rather, they are further emblems of decline and the inability of the tools of law enforcement to keep pace with urban chaos. Indeed, they signal a distension of scale, not the mastering of a fixed space. The car functions most efficiently in *Serpico*, but primarily as a means of picking up graft; otherwise, it serves primarily as an impediment to movement. Further, the relative utility of cars is in sharp contrast to that of the planes and the helicopter we see in *Dog Day Afternoon*. Indeed, this particular approach to space, one that finds it amoebic and most easily traversed through the air, is part of the postmodern emphasis of these films.

In the films that are more central to this chapter, the transition between the world of Frank Serpico and that of Danny Ciello in *Prince of the City* expresses a shift from cops as urban residents to that of commuter cops living in distant corners of the metro area, a change similar to the one foreshadowed by Don Corleone's move to Long Island. This sense of a far-flung force is elaborated in the first scenes of the film, as we see Ciello restless in his suburban bed, and then, after an introduction to the Special Investigations Unit by their identity cards, we find him, in a very different venue, under the elevated tracks in the Bronx. When he learns of a drug delivery, the scene follows the calls of a phone tree, finding the various men spread around the city and beyond: from one detective in a mid-town restaurant, to another in his suburban basement playing ping pong, to another in the basement of the building of the Bronx where the shipment is taking place. The location shifts that follow the phone calls emphasize that proximity need not be persistently physical.

In *Dog Day Afternoon*, the police and news helicopters hovering over the bank where Sonny and Sal hold their hostages represent a further technological solution to the problem of urban sprawl, as well as define an ever-voyeuristic public. The variety of means of traverse suggest the relativity of scale and define it as a concept distinctly related to access to capital. With better networks and devices of transportation, distances shrink. And it is the fact that certain entities can command capital that creates the rhetoric of neoliberalism, a principle that defines the ultimate efficacy and moral correctness of markets, a formulation with only a modicum of real-world applicability, but one which elevates avarice to theory.

Both *The French Connection* and *Dog Day Afternoon* begin by introducing visions of New York that contextualize it as part of an extensive network of social relations, and those representations of connection have implications for its shifting economic status. These scenes are geographically extensive and distinctly fragmented. *The French Connection* (1971) begins with a series of scenes that cross-cut between New York and Marseilles, connecting not only the two geographies but also the two opposing entities of the film: drug traffickers and cops.[16] The film opens with a dissonant jazz soundtrack as we see a small inlet near the Port of Marseilles marked by distinctive houses and small wooden boats. This is clearly the civilized world, but it is not developed in a way that those in the United States would recognize. There are cars but little congestion, no squalor, no vacant lots or empty buildings. Indeed, it is a characteristic picture of European charm. The camera shoots from straight ahead and eye level, as we see a man leaving a bakery, eating a croissant for breakfast. We note him watching two well-dressed men, one who is Alain Charnier, a central character in the film, who soon enters a Lincoln Continental (figure 5.1). This car grabs our attention from the first, since it is garish and out-sized for the streetscape of this city. Its presence shows us an economic connection between France and the United States, as it is indicative of a system of trade that flows from the more developed to the less developed space of Europe. However, such a vision of product flow is not at all indicative of the typical movement of goods, and it is subsequently revealed as anomalous. It is more revealing in its showing us the way in which its owner is not fully of this place, as he mixes his work in shipping with a lucrative business in drug smuggling. Further, its singularity and lack of Europeanness suggest distinctions in scale and consumption between the United States and France. The car, then, in this more involved view of the character, belongs to one who stands outside of conventional systems of commerce.

We see the man next at a more public street, at an outdoor café, where the camera pans back so that we can see the two men and the Lincoln yet again. Soon after, the man, who is apparently a detective tailing these two, traverses the narrow

FIGURE 5.1 *French Connection*: Charnier in his Lincoln in Marseilles.

alleys of Marseilles, enters a bread store to buy a baguette, and, upon entering the vestibule of his apartment building, while gathering his mail, is shot in the head by Pierre Nicoli, the enforcer for Charnier. Nicoli, famously, pulls a piece of the baguette from the dead man's hand, and eats it. The way in which this execution takes place, among the banal activities of everyday life, suggests a certain kind of mercenary attitude, a view that commerce cannot be disrupted by the law. The threat of this investigator is clearly worth much more than his life. The scene also is more abrupt than any that take place in the United States, suggesting the ways in which this type of commerce influences behavior, a consideration that is also germane to *Serpico* and *Prince of the City*.

The scene then cuts to a darker, grainier shot of the United States, of Brooklyn, where we find a man dressed as Santa Claus entertaining a group of African American children, and another man tending a hot-dog cart. The camera moves horizontally but not vertically. This is a world where the frame is filled with action: kids, cops, criminals, cars, noise. There are no artful pans, nor direct cuts to adjust perspective. The two cops, Popeye and Cloudy, soon enter the abutting bar and begin harassing its patrons, physically and verbally accosting them. The scene ends with a chase through the devastation of the borough—empty lots, graffiti, abandoned buildings (figure 5.2). The camera is mobile throughout the chase, not only

FIGURE 5.2 *French Connection*: Popeye and Cloudy in the devastation of what passes as Brooklyn, though this scene is one of East Harlem standing in for that borough.

viewing movement but becoming movement itself. Popeye and Cloudy catch the man, harass and beat him, suggesting the distinction between the street criminals of the United States and the entrepreneurial criminals of Marseilles; not to mention the difference in police work.

The scene cuts back to Marseilles, a calmer place, where we see the same cosmopolitan-looking Frenchman from the opening scene, and find that he is involved in the expansion of the Marseilles waterfront so that it can accommodate larger cargo ships. The desirability of this expansion points to an increase in commerce between France and its global trading partners, a significant assertion within the context of this film. The cross-cut scenes culminate with the Frenchman's entry to New York, complete with car and drugs, thus merging the two strains of narrative, as well as revealing the potential points of resolution: either the New York police will uncover the smuggled heroin, or the smugglers will succeed. It is also intriguing that the ostensible premise for the trip is that Charnier is accompanying a documentary filmmaker who is making a film about New York for French television. That illegal transnational commerce is shielded by the most fluid of global products, information and entertainment, suggests to us how various types and scales of commerce interrelate. That New York becomes the point of sale for the drugs asserts a logic that emphasizes the extent of the New York market. That

New York as an entity is a matter of intrigue for the French entertainment market is connected to its status as a capital for drugs. That is, the fascination of New York for the French audience is, at least partially, its image as a wide-open economic market, and as a place where lawlessness abounds.

Dog Day Afternoon (1975) begins with a montage of the city set to the lilt of Elton John's *Amoreena*. The very structure of the montage introduces the city as a juxta-position of distinctive elements, a region defined by its variety, rather than a loca-tion with a coherent focus. The opening shot finds the Circle Line Ferry in the (apparently) idyllic blue of the Hudson River with a high-angle shot of the ferry leaving the dock. The camera pans back to show New Jersey in the background and the contours of the ferry's boat slip, revealing the city's expanse reaching out into the water, and the city within a larger but still circumscribed geography. The shot cuts to a dog eating out of trash can, and a drug deal on the street with homeless men in the background. These street-level and intimate shots end with a cut to a rooftop-pool in Queens, shot against the Manhattan skyline, as the stationary camera captures a boy jumping into the water. This movement away from Manhattan reveals that borough as a presence but not necessarily a defining or enveloping one. The montage shots are the only images of that island in the film. This is a New York of men working, people watering lawns, families lounging at the beach of Coney Island. It is a region in which the perimeter has become more significant than the center. Fittingly, as we cut to the Triboro Bridge, linking Queens, Brooklyn, and Manhattan, the camera pans up to planes heading toward La Guardia and Kennedy Airports (figure 5.3). The opening credits end as a car pulls up in front of the First Brooklyn Savings bank (which is actually the Chase Manhattan Bank, at 450 Avenue P in Brooklyn). The bank is an undistinguished two-story building set amid many similar buildings in an unmemorable corner of New York's sprawl. This is not exactly anyplace U.S.A., but the emphasis in these shots on a sprawling space that lacks definitional architecture or distinct contours, and which is largely defined by its horizontal mass, is one that recurs in the films of this chapter.

For William Friedkin in *The French Connection*, one of the emphases of his cross-cutting is the very different look and feel of each place, a distinction that is defined and emphasized by his camera work and editing style in each. The *French Connection's* view of Marseilles and the intrigue between the detective and the man we come to know as the drug importer Charnier is defined by long takes from a camera mounted at eye level, shooting directly across from its object in mid-range, generally capturing its figures in classical style, centered and framed from head to toe. There is little camera movement within scenes, merely continuity cuts to locate the detective's point of view. And this general style broadly defines the

FIGURE 5.3 *Dog Day Afternoon*: Planes over the Triboro Bridge.

three scenes in Marseilles, which are also notable for the quietness of the streetscape and the pristine clarity of the natural light.

New York, on the other hand is defined by extreme close-ups, slightly skewed
angles, frequent cuts, and unnatural and garish light. The streets are loud, as is the
music. The New York of the *French Connection* is a place of racial antipathy and
rough policing. Though the cross-cutting that marks the beginning of the film
ceases, the way in which it defines the dynamism and chaos of New York remains
an important emphasis of the film. This is a film that shows the French drug smugglers ensconced in their midtown hotel, so that its Manhattan is something of a
center for the region depicted. But the real action of the film takes place in the
outer boroughs—Brooklyn, and on Ward's Island in the East River, where the
heroin comes to land and to be sold. It is in Brooklyn that it permeates the community and becomes a commodity with real and distinct consequences. It is also a
film of cars, with much driving to traverse the extent of the sprawling city.

Both films show a New York that is vast and diverse, opening out to the world
beyond, both a microcosm and, in Lumet's montage, a macrocosm. Lumet's juxta-
positions offer a sharply conceived idea of the city, and one that can be applied to
all of the films of this chapter, all of which emphasize motion. This view is distinct
and complexly related to the centrality of crime and policing that marks these

films. In these films we see the core concept of New York shift to a city defined by its expanse and by its various means of traverse, including subways, cars, planes, helicopters, and boats. It is a space that ceases to operate from its center; rather, in most of these films there are few if any shots of central Manhattan and the iconic locations of that region. These are overwhelmingly films of the outer boroughs and as such, extend out to systems beyond, to further suburbs, to far-flung regions, and ultimately to the world.

Urban historians, including Robert Caro and Marshall Berman among others, note the change in New York City's landscape from the 1930s to the 1960s, with the building of bridges, parkways, and airports that disrupted the fabric of urban neighborhoods and opened access—in effect reduced distance—between the city and the world beyond. Both write insightfully about the coming of modernity to New York, as its self-contained neighborhoods with their ethnic character and distinctly local commerce are disrupted and, in some cases, destroyed by the "modernization" of the city. This process not only involves the replacement of older structures with massive and faceless housing developments some distance from established neighborhoods, such as Co-op and Lefrak cities.[17] It also involved the physical demolition of whole neighborhoods, as Berman notes in his discussion of the razing of a corridor in the South Bronx for the purpose of building the Cross Bronx Expressway, a part of Interstate Route 95. Such changes are well documented and a matter of the visual texture of these films. Such reconstruction altered the rhythms of everyday life, creating a bareness where a neighborhood used to be, a process we can easily see in the empty lots and unpopulated streets depicted in all of these films. Attempting to accommodate cars also altered the pace of cities, creating as well as a kind of frenetic pace, as walking was replaced by driving cars, which often sat in traffic and encouraged long-distance commutes. Writes Edward Dimendberg, employing language developed by Henri Lefebvre about films noir, a genre that is highly influential for all of these films of this chapter and the next,

> While both centripetal and centrifugal films noir spaces manifest traits of abstract space, each reveals distinct modalities of urban anxiety. For if the former elicits the agoraphobic sensation of being overwhelmed by space . . . the anxieties provoked by centrifugal space hinge upon temporality and the uncertainty produced by a spatial environment increasingly devoid of landmarks and centers and often likely to seem perpetually in motion."[18]

Such a sense of motion and altering of scale is a recurring feature of these films. It is the expanse that these films depict which spawns the need for more effective policing. In a city that is literally moving and extending beyond control, it becomes even more necessary for agents of law to police its borders to control those variable elements always entering this space. In films such as *The French Connection* and *Serpico*, this view of police work is at least noted, if not emphasized. That effective police work is virtually equated with ease of mobility tells us how far our conception of the city has come from the world of the Bowery Boys, where policemen walking a beat defined the profession.

These matters of speed and relative proximity are germane in a New York defined by spatial sprawl and, relative to the white-ethnic populations that define the population of the police stations, cultural sprawl. That it is a polyglot entity illustrates how involved this location is with a far-flung network of people, places, and goods. In their particular and at times peculiar ways, these films gesture toward the cosmopolitan, and at least toward the regional. Whether this takes the form of drug smugglers from France involving themselves in the drug trade of New York, Sonny's doomed request for passage to Algeria in *Dog Day Afternoon*, Frank Serpico learning Spanish to do his police work, or Ciello's largely Spanish-speaking informants, New York is now a place with porous borders that is defined by its multinational population and a flow of goods from without. And while it is arguable, as I noted in my discussion of *The Godfather* films, for example, that the historical process through which these insular definitions and affiliations were already in the process of being distended, as a matter of emphasis, these productions show a city that is literally exploding in all directions, and which is becoming increasingly defined not by its vertically imposing center but by its enormous horizontal sprawl.

This sense of an amoebic city results from the depiction of indeterminate space and shape that marks these films. In many of them, we see no discernable center, few large buildings, and few points of social, governmental, or economic focus. Popeye Doyle lives in a housing project in Brooklyn, a building with little charm and apparently few amenities, a location that is used in the film as a symbol of Doyle's chaotic personal life. Sonny lives in Queens; Ciello lives on Long Island. And in the films where we do see such a center, however briefly—*The French Connection*, *Serpico*, *Prince of the City*—that place seems unable to serve as a post from which all activities can be monitored and governed. The New York of these films is not a series of villages but a sprawl of faceless locales, including a strong representation of urban slums. Unlike the Little Italy of the earlier movies or even Harlem of *Across 110th Street* and *Little Caesar*, there is no center to the world of crime, as this activity seems increasingly organized in a scale that extends beyond the local.

The Little Italy we encounter in *The French Connection* seems somewhat peripheral to the central action of the film, placed in the film as a nod to the past. This lack of centrality is emphasized by the nature of the scene shot there, as well as by the fact that the location never recurs. The one time we see the streets that formerly housed a concentration of Italian Americans in lower Manhattan is near the beginning of the film when Popeye and Cloudy are tailing the two conduits for the imported heroin, Angie and Sal. The trip to Little Italy takes place after a brief stop at Ratner's on the Lower East Side, and before the excursion to Brooklyn that marks the end of the journey, defining it as something of a way station in a broader tour of the city. Little Italy is announced visually with a point-of-view shot, apparently from the front seat of Doyle's car, with a low-angle view of the neon sign of *Café Roma*. The viewer's perspective shifts to one of the unmarked police car as it rides through down Mulberry Street, one of the central streets of the district. The shot is from straight ahead, and it affords us the opportunity to see Sal park and then leave his car to drop off a briefcase. Clearly there is some individual of importance that has domain in this region, but within the context of the film this stop is almost incidental, and the real action takes place in Brooklyn and Ward's Island, where the drugs are sold and where the drugs are smuggled in an imported car.

In *Prince of the City*, Ciello's cousin Nick is a mobster who spends his days in Little Italy, at a social club with other Mafiosi. Nick is a relative center of authority for a time, as his connections save his cousin's life at least once. A corrupt bail bondsman who Danny bugs electronically questions whether he is informing on him and threatens to kill him. Ciello takes the gangster to Little Italy and Nick vouches for him. The shot of Nick giving his blessing is from across the street, framed against the social club, and suggests in its diminishing of Nick and his locale that Ciello will not long be able to rely on this man or organization (figure 5.4). And indeed, as Ciello is found out to be an informant, his cousin's head is found in a trash can on Mulberry Street.

This view of the decentered city has a historical dimension. Jon Teaford explains in his *The Metropolitan Revolution* that as the entertainment districts of major northeastern metropolises declined, so did its core of industry. "The central city was losing its preeminence of metropolitan employment. The outward migration of manufacturing accelerated, eliminating working class opportunities" (130). Jobs, entertainment, and shopping gradually shifted beyond the outer boroughs, to suburbs in all directions. The result was massive middle-class flight. If parts of Manhattan suffered from an erosion of middle-class residents, then Queens, Brooklyn, and the Bronx suffered in greater proportion, increasingly becoming the home to an urban underclass and new immigrants from the Caribbean, Latin America, and Asia. When Walter O'Malley moved his Dodgers to Los Angeles in 1957, he based his judgment in an appraisal of demographic and economic trends.[19]

FIGURE 5.4 *Prince of the City*: Ciello's cousin Nick vouches for him in Little Italy.

The picture of New York City that marks these films introduces it as various and connected to external regions in a multiplicity of ways. Drug use and drug trafficking is largely an outer-borough phenomenon, and even the investigation of police corruption largely takes place in the outer boroughs. *Serpico* shows us its named character moving to Greenwich Village, but his police work is largely in the Bronx and Brooklyn; and his family remains in the Bronx, even as the neighborhood loses vitality. When Serpico is confronted by the legion of corrupt cops who suspect him for his refusal of bribes, the scene takes place in the Bronx, in the shadow of Yankee Stadium, a presence that is distinct in its physical centrality.

It is intriguing that these films all shoot a significant number of their key scenes with characters framed against bodies of water and in the shadow of bridges. It is as though they are discomforted by the constraints of the land mass they inhabit and therefore look beyond it to abutting and more distant land masses. Such a scene, for example, is vital in *The French Connection*, a film in which shots of the Williamsburg, Brooklyn, and Triboro bridges abound. As Popeye and Cloudy seek the car that they are sure holds the heroin, the shadow of the Brooklyn Bridge looms over them in Lower Manhattan. The scene of apprehension takes place beneath the supports of the Triboro Bridge. Bridges become a means of hiding shady dealings, the places of margins, but indicative that the periphery is now where the action is.[20]

Further, the presence of Washington, D.C., as a place easily reached and ever-present in three films—*Serpico*, *Dog Day Afternoon*, and *The French Connection*—suggests the continuous connection between that place and New York. It is an admission of a breakdown of local authority: crimes of the region are subject to the enforcement procedures of the federal government. This suggests a shift in scale. As local governments find themselves inadequate to the demands of organizing the social and business aspects of the city, the larger organs of governance enter. Intriguingly, the intermediary level of the state is barely noted. Perhaps this is a matter of the necessary scale of international trade. Arguably, the increasing pressures to globalize international trade push decision making toward larger and larger entities, from the local to the federal to international groups such as the WTO and the IMF. As David Harvey notes, "The hierarchical scales at which human activities are now being organized are different from, say thirty years ago. 'Globalization' in part signifies an important aspect of this shift."[21] Of course, these films were made just under thirty years prior to this discussion. But with the historical luxury of hindsight, we are able to see how the "urban crisis" and its representation softened the way for a reorienting of scale, away from the local and toward the global. Indeed, in these films, federal enforcement and space seems no more effective than local, and the gesture toward Washington appears as a means of seeking alternatives to a broken system rather than the restitution of authority through invoking a more powerful entity.

The feds cannot protect Serpico; for Sonny in *Dog Day*, the feds offer only an illusion of authority. And perhaps the oddest segue to Washington occurs in *The French Connection*, where that seat of federal enforcement is used by the drug smugglers as a respite from the constant harassment by Popeye and the New York City police; though, of course, the ever-obsessed Doyle follows them. As Sal and Charnier meet on the Washington mall, shot in a mid-range two shot framed against the capitol, they come to a halt and the camera zooms to a speck in the background, which is revealed as Doyle surveying them with binoculars.

This shift in representation emphasizes a rescaling of space and systems, suggesting a crisis in specific and localized authority. It is no wonder that power leeches from this sprawling municipality, since its system and devices of governance are by no means equal to its size, complexity, and range of connections to outside systems. This shift in conception is certainly an element of the broader transition of the national and international economy in the 1970s, as these films provide a reading of a moment of change. In his *Consciousness and Urban Experience*, David Harvey offers a vocabulary for considering this shift, encouraging a view of the city as expansive, and requiring but perpetually resisting means of control from within. Harvey explains that urban space in a discrete regional and national context was necessarily the seat of the market economy to the late nineteenth century and early twentieth century, and therefore subject to being reconfigured and reconceived in the terms of that system. He roots this instrumentalism in a view that defines this by its assimilation of Fordist notions of space and organization, a conception that urban areas are subject to the organizational logic of the early century industrial workplace. This configuration would, then, be the basis of development and wealth. Cities in this period were also conceived of as finite, if expandable, and governable, and it was the job of experts— urban planners, reformers, and politicians—to define them and bring them under control. Thus, New York City could annex Brooklyn, Queens, the Bronx, and Staten Island in 1898, in order to add to its domain and tax revenues; and soon after, as a means of reining in what was now an expansive space into a mass that could be traversed in a reasonable amount of time, the city built its subway.[22]

Such infrastructural and political changes were based on economic considerations of the desirability of large cities and notions of the need for centralized authority; both ideas were lodged in a confidence that urban processes could be rationalized and organized for the greater good of order and general prosperity. Labor markets expanded and housing markets boomed. Writes Harvey, "The growing consensus that space must be, in spite of its evident fragmentations, objective, measurable, and homogeneous (how else could it be ordered for the rational conduct of business?) was accompanied by another emerging consensus toward the end of the late nineteenth century. Writers as diverse as Alfred Marshall and Proust concluded that space was a less relevant dimension of human affairs than time" (15). Harvey explains, as he invokes Karl Marx, that "under capitalism," it was necessary "to annihilate the constraints and frictions of space, together with the particularities of place. Revolutions in transport and communications are therefore a necessary rather than a contingent aspect of capitalist history" (15). The moment to which Harvey refers ushers in the era of the Fordist city. Whether it was through laws of work, comportment, education, and sanitation; or the rationalization of space by planners and of transportation by engineers, the experts of the early twentieth century sought to promote ease of movement, health, and above all, economic vitality.[23]

But by the late twentieth century, the systems of public management were clearly fraying, and this process was nowhere more visible than in New York. Where space had once seemed manageable in relation to time, with the sprawl of work and housing into the distant suburbs and exurbs it now seemed less so. And public systems, from the bankrupt rail lines to the dysfunctional subway, offered neither greater comfort nor reliability. But the city was on the verge of a new organizational logic, one that was far less linear in its understanding of the relations of discrete spaces and in its broader view of civic order. Any number of public functions, from policing, to schools, to transportation, were now increasingly subject to the self-actualizing logic of the marketplace. As we see the sprawl of the city, and understand the ways in which crime is not just a matter *for* the police but now is a problem *of* the police, we are able to recognize this as symptomatic of the breakdown of centralized planning and public systems. Indeed, in this new city, policing takes the form of an unconstrained and authoritarian enterprise, as maintaining order for the sake of the stewards of international capital becomes a priority.[24] Further, the act of policing itself became increasingly privatized, as business districts employed their own forces to assure their clientele that they were safe in a way that public systems could never assure.[25]

In a subsequent volume, *The Condition of Postmodernity*, Harvey goes on to elaborate the end of the Fordist/modern epoch and the beginnings of the postmodern mode of flexible accumulation. Writes Harvey, "I begin with the most startling fact about postmodernism: Its total acceptance of ephemerality, fragmentation, discontinuity. . . . Postmodernism swims, even wallows, in the fragmentary, the chaotic currents of change as if that's all there is" (44). Thus fragmentation and motion become not just a formal strategy for directors of feature films, but rather are deeply involved in a fundamental reconception of space and mode of production (see 147). The city's fortunes reach a nadir as it transitions from the modern to postmodern moment. Its economic base declines as a result of a range of factors connected to the emergence of this new epoch, including the shifting of jobs and manufacture to regions outside of the city, region, and nation.

A remnant of this older city is the subway system. Indeed, one needs only to look at a filthy, graffiti-riddled subway car to know that the film is set in New York, and often in the period of these films. The subway and elevated trains of the turn of the century were very much a marvel and were emblematic of the gains in the management of time and space that were endemic in the modernist epoch. Early motion pictures documented this marvel of motion and modernity, turning their device that captured motion on a device that exemplified its modern incarnation.[26] However, with an increasingly bifurcated class system within the city, as well as a general economic inability to invest in and modernize its existing systems, the subway became a place where few would go who could afford not to. Further, in a space now defined not by its integral structure but by its limitless sprawl, such a system was inadequate not only in its amenities but also in its scope.

The subway occurs in important ways in *The French Connection*. It is the means by which Charnier eludes Doyle in midtown, in the crowded cars and the dimly lit station, both matters of the system's status as a public conveyance. It is also the means by which the hit man seeks to escape from Doyle after trying to kill him, since the subway is accessible to all—even criminals. And it is the pursuit of this assassin that motivates the famous chase scene. In both cases, the subway is decidedly lacking in glamour and has only a modicum of functionality. In the latter scene, the subway literally becomes a space of entrapment, as its public nature allows for the gunman's entry. That a man with a gun can threaten so many appears to be a good argument for privatized and individual systems of transportation. Where once the subway had offered control over space through its ability to traverse it rapidly and thus to save time, it is now depicted, with shots from the inside, as a box that cannot be escaped. Where Popeye can steer his car and expertly avert pedestrians, the train is a dumb beast, hurtling toward its death, unable to avert even stationary objects, such as other trains. When we ride with Doyle, we feel the thrill of avoidance; in the train we experience the inevitability of impact.

THE EMERGENT CITY AND THE RHETORIC OF NEOLIBERALISM

Neoliberalism in its theoretical form defines a world that has been reduced to the drive for economic accumulation. It assumes that the desire to gain financial resources is the common human goal and that the best thing that any governing entity can do is to allow for the logic of that common quest to organize all phases of life. Its most famous advocate and commentator is Milton Friedman, who equates the freedom to acquire with the idea of freedom itself.[27] Not only do these films extend and distend space as a means of disrupting conventional notions of related areas. This group of films also places issues of the acquisition of wealth at its center. All of them are defined by protagonists or antagonists who attempt to place some strictures on the means by which wealth is acquired, but that act of constraint is only made necessary by the representation of an extraordinary drive to acquire wealth. The action of each film revolves around questions regarding the morality and/or legality of acquiring money in ways that might appear unacceptable, whether through the sale of drugs, by shaking down criminals, or by robbing a bank. But within the four films, efforts to restrict certain modes of acquisition, even if successful, reveal the problematic nature of such efforts. We can see the tensions between an older vision of economic acquisition and distribution and that which asserts the logic of the market and the necessary brutality of uneven development. If criminals prosper, why shouldn't cops? Why should Doyle live in a housing project? Such plot constructions suggest a free-wheeling social structure where claims to authority are at least mitigated, resulting in a leveling that emphasizes acquisition. Indeed, rather than actors for the state, the policemen frequently see themselves as Friedmanesque free actors in an unfettered capitalist economy, selling protection and security. In the three films about cops, it is clear that the points of view defined in the films do not offer a sympathetic view of criminal behavior. But it is also true that each offers a means of seeing such behavior as inevitable.

Neoliberal theory is utopian and ideal; but, as a means of explaining economic practice, it fails to iterate the many devices that enable and restrict commerce. The notion of an unconstrained market place is largely a device of U.S. economic hegemony in a world system where the United States sacrifices its productive industry in order to remain the financial center of the world economy.[28] As such, the rhetoric of freedom and free trade expresses a conscious governmental shift in the 1970s to allow mass-produced consumer goods from lower-wage nations to flood the U.S. market, an event that drove up the U.S. trade deficit and largely eliminated industrial workers as part of the middle class. This system, then, resulted in the ascension of finance capital, as Wall Street became the financier of choice for those nations and corporations running surpluses, since propping up the dollar's value was ultimately in the interest of those who held a profusion of that currency.[29] And as wealth in the United States became more and more unevenly distributed, the need for harsh policing took on a certain attraction. Thus, in New York, the liberalism of the Lindsay era soon gave way to the repressiveness and rhetorical excesses of the Koch regime and the more material repression of the Giuliani administration.[30]

As various commentators have pointed out, New York City was the proving ground for the broader transitions that took place in the U.S. economy and politics during the Reagan administration.[31] By defaulting on its debt, the city government was in effect placed in receivership, with its finances largely controlled by bankers who were outside of the democratic process and who defined their primary obligation as one to financiers. Those transitions included a movement away from democratic governance, a move that built upon the modernist fascination with the centrality of experts outside of the electoral process. But now, rather than reifying the ideal of efficiency, as the urban experts of the modernist regime had done, the rhetorical ideal that drove these nondemocratic overseers was that of markets that were not constrained by government control; in effect, the ideal was for business to proceed toward its goals of maximum profitability unencumbered.

These films are both documents of the onset of this era and indexes of its excesses. It is difficult to see the outer-borough neighborhoods of *Serpico* and *Prince of the City*, for example, without seeing the ravages of a city that has allowed its infrastructure to wither, a fact that was a matter of the limits of the city's finances in the sixties and early seventies, but that was more a matter of policy in the eighties and nineties. This vision of a city of peripheries is a matter of the decentering of its system of social safeguards and devices for economic mobility. Heroin becomes the drug of choice both as a means of supporting a habit and as an index of the hopelessness of those on the perpetual social periphery.

These films show a New York City that offers little hope to those of limited means. But as we consider the distension of space and the related disruption of systems, we can see in these films the beginnings of the program that officially became policy after 1975. Fiscal chaos allowed for adjustments that became something of a prototype for the World Bank and International Monetary Fund in the 1980s and 1990s. Those organizations, in return for necessary capital, required the dismantling of the public sector, the discouraging of trade unionism, and a general imposition of the logic of the market in loans to countries in Africa, South America, and Eastern Europe.[32] In a way that anticipated those developments, in return for necessary capital, the city was forced to allow a small group of bankers to oversee its budget. As part of this structural arrangement, repayment of its debt took precedence over all other civic responsibilities. Thus, the city's payroll and services shrank accordingly, with a resulting dislocation of those at risk and a continuing decline in all manner of city services, including health care, transportation, policing, and the providision of shelter.[33] Writes William Tabb in *The Long Default*, "New York City continued to have an elected mayor, but the Emergency Financial Control Board (EFCB) reviewed the city's operations and approved all city contracts. . . . From this point on many aspects of New Yorkers' lives . . . were decided not by elected officials but by the government. New Yorkers had become disenfranchised and the political process had become an empty ritual" (28).

All of these films, with the exception of *Prince of the City*, were released prior to the city's default and the resulting restructuring of its debt and means of governance. But the fiscal and social problems they address were well in evidence in the 1960s and certainly a fact of the latter years of the Lindsay administration.[34] Though none of the films offers nostrums that may fix what ails the city, all at least outline conditions that a group of experts with a view of the necessities of the open market might agree upon as needing reform. The films portray the weakness of a city government and the failures of representative government more generally, as they make cases for alternatives. All of these films tend toward the validation of the authoritarian, or at least the nondemocratic. For example, in *Serpico*, an important aspect of the film is Serpico's inability to find higher-ranking police officials who are willing to investigate the department. Since it is not within the power or desire of elected officials to address the cancerous problem of police corruption, Lindsay appoints a five-man committee chaired by Whitman Knapp. This act is seen as a victory, and, relatively, it is one. And the hearing at end of film is the film's ambivalent climax (figure 5.5). As Serpico speaks in a formal and well-appointed hearing room, a tracking shot moves around the speaker to sweep the room from right to left, and before the arc can be completed the shot cuts to a close-up of Serpico speaking into his mike. He asserts that the need for the

FIGURE 5.5 *Serpico*: Serpico Testifies.

formation of "an independent, permanent, investigative body dealing with police corruption, like this body, is essential." The film's end titles tell us that Frank leaves the police force in 1972 and moves to Switzerland. The camera movement of the scene in the hearing room shows us the incorruptible police officer at his most heroic, providing us with a visual sweep that confirms his gravity, wisdom, and centrality in a moral universe that is not New York City. The film valorizes Serpico's suggestion, even though it fails to come to fruition. But as the audience falls into the logic of this cure for the disease the film has articulated, we are moving further and further from a democratic means of government, as well as admitting the inevitability of police corruption. In effect, it sets him up to go to Switzerland. And while it is difficult to see a heroic presence in the Serpico mold in *Prince of the City*, this film also reverts to bureaucrats and commissions as a means of righting the wrongs of police corruption. In *The French Connection*, on the other hand, the degree to which we can sympathize with Popeye's obsession with drug dealers and traffickers is the degree to which we feel that his authoritarian acts are justified by the immorality they prosecute. Indeed, Popeye's tactics would have found a home in the Giuliani regime of the 1990s.

But nonrepresentative government or a police state are only means to an end. In New York, this type of government is designed expressly to promote the neoliberal concept of freedom, which, in the parlance of that system, involves laissez-faire governance, including the dismantling of public services, as well as a termination of other institutional apparatuses that impinge upon the purity of market relations. As I noted earlier, all of these films assert the centrality of a basic human impulse of acquisition. In *Serpico*, it is that impulse which creates the culture of criminality. On one hand, criminality is depicted as an urge to violence, as in the rape we see early in Serpico's career; but the urge to acquire defines the world of large-scale drug dealers and the world of corrupt cops, an impulse far more prevalent and far more comprehensible.

That Serpico lives outside of this logic is notable. And although the figure of this lone uncorruptible cop is attractive and a compelling figure for an urban romance—which this film most certainly is not—the preponderance of evidence presented here is that corruption is systemic, inevitable, and beyond the control of any existing power. In a defining scene, after Frank has moved from partner to partner and been forced to assert repeatedly his nonparticipation in graft, he meets with a group of officers on a hill in the South Bronx, at Joyce Kilmer Park on 161st Street and the Grand Concourse, with the old Yankee Stadium in the background (figure 5.6). As Serpico approaches the crowd of officers lying and sitting on the grass, they arise to meet him. They ask for an explanation of his position and what has happened to the money that has previously been meant for him; a mid-range shot finds Serpico encircled by his fellow cops. Their leader, named Al Sarno, asserts their initial problem: if Serpico has not taken his share, then his former partner has received double. So the issue is not so much that his nonparticipation constitutes a threat, as it is that his former partner Rubello may have ended up with more than his share of the payout.

That the other officers did not know about Serpico's refusal of his "share" defines a breakdown in system. A resolution is offered: everyone makes his own

FIGURE 5.6 *Serpico*: Serpico in front of Yankee Stadium with his dirty cops in Joyce Kilmer Park.

collections, as the camera cuts to close-ups and two shots of the other cops, but as the scene goes on, the other cops' faces become increasingly distorted by a fish-eye lens. As the scene ends, they all scatter in different directions as Serpico holds his ground. While taking this money is clearly wrong, just as we are shown that it is morally wrong in the previously discussed scene of the Knapp Commission hearing, it is clear from the visual composition of these films that Serpico defines a moral center that cannot hold. In Lumet's view, and one he reiterates in later films such as *Prince of the City* (1981), corruption is a kind of social cancer, and once it enters the public body, it cannot be eradicated. The avarice of the officers is notable. It takes precedence over virtually any other drive: that for respect, as in the case of Serpico's partner being cursed as a bag man by a child in the Bronx; for safety, as these men will jeopardize their lives for a payoff; and even their desire for certain foods, as in one of our early confrontations between Frank and a partner over Frank's desire to choose his own preference of lunch and to pay for it.

The systemic nature of corruption and its rooting within the police force becomes, in effect, an assertion of the inevitability of avarice and, at least by inference, an argument for privatization. Indeed, in a neoliberal formulation of the relative value and relative cost of public safety, the reason that police officers engage in graft is that their work in the public sector is not remunerated at a market rate. They see the financial possibilities of their position and seek out further profit; in effect, they become private contractors, assuring safety for those who offer a direct payment for their services. And to some extent the proliferation and increase in scale of corruption among urban police officers, and those in New York City in particular, is symptomatic of the city's ever-increasing financial despair during the 1960s and 1970s, a condition that limited salaries and diminished working conditions. The visual language that places Serpico against the mob puts him, in reality, against the inevitability of the reign of market relations, however distorting that regime may be. His position, then, suggests the further decline of the public sector and of collectivity in general.

It is also worth noting that at the point when this film was shot, in the spring of 1973, Yankee stadium, highly recognizable backdrop for this scene, had become an icon of the city's relative decline, as the team, which was now a club that failed both on the field and at the box office, sought extensive renovations for its stadium. Ultimately, the city bought the stadium and paid for the renovations. The stadium closed in September of 1973, and reopened in 1976. George Steinbrenner bought the team from CBS in early 1973, and the Yankees won the American League championship their first year back in the renovated Yankee Stadium. That the fiscally declining city of New York underwrote renovations of this largely private facility, thus subsidizing what had the capacity to become, and indeed did become, one of the most lucrative sports franchises in the world, suggests a further erosion of the public sector and a corollary to the rise of neoliberalism. Such a use of public money anticipates the massive public subsidies gained by U.S. manufacturers from state and city governments when they threaten to close down operations in a given location.[35] Thus, while the purity of market relations are a political mantra, bailing out Chrysler, the airlines, or rapacious lenders of undersecured loans is well within the purview of government.[36] While the ideology of that worldview asserts the necessity of unimpeded markets as a means to "freedom" and general prosperity, to some degree this rhetoric has been in the service of reestablishing the preeminence of a class of plutocrats, a restoration that at least partially succeeded. In the example of Yankee Stadium, we can see this disposition in action.[37]

And while *Dog Day Afternoon* does not dwell on avarice, it also includes its significant neoliberal discourse. The film provides a dialectical approach to space that asserts the film's moment as occurring between the constrained spaces of the Fordist city and the fragmented and sprawling spaces of the city of the future. A title informs us that the film takes place on August 22, 1972, the date the bank robbery that the film portrays takes place. But by fixing that date, the production opens out to a broader area of historical event and in particular, the major shifts in world currency policy in 1971 and 1972. When we see the beginnings of the robbery, the very obscurity of the bank and its location provide a view of a decidedly unglamorous New York City, and the bank, rather than a center of global finance, is a backwater for capital, a place that will be consolidated out of existence in the next twenty years, as freestanding savings banks are swept up by large and diversified national and international entities.[38] When Sal walks through the door, the scene is shot from the bank-manager's point of view, as we see Sal approach his desk. Soon, we watch from the sidewalk as Sonny enters the building.

The bank is the very image of a place outside of the pressures of global development. Its lack of a connection to a recognizable system of banking, as well as its neighborhood status, place it in an era that is about to come to a close. Shots of it, from the first, circumscribe its location. The framing of the front entrance to the bank through straight-ahead, mid-range shots recur throughout the film and thereby reduce our sense of context. Similarly, the shots inside the bank emphasize its claustrophobic qualities, framing individuals against walls, the restricted space defined by the bank's interior pillars, and even in the way in which the crowd and the police restrict the space in front of the building. This spatial sense of the bank existing in a corner of the city away from other places and functions is heightened by the introduction of the city police, who promptly cordon off the area. The sense of being trapped is a function of the way in which the film shoots the restricted space inside the bank, as well as the way in which the crowd and the police restrict access outside.

Dog Day Afternoon juxtaposes the helicopters of the police and television stations with images of a neighborhood that seems locked away in another time. Similarly, it brings a populist bank-robber tale into the present.[39] Sonny's act of criminality is to acquire the money for his gay lover to obtain a sex change operation. In this variation on legends such as Bonnie and Clyde and Billy the Kid, Sonny, though well intentioned as he is, is not interested in easing the lot of the dispossessed. His goal, in a social corollary to neoliberal concepts of the individual, is to achieve happiness for himself and his lover. Finally, in a transition to a view of New York that explicitly shows the ways in which even this corner of the city is connected to a world beyond, Lumet's shots juxtapose a view from above that finds the police van traversing the streets on its way to the airport with shots from inside the van, in its closeness and darkness. We also see the van being harassed as it moves through Brooklyn, as we feel the tension of Sonny and Sal through the point-of-view shots that reveal people in other cars screaming homophobic insults and beer cans launched in the direction of the van. When it finally reaches the open space of the runway at Kennedy Airport, presumably on the way to Algeria, the van and the hostages seem to have entered a world with a very different configuration, one defined by the apparent closeness of what seemed like remote spaces. Sonny's whim briefly appears a possibility. But the forces of the federal government intervene at the last minute, killing Sal and rescuing the passengers.

DRUGS AND COMMERCE

There is no way of looking at any of these films and seeing them as rationalizing the crime they portray. But they do reduce the moral distance between cops and criminals. The films also define contemporary law enforcement, and explicitly in its New York settings, as structurally ineffective. That is, the reason that cops cannot stop crime is that the domain of criminality has so expanded in scope that the relatively understaffed police force is unable to effectively restrict it. In these films, the scope of antisocial behavior has burgeoned, as has its potential number of actors. Christopher P. Wilson explains in *Cop Knowledge*, "In the aftermath of the standoff in the streets of the 1960s, the post Vietnam decades were a period in which metropolitan police departments, particularly in the larger rust-belt cities, found themselves faced with fiscal crises, resurgent scandals, and public ridicule, and of course, escalating crime rates that, simply put made it seem as if the police were not the answer" (141).

Three of these films, *Prince of the City*, *Serpico*, and *The French Connection*, are more or less concerned with a burgeoning drug trade that has its origins in places far from New York City. *The French Connection* is, of these three, the most focused on that enterprise and most effectively creates at least the basis for an argument for the inevitability of its relative success. *Serpico* and *Prince of the City*, while about police corruption, a fact of law enforcement since the drug trade began, show us a world where the cash generated by drug transactions creates an economic climate where traffickers and large-scale dealers cannot afford not to pay off cops, and in which cops are hard-pressed to pass up the copious amounts of money available to them. Indeed, the Knapp Commission investigations that this film is plotted around concluded that the extent and money involved in the drug trade made police corruption all the more prevalent.[40]

If we look at these films intertextually, we can see how they offer complementary views of the situation of drug-related crime in the 1960s and 1970s.[41] The *French Connection* refers to a network of financial relationships among Turkish opium growers and exporters, French and Corsican drug processors and shippers, and U.S. drug importers and distributors. "By 1972 French heroin processed from a Turkish morphine base was estimated to account for 80 per cent of the total amount entering the United States."[42] The character on which Popeye Doyle is based, Eddie Egan, was instrumental in disrupting this supply chain in the early 1960s. But the demise of trafficking from Turkey via Marseilles had little impact on the amount of drugs that made their way to New York and the United States. Indeed, in the Vietnam and post-Vietnam era demand and supply rose geometrically. The shifts in the global routing of drugs follow the model of any number of international commodities, as the focus of the industry shifted as supply and cost became problematic. Poppy cultivation switched regionally to countries such as Afghanistan, and trafficking, rather than routing through Corsica, made its way through Turkmenistan and Kyrgyzstan.[43] Opium, like textiles, was a commodity that provided only relative wealth to those in producing counties. Its value was substantially enhanced by the factors of the markets in the developing world. Thus, while a poppy farmer in Afghanistan might achieve relative prosperity, the drug importers and wholesalers in the developed world made fortunes.

It is that desire for wealth that motivates figures such as Charnier, who is already quite prosperous. In order to apprehend such a smuggler, Doyle must become obsessed. *The French Connection* portrays Doyle as a maniac, unloved by cop and criminal alike. Doyle has become obsessed with the chase itself and far more concerned with the apprehension of the smugglers than with the goods. In viewing the extensive cat-and-mouse game in which Doyle is involved, it appears that all of the advantage belongs to the criminals. There are many drug dealers and, apparently, a not very extensive network of those involved in apprehension and interdiction. Within a world where cars and cameras are shipped freely from place to place, where casual business meetings may take place hundreds or thousands of miles from a base of operations, the reach of cops in their cars—defined by their squalid stations and made to appear and feel powerful only by their ability to harass users and small dealers—is limited. Doyle's obsession is either an illness of his trade or an illness that has led him to his trade. To some degree this obsession is comprehensible; for example, after the chase that marks the culmination of the first scene in Brooklyn, and then after the next cut to Marseilles, Popeye and Cloudy go to a club after work for a drink, and there encounter a table of people that Doyle is sure are suspicious, including some who he knows are criminals and some who he suspects. The camera cuts back and forth between the fully lit table of criminals and the two cops, shot in a two shot in shadows and whispering. The intensity of Doyle's reaction, and then the image of him pacing outside of the police car as he awaits their exit from a hotel, define him as always possessing a desire for the chase. And while he is clearly a man possessed—the people he suspects are indeed criminals—he is relatively unable to disrupt the flow of drugs at the top of the chain of supply.

In *Serpico*, we see the beginnings of the massive corruption wrought by the burgeoning of the narcotics trade. Frank serves in a narcotics unit at the end of the film, when his partners allow him to be shot in the face. This seems like a logical culmination of his assignment. From the first, the association between working undercover in narcotics and accepting large bribes has been assumed. Indeed, when Serpico is reassigned to this unit in Brooklyn, he asserts its potential to disrupt his anticorruption work. This is affirmed soon after he begins his tour. Says his fellow narcotics officer, in shadowed full close-up, with malice in his voice, "Down here 800 a month is chicken feed." As Serpico's pensive face in profile fills the frame, he goes on, "Last week we took $120,000, split it four ways. That is serious money and with that, you don't fuck around."

In *Prince of the City*, the connection between drugs and corruption is even more explicit. This film literally begins where *Serpico* ends, a fact easily explained by the centrality of director Sudney Lumet in each project, as Ciello's unit appears to be either the group that took the $120,000 or is just like that group. As we see our protagonist go through the pain of informing on his associates, and then closer and closer associates as the film proceeds, it is nearly impossible to find even one cop who stands outside of the network of corruption—including the informant. In fact, by the end of the investigation fifty-two out of seventy at the Special Investigations Unit cops were indicted. As we watch Ciello's three instances of admitted corruption exponentially increase, the rule of law becomes less and less the way of the world and increasingly seems an arbitrary convenience asserted by those with the power to do so. Ciello consorts with the mob, shakes down junkies and prostitutes, robs, procures drugs, and uses his power capriciously. He is Machiavelli's prince.

It is no accident that, as cops increasingly cross the line into corruption, motivated by the fact of drugs pervading New York, that the spatial configurations which define these films become all the more fluid. For example, a key scene in the later investigations of *Prince of the City* is when Ciello, awakened in the dark in his bed, responds to a snitch's cry for drugs and drives from his home all the way back to New York in order to find junk (figure 5.7). We have a sense that this is a considerable trip in the rain, in the middle of the night, but the narrative makes the transition from the suburbs—Ciello closes his electric garage door as he pulls away—to the squalid streets of New York. In *Serpico*, Frank's work in the narcotics unit maximizes his mobility, as he moves from neighborhood to neighborhood almost without chronological transition.

Heroin and cocaine become the devices that anticipate the logic and methods of globalization, and as that process develops, drug prohibition becomes all the more ineffectual. Explains Paul Stares, a senior fellow with the Brookings Institute,

> Revolutionary advances in communications, transportation, and information technology have made it possible for goods, services, people and ideas to travel across international boundaries with unprecedented speed and efficiency . . . The drug trade, as a consequence, has increasingly become a

FIGURE 5.7 *Prince of the City*: Ciello drives in the rain to meet his snitch.

transnational phenomenon, driven and fashioned in critical ways by transnational forces and transnational actors. Thus, the global diffusion of technical expertise and internationalization of manufacturing have made it possible to cultivate and refine drugs in still be within reach of distant markets.[44]

Drugs constitute the commodity that produces an inexorable chain of production, distribution, and consumption. They are the consumer item that users must have. As such, they serve as an example of the inexorable logic of the marketplace. No commodity that has such a desiring clientele can ever be effectively interdicted, and it is the logic of this position that pervades the corrupt and futile efforts at policing that inform these three films. The libertarian position on drug prohibition is instructive for considering these films, as well as the ways in which drug trafficking is involved with broader issues of international commerce. In this view, the cost of prohibition is far greater than the benefit. Further, this public war on these substances produces an increase in the size of government and often results in unwarranted intrusions into the lives of individuals.[45] These films of New York serve as an intriguing assertion of the decline of the public sector as they provide a complementary vision of the inevitable reign of market relations. As such, they move their audiences toward a reconception of the role and place of the financial capital of the United States, showing its sprawl and connection to far-flung places, as well as its permeability to people and goods from without. In examining these films, we are able to see how visions of urban space become broader organizational strategies that have the power to link plot and history. Indeed, this emphasis on sprawl and on a decentered urban space, and even on means of traverse, suggest a shifting concept of the city. And that idea lends itself well to emerging discourses of the global and an altering scale of commerce.

6

Vigilance!

ALONG WITH ISSUES of policing and the various representations of physical and cultural sprawl that marked New York City and its image in popular culture in the mid-seventies, a cycle of films emerges that overlaps those of the previous chapter, as well as more generally moves the chronology of New York films forward. These productions also concern themselves with crime, but the acts of violence depicted are more random, and apparently endemic, street crime. In *Death Wish* (1974), *Taxi Driver* (1976), and to a lesser degree in *Marathon Man* (1976), we see a city that is spatially and thematically related to that which we saw *in The French Connection*, *Serpico*, *Dog Day Afternoon*, and *The Prince of the City*. It is a place with any number of menacing people, a world of drug use, sexual assault, and a police force that is unable to bring stability to the volatile mix that defines New York City. But in the films of this chapter the problem of violence and the inadequacy of the official response are addressed by individuals making the law a matter of individual concern and resorting to violence in order to stem violence; in effect, these three films assert the efficacy and broad social acceptability of personal vigilance.

These films alter the representation and explanation of urban crime from one that asserts the immanence and inevitability of neoliberal principles to that which asserts the efficacy of neoconservatism. Though they do not necessarily take neoconservative writings and policies explicitly into account—some of those writings, such as Daniel Patrick Moynihan's treatise on the African American family, *The Negro Family: A Call to National Action* (1965), well preceded them. But, since neoconservatism was still in its formative stages in the first half of the 1970s, they can be seen as anticipating the more formal coalescence of that political trend. As such, the films are part of the response to social conditions that spawned this political tendency. The movement originated in the conservative wing of the Democratic Party, a group that largely rejected the social mores of the counterculture, and what they felt was a foreign policy that was "soft" on Communism. Among its leading figures were Irving Kristol, Gertrude Himmelfarb, Seymour Martin Lipset, Midge Decter, and Norman Podhoretz. All had been Trotskyites in their younger days, though there were many neocons that had not been, including James Q. Wilson, Jeanne Kirkpatrick, and Michael Novak.[1] And a significant number of neoconservatives, including Decter, Kirkpatrick, John Podhoretz, Elliott Abrams, and William Kristol, had some role—formal or informal—in the Reagan administration in the 1980s.[2]

Neoconservatism and neoliberalism are related approaches to governance and economic order: both largely believe in the efficacy of the market and in limiting government. But whereas neoliberalism, as in the case of the rhetoric of laissez-faire drug policy, is an approach that emphasizes a philosophy of libertarianism, neoconservatives recognize that free-market economics may also result in social chaos on every scale—from the local to the global. As a result, neoconservatives emphasize the role of government and individuals in imposing and maintaining social order, and indeed, reserve the moral imperative to employ force. Such a view may entail an interventionist foreign policy and an advocacy for restrictive laws that constrain social behavior. This last idea is important for our purposes, since it dispenses with the idea of victimless crimes. They also endorse harsh and proactive policing as the rightful domain of the state, as well as recognizing the role of the individual in defending his or her own person, family, and property. As such, neoconservatives are decidedly against restrictions in gun ownership.[3]

Irving Kristol famously wrote in his autobiographical *Reflections of a Neoconservative*, "a neoconservative is a liberal who has been mugged by reality." The fit of this quote to these films is extraordinary. The three, in their emphasis on morality, vigilance, and violence take up the neoconservative argument for maintaining order in urban spaces as a necessary moral imperative and as a precondition to their gentrification. Neocons emphasize individual volition and responsibility, the necessity of a clearly articulated moral and social order, and the need to violently expunge those who would infringe on that order. It is this emphasis on a singular vision of order that grafts neoconservatism's foreign policy to its domestic one. In foreign policy, for instance, write Bill Kristol and Robert Kagan, discussing "National Interest and Global Responsibility," "the maintenance of a decent and hospitable international order requires continued American leadership in resisting, and where possible undermining, rising dictators and hostile ideologies; in supporting American interests and liberal democratic principles; and in providing assistance to those struggling against the more extreme manifestations of human evil" (64). Indeed, the unproblematic layering of descriptive tags with the clear assumption of their perpetual good or perpetual bad content—American interests and liberal democratic principles versus dictators and hostile ideologies—provides a map that allows us to see the very wide range of possible military interventions that those of this world view could justify undertaking.

Similarly, the most famous neocon treatise on domestic policy focuses on urban life in particular, and was the model for the Giuliani-regime policing strategy in New York City during the 1990s. In their "Broken Windows: The Police and Neighborhood Safety," published in the *Atlantic Monthly* in 1982, James Q. Wilson and George L. Kelling lay out the argument for the preemptive policing of urban regions. The writers, professors of government (Wilson) and of criminal justice (Kelling), argue for the efficacy of police patrols, not for the arrests these officers may make but for the sense of security and general presence they provide: "The essence of the police role in maintaining order is to reinforce the informal control mechanisms of the community itself" (2). This means that to preserve a given community, police must engage in symbolic acts of suppressing petty crime and nuisance—vagrancy, public drunkenness, vandalism. The authors lament the proliferation of such activities and tie them to a breakdown in moral structure that took place during the 1960s. They write, "The police cannot, without committing extraordinary resources, provide a substitute for that informal control. On the other hand, to reinforce those natural forces the police must accommodate them."[4] Thus, as in foreign policy, acts that cause no direct harm but that constitute a nuisance or suggest the prospect of escalating threats and disorder must be addressed by the institutions with the appropriate social authority.

Of course, a significant percentage of those identified with neoconservatism were New Yorkers. This is not to say that they were deeply involved in city politics; but it does suggest that they were also something of a political vanguard within the city, as well. It is relatively easy to plot these films as part of the post-Lindsay era, and as participating in the transition to the neoconservative-tinged policies of the Koch administration, which began in 1977 and lasted until 1989. The films portray the dashed hopes of the 1960s and early 1970s, and offer visions of the city and its citizens that see the need for increased social control, even if that does not include an increase in government-sponsored means of enforcement.

These films, if approached with greater historical specificity, are documents of the days of the Abraham Beame administration and are sandwiched around the moment of financial default. Beame was a former city comptroller whose election marked the return of the machine Democrats to the mayor's office. His administration was remarkable for its relative lack of vision, and relative lack of power. The police force continued to shrink as crime continued to burgeon. Robberies, for example, almost quadrupled between the mid-sixties and early 1970s. Police protested frequently and staged picket lines designed to embarrass the chief of police, Michael J. Codd, and the mayor. "When Muhammed Ali and Ken Norton met for the heavyweight championship fight at Yankee Stadium that September [1976], a mob of militant cops showed up, hoping to get some free world-wide publicity. . . . Fifteen hundred off-duty cops roamed about like high-school kids at a pep rally, shouting, among other slogans, 'Beame is a shrimp'; 'Codd is a fish.' Three high-ranking chiefs were knocked down as they alighted from their vehicle."[5] Such behavior did not exactly enhance the standing of the police force; but the Beame regime did little to restore confidence in city government in general.

In all three films, vigilance is posited as the response to the failure of policemen in cars, as well as to the decline in community-enforced rules of comportment. Gangs and muggers are featured in *Marathon Man*, child prostitutes in *Taxi Driver*, and marauding youths and all manner of muggers pervade *Death Wish*. In at least in two of the films—*Marathon Man* and *Taxi Driver*—it is the residue of a failed foreign policy, one that was not sufficiently tough minded, that contributes to the particular disruptions the movies trace. In *Marathon Man*, the failure of government to pursue Nazi war criminals and their ill-gotten treasures after World War II results in the return of Christian Szell to New York. In *Taxi Driver*, Travis's involvement the Vietnam War triggers his erratic behavior. The film suggests that his personal chaos results from the U.S. government's failure to dedicate sufficient means to vanquishing an enemy that it had vilified. These films elaborate the connection between the neoconservative notion of ethical and militarily conclusive behavior abroad, and the need for proactive and affirmative policing at home. In what appears as a precursor to the political slogan of the Bush era, not fighting enemies abroad results in domestic disruptions. And while these films stand as the strongest assertion of the need for stronger policing and the imperative of self-defense, such assertions are also definitional for a number of later films of New York, such as *The Warriors* (1979), *Fort Apache, the Bronx* (1981), and *The Wanderers* (1979). These later films move toward the surreal—particularly *The Warriors*—and, unlike the films of this chapter, are substantially of the outer boroughs. And it would be a glaring omission to neglect to mention that the ever proactive Harry

Callahan (or Dirty Harry), in *Dirty Harry* (1971), *Magnum Force* (1973), and *The Enforcer* (1976),was busily at work on the streets of San Francisco at the same time that our subway vigilante was cleaning New York's underworld in *Death Wish*.

Unlike the films of the preceding chapter, however, these films envision the space of New York in a far more focused way, dwelling almost exclusively in Manhattan and each in a particular region of that island. Each also complements that focus with a more fleeting reference to regions far from Manhattan. *Taxi Driver* has the pall of Vietnam on it; the other two films place important elements of their narratives in distant lands: *Marathon Man* in Paris and *Death Wish* in Hawaii and Tucson.[6] But the means of connecting New York and far-flung locations is elaborated differently than in the preceding chapter. In the earlier chapter, the films developed connections between New York and regions that were causal and largely economically motivated—drugs from abroad entering New York in *The French Connection* and in *Serpico*, for example. In these films the connections are temporal and thematic. That is, these other places connect to Manhattan as a matter of the residue of their history. Vietnam is present because of the U.S. role in that nation. Nazi Germany is present as the result of World War II and its aftermath. In effect, the films compress time in order to re-elaborate spatial connections. They largely feature the landscape of Manhattan during the portion of the films that is set in New York; though each of the films references that relative location, to varying degrees, as the nexus of a historical/geographical continuum, and arguably the terminus of that process.

This recentering of Manhattan that takes place in these films points toward New York City's postindustrial fruition, as well as its gentrification. While emphasizing the role of the U.S. military in foreign policy, neoconservatives tend to resist notions of the fluidity of space and culture. That is, since neoconservatives valorize a world of rules and discernable hierarchies that will provide the necessary order for a commodious social life, it is necessary that these rules have a clear basis in a notion of ethics. This reassertion of the centrality of the core of the New York region is a matter of defining space as the container of culture. But each of these three films, in a postmodern way, sees Manhattan as a crossroads that must import its redeeming system of culture from viable external models. In *Death Wish*, the mythical West serves a paradigm; in *Taxi Driver* it is the culture of the military; and in *Marathon Man* it is a reborn Jewish militarism. But all are grafted onto the culture of Manhattan, which is characterized as paradoxically cosmopolitan and porous, while at the same time centered and specific. Such apparently contradictory assertions capture the divergent threads of neoconservative rhetoric, a discourse that attempts to recuperate contemporary culture as it situates itself in the idealized past.

The centered spaces in these films show the confines of an aspect of Manhattan as intimate space. Each film calls upon the individual to take the issue of violence against himself, his family (*Death Wish*), his assumptive family (*Taxi Driver*), and his nuclear and ethnic family (*Marathon Man*) as a personal one requiring a personal response, and thus refers to the ethos and mythos of the frontier, of imperialism, and the failures of appeasement. These more specific assertions are joined with a more general conservative ethos of individual empowerment. In doing so, they ask viewers to at least note the social analogies between late twentieth-century New York and late nineteenth-century Arizona, Texas, or Wyoming; between the children of Vietnam and those from other places in the United States prostituting themselves in Manhattan; or between the persecution of Jews of Europe in the 1930s and 1940s and those afflicted by violence in Manhattan. Such comparisons ask viewers to conceive of New York as a place that is involved in a range of spatial and temporal networks. And indeed, such analogies are apt re-elaborations of the trope of the city in decline. In this model, as the reasons for decline are cultural, so are the means proposed for their redress. Mirroring what we have seen in other chapters, these films assert, in varying degrees, that the cleansing and redemption of the city has a decidedly racial aspect. But more explicitly, they tie that redemption to violence that is defined as a social good, as an ethical act. The means of justification are tethered to the mythos of U.S. history, as a reassertion of the broad belief in U.S. exceptionalism and the code of the frontier. This appeal to nationalism, then, becomes the dialectical other of the global, revealing how the local and the global always interact; in effect, articulating what many have called "the glocal."[7]

Intriguingly, it is the vision of New York as place that is both specific and cosmopolitan; that defines a discourse of globalization which skirts issues of economics, though the effective social philosophy does have economic implications. Asserting the warlike aspects of New York resituates it not simply at the center of U.S. economic life, but as a free-floating entity subject to multiple cultural influences and cultural definitions. As such a specific space, New York's locus of meanings emerges from its involvement in multiple narratives and its powers to serve as a central point of communication.[8]

And, of course, to see New York as a repository of individualism and self-protective and assertive violence, on one hand, brings to the fore one of the central themes of neoconservatism; and on the other, provides one of the necessary preconditions for gentrification. These complementary assertions, then, vault it out of the seventies and project ahead to the eighties and nineties. All three films point to the clearing of specific spaces within Manhattan where formerly the activities of those who would gentrify were threatened. And though it's difficult to affirm the ultimate fates of our protagonists, all three—Travis Bickle (*Taxi*

Driver), Babe (*Marathon Man*), and Paul Kersey (*Death Wish*)—tame strategic spaces of the island: Bickle's 12th Street corridor, Babe's Central Park Reservoir, and the Upper West Side. With the three, the aggregated result of these films is a kind of symbolic violence that stands as a warning to all who would visit class resentment on those who prosper and transform central Manhattan.

In his study of vigilance, Ray Abrahams explains that

> Vigilantes typically lay claim, at least temporarily, to the state's own mantle of authority. If only for this reason, their relation to the state is bound to be awkward. Vigilantism typically occurs in "frontier" zones, where the state is viewed as ineffective or corrupt, and it often constitutes a criticism of state machinery to meet the felt needs of those who resort to it. It is a form of self-help, with varying degrees of violence, which is activated instead of such machinery, against criminals and others whom the actors perceive as undesirables, deviants, and "public enemies."[9]

Such a definition is indeed clarifying in locating the spatial politics of these films. All three find their protagonists in "outposts of civilization" that require the proactive interventions of a few good men. That these outposts are in central Manhattan makes perfect sense in the context of this study, since we have seen the rhetoric of anti-urbanism and the city in decline grow increasingly strident over the previous half decade or so. Further, such rhetorical certainly had a basis in materiality. New York's middle-class presence and the types of jobs that went with that constituency had been declining for at least two decades.

But it is the confluence of incipient gentrification and the rhetoric of the frontier that makes these films salient historically and effective viscerally. Indeed, the frontier concept becomes a vital means of defining their emphases in two directions, making them both about the need to clean up New York City and the need for the assertion of American might and domain in the world beyond. All of the violent redeemers, then, suggest both the need for a reaffirmation of American might and that cleaning up the cities of the United States is conceptually connected to cleaning up the world, a formulation that takes us back to the neoconservative core of each film.

But the resonant action and the elaboration of the frontier metaphor has its basis in Manhattan. And, indeed, to employ such a metaphor aligns these films with the very language of gentrification as it took place in the 1970s and 1980s. As Neil Smith explains, the commonly employed term "urban pioneer" valorizes the process of gentrification and makes the displacement of existing populations both a noble deed and part of an inevitable historical continuum.

The term "urban pioneer" is as arrogant as the original notion of the pioneer in that it conveys the impression of a city that is not yet socially inhabited: like the Native Americans, the contemporary urban working class is seen as less than social, simply a part of the physical environment. . . . In the end . . . the imagery of the frontier serves to legitimate and rationalize a process of conquest, whether in the eighteenth- or nineteenth-century West, or in the twentieth-century inner city.[10]

This notion of the urban pioneer applies in varying degrees to all three protagonists and emphasizes their violence as purposeful in the process of redeveloping central Manhattan.

THE GHOSTS OF THE PAST AND THE NEED FOR VIOLENCE

New York in these films is defined as a place that suffers the accrued ills of the 1960s. It is also pictured, more broadly, as a historical crossroads that illustrates the failures of the policy that led to diffusion, both personal and governmental, of social responsibility. Neoconservatives, while not defining violent intervention as the most desirable means to social cohesion, do recognize it as a means to an end. In the context of the cold war, it was an element of their residual anti-Staliinism and general anti-communism; militarism and direct intervention was a way to undo the inertia and moral relativism that defined the doctrine of détente.[11] The notion of a moral need to act is at the core of neoconservative readings of Leo Strauss, a leading intellectual force in the definition of the movement. Strauss, a long-time professor of classics and social philosophy at the University of Chicago, numbered many prominent neoconservatives among his students, including Allan Bloom, Paul Wolfowitz, and many others who are not so widely known.[12] This view of morality as a fixed entity serves as a means of redressing the twin evils of modernity: historicism and relativism.[13] That is, on the one hand, Strauss critiqued the notion that historical events possess a logic of their own and humans can only sit back and watch them unfold. On the other hand, he viewed liberal democracy as the ideal social state and felt it a moral obligation to maintain or restore individual rights.

Strauss's vision of the need to confront what he believed were the failures of moral tolerance could also be applied to domestic policy, and not only by the criminologists James Q. Wilson and George L. Kelling. For example, the historian Gertrude Himmelfarb's work and analysis of the Victorian era and its after-effects decried the state of contemporary civil society. According to Himmelfarb, the residue of Victorian morality obtained in the Anglophone world until after World War II and then began rapidly to dissipate.[14] She saw the decline of social decorum in the 1960s as only a further plunge into the chaos and relativism that had begun more than a decade earlier. And since comportment is necessary for the good society, its enforcement becomes a necessary historical intervention. Similarly, Jeanne Kirkpatrick saw the need for moral absolutes emerging in the 1960s in response to the highly influential counterculture. She writes, "The counterculture . . . constituted a sweeping rejection of traditional American attitudes, values, and goals."[15] And though Himmelfarb and Kirkpatrick finally focused on different dimensions of U.S. life—the former on domestic affairs, the latter on international relations—both preached an intolerance of disruption and the need to return to a traditional and hierarchical model of social organization.

The neoconservative imperative is the rewriting of a historical narrative of decline by materially intervening in the dystopian present. Intriguingly, the possibility of this rewriting is enabled by the postmodern vision which emphasizes that historical sequence is both malleable and discontinuous. And indeed, it is this vision of history as having veered in the wrong direction and requiring violent intervention that informs all three of these films. Both *Death Wish* and *Marathon Man* have key sequences either at or near the beginning of the film in which powerful images of the recent and more distant imperial adventures of the United States are invoked and largely naturalized. In *Death Wish*, the opening scenes takes place in Hawaii, as our architect and his wife frolic on an idyllic beach on which no other human can be seen, bringing to mind colonial narratives of unpopulated lands and the conception of such places as needing the touch of civilization that only white people can bring. Reciprocally, as figures like Theodore Roosevelt asserted, such lands have the power to reinvigorate the spirit and culture of the conquerors as they create necessary physical ardor and a redefinition and reaffirmation of national purpose.

In *Marathon Man*, we find Doc, Babe's more successful older brother, in Paris involved in some type—we never quite know what—of counter-, or counter-counter-intelligence. This activity is part of the residue of World War II and a feature of the moral chaos of the cold war. That his actions are indecipherable except from a perspective of pragmatism and self-interest tells us about the failures of morality and policy that marked the 1960s and 1970s, as the moral distinction between the "good guys" and "bad guys" had been obscured by a kind relativism. In *Taxi Driver*, it is only the reference to, and residual effect of, Travis's time in Vietnam that informs his beliefs and actions. This reference is a matter of dress and era, but is barely expounded upon. In the shooting script there are two oblique references but also little elaboration. But again, that which afflicts Travis is the moral confusion surrounding that conflict, a sense of his inability to execute a morally desirable result.

The opening scene of *Death Wish*, as we have seen, shows the fruition of the dream of nineteenth-century empire as a contemporary Hawaiian paradise. The island, once remarkably defined by architect of U.S. naval power and imperialism, Alfred Thayer Mahan, as the Gibraltar of the Pacific, now stands as a testament to the power of U.S. empire to assert its domain. Our initial shot, and one referencing this process, shows architect Paul Kersey, played by Charles Bronson, and his wife Joanne, played by Hope Lange, inhabiting a vast and sprawling seascape in which no other person appears. In this scene they discuss having sex on the beach, but Joanne demurs––because they are "too civilized." When they return to their hotel, we see them at an ersatz luau, as natives dance and sing. This question of relative civilization is one that recurs throughout the film and ultimately is one that is responded to in a counterintuitive way; since it is the colony that exudes the qualities of physical beauty and peace, while mainland New York is the site of violence and chaos. Between is Tucson, Arizona, a beautiful but populated physical space that men bearing arms have tamed.

When Paul and Joanne return to Manhattan, the camera takes pains to show us the ravages of civilization with shots that alternate between panoramas of urban grit and chaos, and subjective views of the Kerseys in their cab experiencing traffic, pollution, and later, violence. These perspectives suggest that notions of civilization have become inverted by the ravages of urban living. This film is clearly not about the doings of people on the margins in the outer boroughs, but about those in the center of Manhattan—like the Kerseys—who are at least contiguous to people of wealth and power. From the first, Manhattan is invoked, in the words of one of Paul's co-workers, as a "war zone," and by another as a place to work but only by commuting from "someplace else." This advice is offered earnestly, in intimate two shots with Paul, or in close-ups that feature the speaker turned fully to the camera to emphasize his sincerity.

Soon, Joanne is killed by barbarian and atavistic adolescents, who beat her as she tries to save her daughter from being raped. This is shown with a point-of-view shot from Joanne, and it is the sight of one of the attacker's pants sliding below his knees that spurs her to act. It is also worth noting that as they accost these women, the intruders also spray-paint graffiti on the walls. These young men are the vision of Himmelfarb and Kirkpatrick's social nightmare, exhibiting the behavior that Wilson and Kelling defined in "Broken Windows" as socially corrosive. "Graffiti, even when not obscene, confronts the subway rider with the inescapable knowledge that the environment he must endure for an hour or more a day is uncontrolled and uncontrollable, and that anyone can invade it to do whatever damage and mischief the mind suggests" (2). It is not at all a stretch to see these adolescent thugs as also spray-painting the subways, and any number of other spaces of the city. Indeed, we first saw them thrashing around the supermarket, annoying patrons and damaging the food. Their engaging in rape and murder would clearly have been averted by a policing strategy that took their more benign but clearly aggressive earlier behaviors more seriously.

The police are ineffectual: overburdened and barely interested. Paul's forays to the police station are shot from skewed angles in which Paul is only eventually found within the camera's sweep of its field of vision, emphasizing his relative unimportance. Paul reverts to less civilized behavior, as he confronts muggers with a sock filled with quarters. The city he now sees, and that we see, is one in which danger lurks in every unilluminated crevice. New York has become the very definition of uncivilized, a place where the barbarians rule. In the largely late nineteenth- and early twentieth-century architecture of Kersey's Upper West Side neighborhood, street configurations, and even the subway system, do not at all take into account the decline in public comportment that marks the later twentieth century. Indeed, as Himmelfarb would agree, these vestiges of the Victorian era tell us much about public safety and demeanor during that period and the aftermath it influenced.

This sets up Paul's trip to Arizona, one which, in the postmodern way, occurs with a cut to the airport tower in Tucson. The airport, when shot from Paul's perspective, is an ersatz Old West setting; when shot from the point of view of his host—Ames Jainchill, played by Stuart Margolin—it is a clean and featureless modernist space. Ames wears a cowboy hat and exudes the Western spirit. From his twang to his hat and safari suit, Ames (and Tucson) express a synthesis of the modem and the residue of an idea of the historical West. It is this synthesis that marks the site of postmodern emphasis within the film, as well, which informs Paul's resurfacing as a New York vigilante. The frontier has been flattened, mythologized, and recast as the frontier ethos, a notion of the good apparently tied to place and tradition. We have to remind ourselves that Paul and Ames are real estate developers, even as we hear the lowing of cattle and the shot tilts down from the setting western sun to the cattle and cactus. As the two men walk the terrain where the development will be built, the camera zooms back to show us the sweep of the land. As they discuss the project, Ames elaborates his plan to build along the contours of the hills, "with the land" rather than altering its natural shape. Paul protests that this results in too much wasted space. Says Ames in close-up: "There's no such thing. There's space for life, space for people. I'm not interested in building something that will be a slum in twenty years." And as he says this, we can only think of the housing projects of Manhattan.

This disagreement defines a rupture between schools of architecture, and one that the film is able to apply to many issues—to civil authority, gun rights, even economic freedom. Paul's vision of imposing square shapes on a rolling land and making the emerging cities of the western United States virtual reproductions of those in the East suggests his restricted training in the confines of modernist styles and implies the culpability for those forms in creating the uncivilized cities of the East. In order to devise a newness of spirit, thought, and space, an alternative mode of building must take place—one that allows people, as Ames says, not to hear their neighbors flush their toilets. But, of course, this mode of building cannot be imposed on cities such as New York. As the scenes in Arizona proceed, we move topically from buildings, to law and order, to self-defense, and then to guns as the closely connected definitional elements of the Western way of life. From their interaction at the building location, the film next has Paul and Ames attend a Wild West show in "old Tucson." Old Tucson is a movie set that trades on the idea of the West as depicted in Western films. While Ames notes that it's for tourists, he does bring Paul's attention to the drama of the marshal and the four bad men who seek to kill him. The scene proceeds complete with a voice-over narration to inform the crowd of the nature of the drama they are watching. Unlike the cops of New York City, this marshal is everywhere, killing the four. The announcer tells us about the West as the triumph of "honest men with dreams." Throughout this drama, the camera intermittently cuts to a tight shot of Paul's face, which shows that he is quite moved by this spectacle. This vision of the law enforcement community as intrinsically part of the broader populace is what is missing in New York, as we see our bureaucratic, car-bound policemen in their bunker-like stations. Again, it is a vision of organic connection between the land and social structure that leads to this sense of responsibility. And indeed, it is Paul's personal stake in public safety that justifies his actions.

The culmination of Paul's visit to the West is his foray to the local gun club. It is here where Ames further indoctrinates Paul into new ways of looking the world. As they enter the club, they are shot from within the structure, providing a feeling of arrival. Decrying the gun control people ("half the nation's scared even to own a gun"), Ames argues for the utility and naturalness of firearms, comparing a gun to a hammer, "just another tool." As they speak in relative intimacy and approach the indoor gun range, but still a bit divided in a mid-range two shot, with the post that connects to a pulley for the targets separating them. Ames goes on to tell the New Yorker that it is the prevalence of guns that makes Tucson safe. "Muggers operating out here, they would just plain get their asses blown off." Paul even shoots an antique pistol, solidifying his connection to the historical West (figure 6.1). He is an able target shooter, who seems to enjoy himself. It is this pistol that

FIGURE 6.1 *Death Wish*: Paul gets comfortable with his pistol.

he takes home and with which he embarks on a mission to take back Manhattan from the forces of darkness. He is an embodiment of the frontier, as he seeks out those who would do harm to others. That we have personalized Paul's imperative creates a visceral argument for the re-vision of the contemporary East as the mythic West.

In *Taxi Driver*, Travis's service in Vietnam is not heavily emphasized, but it is definitional. Travis's khaki jacket with his battalion insignia is a recurring feature of his wardrobe. It appears in his first scene, as he enters the taxi office in slow motion, and the camera watches him do a half spin toward the personnel man, to the sound of portentous music by Bernard Herrmann. As he tells of his honorable discharge, "May, 1973," and his inability to sleep, the words, along with the music and images point to the degree of disturbance he experiences. There is clearly something missing in this character, and that he is drawn to women, or girls, whose innocence he feels psychotically compelled to protect is both a metaphor for the Vietnam War and the explanation that it is a conflict to save those who are being compromised by the evil and interventionist Russians and Chinese communists (figure 6.2). It is also conceivably a result of the psychic scars of service, of being in a situation where young women were often the targets, however inadvertent, of violence.[16]

His view of New York as diseased and out of control is the expression of his madness, but it doesn't seem to be its root. The figure of Charles Palantine, the presidential candidate, is symptomatic of the amorphous centrist politics that mark both interventionist and non-interventionist foreign policy. While some

FIGURE 6.2 *Taxi Driver*: Travis drives at night in Times Square.

view the candidate as a prototypical liberal, this is far from clear. Indeed, in his script Paul Schrader takes pains to note that he is "not a Hubert Humphrey-type professional bullshitter" (www.awesomefilms.com). When Palantine in his campaign speech declares that the many have unjustly suffered for the few, that sentiment along with his recurring aphorism, the "people will rule," strikes a note of faux populism. This speech is the moment when Travis, with khaki jacket and Mohawk haircut, stands just off from the crowd, apparently intent on assassinating the candidate. Given Travis's extreme, if twisted, moralism, it appears as though it is Palantine's message that makes him a likely target. The campaign slogan, "We *are* the people," emphasized throughout the film, is tautological. But it is also solipsistic in a way that contrasts directly with Travis's ethos. That is, Travis sees his mission in life to rescue those who are lost, such as Iris or Betsy; those who express a kind of innocence that, in his view, makes them subject to exploitation. We can only surmise that the vague liberalism espoused here by the candidate is antithetical to Travis's aggressive, and psychotic, interventionism. And arguably, this is precisely the vision that was lacking in Vietnam and is lacking in Manhattan, both places that need a redeemer who will not allow the conventions of law and custom to stand in the way of resolute actions.

But crime persists in Manhattan and, in this conservative rendering, the United States is thwarted in Vietnam by a lack of will to do what is necessary, by myopic politicians and guardians who cannot see the terms and depth of the moral problems of their immediate worlds. That Travis's killing spree makes him a hero suggests the general need for a different kind of populist hero from that defined by Palantine—that of the populist vigilante, a figure more like Travis and Paul Kersey. Thus, Manhattan and Vietnam are linked both by their social chaos and their definitional relation to U.S. politics.[17]

In *Marathon Man*, Manhattan is again defined as the place where the unresolved issues of history come to reside, thus elaborating New York as both a temporal and geographic crossroads. But this vision is personalized, as the graduate student Babe finds virtually all of these currents directed through him. And since he is a conduit for all manner of unresolved historical tension, he must take matters into his own hands. His gripe with the Nazis, the autocrats of the McCarthy era, and even with the surreptitious and specter-like double agents who work for the U.S. government, concerns their willingness to remain in a state of irresolution. Babe, gun in hand, feels compelled to act as a means of avenging the death of his brother and father. But thematically, the narrative returns repeatedly to the question of history. Indeed, we find out that Babe is a historian, as was his father, who killed himself after being dismissed from his position at Columbia during the 1950s. And as the cold war was the continuation of many of the unresolved strains of World War II, so is the 1970s a synthesis of those persistent aspects of history and culture. Babe studies history to relive his father's life. His brother Doc engages in espionage to avert the questions of ideology and affiliation that made one suspect in the 1950s; as a doer and not a thinker, he is apparently beyond the controversies that afflicted his father and that might afflict his brother (figure 6.3).

This vision of Manhattan as a historical crossroads frames the film. In its first scene, we find a fairly typical New Yorker, driving his car in an aggressive and irritated manner across upper Manhattan. He encounters an older Mercedes unable to start and blocking the street. As he screams at the driver, that man answers in German. The driver responds in his own brand of German, which is obscenity-laden Yiddish. The man in the Mercedes screams back, "Alt Juden," as the other driver calls him a Nazi and a Kraut, smashing his car against the other car's bumper. The camera intermittently cuts to on-lookers who gape but do nothing, exhibiting a kind of wonder and passivity. Many of these figures are orthodox Jews on their way to synagogue to observe the Yom Kippur holiday. The two men eventually race down a street, filling it as they ride side by side cursing at one another, invoking the historical antipathies of Jew and Nazi. The camera cuts back and forth between the two, providing a kind of equivalency. As they scream, an oil truck backing out of a driveway blocks the street. We see the horrified expression on each face as they crash into the truck and explode into flames.

Though they kill no passers-by, they do pose a threat, and this Upper West Side location is no accident; on the Jewish holiday, many of those people wearing

FIGURE 6.3 *Marathon Man*: Babe and Doc eye their father's gun.

yarmulkes evince an unwillingness to engage the threat. This reluctance creates the precondition for Babe's ultimate acts of violence. That these men are menaces within this particular locale suggests the residual power of Nazi anti-Semitism and its unresolved hatreds. Even as the two cars explode into flames, they continue to pose a hazard. It is also revealing that we see no police; an onlooker takes pictures but does nothing; and then more men and women on their way to High Holy Day services inexplicably run toward the fire. We see a key on the German's wrist and then, as he is consumed by flames, it drops into the fire. As the flames burn, we cut to an image of our protagonist, Babe, who is running around the reservoir at Central Park. That we go from one enclosed space on the island to another, but one which is circular, provides us with key geometric images of the film: Babe runs in circles, but perhaps should not. Manhattan represents a dead end, but perhaps need not be.

From Manhattan we go to Paris, where we find Babe's brother, Doc, who is involved in smuggling and some kind of surreptitious, quasi-governmental work. Clearly he is at the center of some plot, as he is almost blown up by a bomb on the street, almost strangled in his room, and his associate is garroted during the opera. But the precise strains of these earlier but recent histories do not become clear until almost forty minutes into the film, when it moves to the jungles of Uruguay and we encounter the center of the narrative, Christian Szell, a former concentration camp doctor and a notorious torturer of Jews, whose teeth he extracted and converted into the diamonds that are kept in a safe-deposit box in Manhattan. As

FIGURE 6.4 *Marathon Man*: Szell in the jewelers' district.

we see Szell travel upriver in a skiff, we see how easily connected even remote places are to centers like New York. As he arrives at JFK, this is not only a city in decline but also a nation in decline. Jokes Szell as he leaves the airport, "They used to think that God was on their side but now they may not be so sure."

In this film, all manner of urban threats and violence form around Szell, who is seeking to recover his diamonds. Babe is mugged in Central Park by two of Szell's flunkies. Doc is stabbed by Szell himself. Though it is true that Babe's neighbors torment him and that they have no particular connection to Nazi Germany, their threat is vaguely comedic in relation to the menace of Szell and his associates. Szell personifies the ghosts of the past and there is no authority—city, state, federal, or international—who will apprehend this man. That he invades Manhattan is an index of a different type of danger that lurks in the city (figure 6.4). Babe must cease to be the man of books and of marathon running and become the man of violence to vanquish this ghost—who is also known as the Weise Angel. That he is explicitly named as a specter points to the necessity of his elimination. Eventually, Babe does defend himself with his father's gun and is at least partially responsible for the death of Szell. The film's vision of direct and decisive action leaves little doubt as to the road of historical redemption. Intriguingly, this vision of vigilance as regenerative is one that recurs in all three films. Manhattan, in all of these films, becomes the place where the unresolved tensions of the past come to bear and can be relatively resolved, allowing for a process beyond that which originates in the past.

SAVING MANHATTAN, SAVING THE WORLD

Michael Peter Smith, in his thoughtful and elucidating study *Transnational Urbanism: Locating Globalization*, argues that the discourse of economic globalization tends to subsume all other notions of social process and therefore may become a reifying term that reduces the specific actions of individuals and groups in a particular place at a particular time. On the other hand, rather than seeing localism as the "other" of globalization, he finds local definitions of place and culture as deeply involved with "transnational networks of meaning and power that now regularly cut across territorial boundaries of local and national political space" (106). Manhattan in the 1970s serves as a specific historical crossroads, a crossroads with distinctive qualities as a location where unresolved political tensions of the past come to a point of crisis, The films also inscribe it in an emerging narrative: one in which individuals with appropriate beliefs can seize control of its contested spaces, thus redefining and redeeming the spaces of the core of the island.

This act of assertion is defined in all three films as a necessary precondition for the safety and sanctity of the citizens of the island. The Manhattan we see in these films is not so much physically decimated as it is morally so, a place where aspects of a geographically remote world impinge, a place where policing has failed. Unlike the films of the preceding chapter, these are far more Manhattan-centered, and all project toward a future where Manhattan serves as an upscale nexus of the region, as well as a city with a distinctive role in the world economy, a center of trade and information-based services. This view is to some degree related to the films' focus on matters of morality. Perhaps this obsession is best captured by Travis Bickle in *Taxi Driver*, who, though truly a disturbed character, does make a case for the fact of the world he sees it. This world is one of decay and menace. When asked by presidential candidate Palantine what he would like to see changed, he replies, "Whatever it is, he should clean up this city here, is like an open sewer. It's full of filth and scum. . . . He should just flush it down the fuckin' toilet" (figure 6.5). Travis's rant is indeed pathological, but it also contains aspects of a world seen. And it is a world that viewers recognize from the news, from other films, and from television shows. If it is not poverty and structural disinvestment that plague Manhattan, then a more commodious place can be summoned by morally uplifting those who reside on the island, or by expelling those who cannot be uplifted. And, indeed, such embedded logic points to conservative notions of individual responsibility, a concept that is also at the heart of vigilance.

All of these films' protagonists serve as avatars of gentrification, a process that is implied rather than asserted, and which inferentially becomes part of the moral imperative of these films. That is, these films focus on the three areas of the city

FIGURE 6.5 *Taxi Driver*: Travis drives candidate Palantine.

that are in the process of becoming important areas of residence for the emerging class of affluent Manhattanites. Paul's world is centered on the Upper West Side. Travis's act of violence occurs on 12th Street in the area of Manhattan that borders the Lower East Side, and Babe is an "urban pioneer" in the area of the Upper West Side that abuts Columbia University, though he also clears Central Park of Nazis. All of these spaces serve as important symbolic areas of violence, as they define a core of the island that will become gentrified in the next decade. All target nuisances of a variety of types, and that they stand up for decency, within the context of these films, asserts a kind of resilience.[18]

Paul's apartment sits at the northeast corner of Riverside Drive and 75th Street, an area that had been relatively middle-class in the 1960s but in a building that had been a luxurious residence when built in the late 1920s and that is one today.[19] Though the source of violence is different in each film, each type is pressing and compelling, and must be exorcized before the city can become re-elaborated as a center for the affluent. Indeed, one of the more time-bound sentiments is one that is repeated in *Death Wish*, as Paul is told by both his son-in-law and a fellow architect in his firm that one may work in Manhattan but should live somewhere else. Such a comment reflects the trends of the preceding two decades, as the 1950s, 1960s, and early 1970s saw the decline of white collar professionals in Manhattan. Writes demographer Richard Harris: "The trend towards inner-city gentrification has increased since the late 1970s. The fiscal crisis of the early and mid-seventies brought cuts in city services, which surely might have made a suburban home

seem doubly attractive to those able to commute. A local economic recovery began
in 1977, and the pace of gentrification has been rapid ever since."[20] As these films
define a demographic nexus in the history of Manhattan, the moment between
decline and renewal of the city's stock of middle-class and upwardly mobile professionals, their sociological commentary is historically evocative. All three redefine
the terms of the threat to the "civilized," and in doing so marginalize the poor and
the nonwhite residents of central Manhattan.

Death Wish offers a city of enclosed and discrete spaces, but these areas lack the
cohesion we saw in the ethnic neighborhoods of chapter 3. This is a city of relatively low density and some degree of interpersonal relationship: those relationships, however, are amicable but lacking intensity. Joanne is mugged because the
clerk at the neighborhood grocery store has left her address in an unattended box
of groceries. There, she is referred to by her name and is obviously known to those
who work there. After the mugging, as Paul contemplates revenge, he enters a
bank to ask for the rolls of quarters he uses as a blackjack. He is shot in close-up
and addressed by name. He is known to his newsman, his doorman. He has close
relations with his fellow workers, who are interested in his life beyond work and
with whom he shares conversation regarding general matters of politics and urban
life. Where the films of the previous chapter largely defined an outer-borough
world of depopulated neighborhoods and criminal anonymity, a city to avoid,
Paul's world is, in ways, similar to those of the Little Italy of the 1920s and 1930s in
the *Godfather* films, one of bounded spaces and interpersonal relationships. It is
different, however, in the degree of affiliation and also in the threat of crime.
While the provenance of Vito Corleone was a vigilance organization operating
within a particular geography—"You go to the police instead of to me," says to Don
to the funeral director in the opening scene of *The Godfather*—Paul's friends are
not his family, and his sense of geography is not nearly so definite nor circumscribed as Vito's.

This connection to that representation of an earlier Manhattan provides a
means of seeing what is lacking in the world depicted here. Though our spatial
sense of the city is relatively intimate, that intimacy, once breached by outsiders,
presents dangers of proximity. That is, this is fortress Manhattan but the gates are
porous. After the death of his wife and his trip to Arizona, Paul fights back in a
range of spaces that begin with his block, extend to the nearby Riverside Park, and
then eventually include the subway station near his office on the East Side in Murray Hill (figure 6.6). It is as though he finds threats that have invaded his personal
space. But his definition of that space becomes more general as the film goes on. It
moves from his house to recreational space abutting his house to his office. As the
film proceeds, the circle of Paul's sense of his life enlarges and demands greater

security. Thus, in the beginning he only accosts those who accost him. Later, he lures muggers to him. Finally, he seeks them out. Paul not only resolves to protect himself but others like him. He does not, however, venture to Harlem or to Brooklyn.

And though the narrative as a whole and the character of Paul in particular seem extraordinary, it is difficult to watch this film without considering its inspirational impact on the notorious Subway Vigilante, Bernhard Goetz, who in December of 1984 shot four African American teenagers who he felt were about to rob him as he rode the Number 2 train leaving 14th Street. Goetz was compared to Kersey and apparently took the figure as an inspiration. Like his fictional model, Goetz became something of a hero and sparked a general appreciation for "people fighting back," as well as bringing even greater attention and support to vigilance organizations like Curtis Sliwa's Guardian Angels, a group of volunteers who wore red berets and patrolled New York City's subways.[21] Subsequently, the film inspired four sequels, and a remake directed by Sylvester Stallone is planned but at this point seems indefinite.[22]

In following the neoconservative vision of the decline of comportment as the key to urban crime and broader dissolution, but not wishing to be too overly racist, *Death Wish*'s muggers are disproportionately white, reasonably well-dressed, and many wear the accoutrements of the counterculture. That is, we see floppy-brimmed hats, a leather jacket with an American flag decal on the back, and long hair as muggers' adornments. And rather than limiting interaction with their

FIGURE 6.6 *Death Wish*: Paul takes vengeance while on the subway.

victim, most are rude, and accost him by cursing at him. For example, the first mugger he beats back with his sock full of quarters is a thirty-or-so-year-old white man. He seems not so much desperate as depraved: "Turn around son of a bitch." When hit, he looks personally insulted and runs away, proving his cowardice and confirming the view that muggers are simply moral deviants. This first mugger becomes something of the prototype, which gives distinctive meaning to the exchange between Paul and his son-in-law as they stand in the snow at a train station in Long Island, having just visited Paul's severely disrupted daughter. They never quite face each other and maintain an excess of space from one another. Says Paul, "What do we call people who run in the face of fear?" Answers his son-in-law, "We're not pioneers any more, Dad." "What are we? What do you call people who, when faced with a condition of fear just run and hide, they do nothing about it." "Civilized," responds his son-in-law. With a simple, "No," Paul ends the conversation. But at this point the architect almost perfectly reiterates Ames's social philosophy, as he reintroduces a key term of his first conversation with his wife. Ames, in Tuscon, defines civilization as the willingness to resist those who would encroach on one's individual freedoms—and by any means necessary. Paul renounces a doctrine of mutual social responsibility for its ineffectiveness and impact on the individual, and thus mouths an inherently anti-urban philosophy—and a notion of the acceptability of violence as a means of response and of preemption.

This vision of redemptive and necessary violence at least informs *Taxi Driver*, though Travis's social marginality complicates it. Although Travis finally brings his obsession to bear on Iris, who walks the streets just below 14th Street on Second Avenue, he begins the film largely in midtown, and it is in this region that we develop our sense of locale. In *Taxi Driver*, the basis of decay is undoubtedly sexual desire.[23] And that desire pervades the city, from the space of Travis's cab, to 42nd Street, to the apartment where his passenger, played by Martin Scorsese, eyes his wife with another man. Travis too is afflicted by desire. He haunts the porno theaters because he can't sleep and confuses their sexual display for mass entertainment. Indeed, as it did in *Midnight Cowboy*, 42nd Street plays a major role in the first part of the film, and while it does define a kind of despair, it is not simply inhabited by the marginal, though such characters do proliferate there. Indeed, the film divides into two phases: the Betsy phase, when he stalks the blonde campaign worker Betsy, played by Cybill Shepherd, and the Iris phase, when he stalks the child prostitute. As such, the focus of the film's geography changes and so does its tone and the sense of the city.

In the uptown phase, the film's view of the Palantine campaign headquarters at 63rd and Broadway near Lincoln Center, and its perspective on Times Square, is intriguing. The office is pristine, open to the street, and a bustle of purposeful activity defines it. This is notable for its distinction from the city of the night that Travis traverses as a driver. When he discovers Betsy in midtown, he not only notices her but is also drawn to the relative sterility of her context. If this is a city in decay, it is, in this uptown geography, more a spiritual corrosion than a physical one. While other districts define a city of menace and desires, of prostitutes and pimps, the world of Betsy and the headquarters stands in sharp contrast.

The Palantine headquarters, like so many places in the film, is significantly located by Travis's point of view, though initially it is Travis who is spied from the office and noted as an odd and disquieting voyeuristic presence. That this point of view often becomes the viewers' shows us what he lacks and what he desires. His longing gazes of Betsy reveal a perverse desire for normalcy even as he purports to rescue her. This rescue, though, is from the sterility and banality of her existence and commitment to the fatuous Palantine. That Betsy is dissatisfied is affirmed by her interest in and romanticizing of Travis. In his various forays into Betsy's space, Travis is marked as an intruder. The camera typically shows him entering, shooting from the inside out, and he is typically off center in the frame. In his first entrée into the office, we get a reaction shot of Betsy and Tom, another campaign worker with some authority, showing discomfort and questioning his presence. We see Travis as out of place in the apparently "normal" world of her office. He leans toward her and is inappropriately familiar: "You are the most beautiful woman I've ever seen." The man without a high school diploma would probably have little in common with this woman or the others involved in the political campaign. The dislocations of Vietnam and the relative social chaos that prevails in Manhattan have resulted in a loss of bearings. But it is the trip to the porno theater—the Mystic Theater on 42nd Street and Eighth Avenue—while on their date that reveals to her the distance between herself and Bickle. At that point he ceases to be interesting and instead becomes frightening. After this rejection, Travis becomes fixated on killing Palantine and saving Iris, which makes sense when you consider those acts in spatial terms. The world of Palantine is that of false prophets, those who declare that they will alter the world but really just modify it to make it work better for those who are already privileged. Travis is far more a creature of downtown, who operates in far less nuanced notions of good and evil than those defined by Palantine and his acolytes.

This is reaffirmed by Palantine's major campaign speech and Travis's reaction to it. This speech takes place at Columbus Circle, which Palantine refers to as a "crossroads of history." Since Columbus never came to New York, this central location within Manhattan can only be understood in those terms as referring to a European, and then a variety of the people of the world, seeking new lands and resources, finding their way to America. Palantine seeks to renew the promise of self-government. Indeed, this notion aligns with the notions of the frontier and imperialism we find in *Death Wish*. He says, "No longer will we the people suffer for the few." But his appeal is to "change" and to an ethos, and not a set of policies: to make America a place of the "right and the good." But such soft populism tells us little of the content of these terms or the road to their realization. In this model, leaders are empty vessels to be filled up with the collective will. The effect of such rhetoric is stasis, as leaders reflect back that which is already there. Travis, on the other hand, is a man of action, one who seeks to turn complacency into some heroic ideal of reaffirmed purity and innocence. Columbus Circle is indeed a crossroads, but it is the nexus dividing two distinct ways of looking at America: Palantine's is that of amorphous collectivity and Travis's is that of mad, but radical, redemption. When the camera cuts to Travis, he is in mid close-up, with a Mohawk haircut, standing alone in fence by the corner, clapping out of rhythm. The world in which he intrudes is that of the mundane, that of the normal. For Travis to do his work he must eradicate passivity and complacence—and its symbolic leader. As the speech ends, Palantine and his body guards enter the crowd, though the guards insulate him from it. Travis approaches him, goes for his gun, is spotted by the secret service agents, and runs off.

Travis's mission then becomes more clearly defined in his rescue of Iris. Iris's iconic figure is not a presidential candidate but a pimp. Though Sport the pimp and Palantine the candidate exercise the same hypnotic effect on their minions, Sport is seen as socially marginal, is not protected by body guards, and his acolyte is a twelve-year-old girl. These distinctions make Iris a far better object for Travis's obsession and make him a hero rather than a pariah. But the fact that his act of madness makes him a hero suggests not only how wrong Palantine is, but how ready the city and the nation are for a charismatic man of action; or, maybe for a former screen actor who was in a few Westerns and hosted *Death Valley Days*.

Much as *Taxi Driver* locates Travis both at Columbus Circle and the Lower East Side, *Marathon Man* is also a film with a distinctive geographic focus: Central Park, another focal spot in central Manhattan and a place that Travis has stood on the edge of during the Palantine rally. Beyond that general location, it dwells on a spot within the park, the reservoir where Babe runs and where he ultimately has his confrontation with Szell. The reservoir is between 86th and 96th Streets, and has a running path that became popular with joggers when Americans became fitness-conscious during late 1960s and early 1970s. The film strategically expands its size and centrality, defining it as a large hole that seems to locate the center of the island and perhaps a vision of the center of the world. As Babe circles it in the first scenes in which he appears, it looks positively oceanic. To some degree this view is connected to Babe's fledgling career as a runner. But to a degree its size is related to the way in which it defines Manhattan as a specific entity that marks the nexus of a variety of geographic and historical currents. As we see Babe run, he conjures images of the great Ethiopian marathoner Abebe Bikila, who in 1968 was involved in a car accident that left him paralyzed below the waist. That it is Bikila, rather than 1972 marathon gold medalist Frank Shorter, who actually grew up in New York near to where the character Babe lived with his family, is indicative.[24] The heroic presence of Bikila inspires Babe, whose summoning of the Ethiopian mythologizes that runner's achievements and hardships. It also makes marathon running a kind of exotic endeavor, despite Frank Shorter and Bill Rogers (another prominent U.S. marathoner), both world-class marathoners at this time and children of relative privilege who attended Yale and Wesleyan Universities, respectively. It is one in which outward-looking Americans might involve themselves. Indeed, it becomes another way of making Babe's actions both place-specific and cosmopolitan.

The image of Bikila emphasizes the ways in which Manhattan, and the park in particular, is a specific place and the center of a global network of activities. It is not only the reservoir and Babe's running that define its centrality. John Schlesinger takes pains to emphasize its Europeanness, as well as its references to other times. It is a central site for the courtship between Babe and his apparently Swiss love interest, Elsa—though we are led to believe that she is an impostor. As they develop their relationship, she increasingly becomes involved in his running workouts, ensconcing herself by the pumping station and timing him. They traipse around the Central Park zoo, where she teaches him French and they watch the glockenspiel, at the time an enhancement recently donated by the Delacorte family and a device that provided a decidedly German feel to its environs. As they sit by the pond in front of the Dakota apartment building, a high-angle shot diminishes them in scale as the scene recalls a respite in the shadow of a medieval castle, with the pond becoming a moat. It is at that point Szell's two henchman appear, two middle-aged sweaty former Nazis, who accost them, seeking the key to the safety deposit box that holds Szell's diamonds. That the park has become the place where, in the 1970s, Nazis go to seek their prey, and that mugging has become their violence of choice, suggests the ways in which the forces of the history and the methods of urban decay converge. It is that morass of forces that come together here which requires vigilance.

There are certainly many references to Jews and assertions/assumptions of their ethos that mark this film. The brothers Henry "Doc" Levy and Thomas "Babe" Levy, played by Roy Scheider and Dustin Hoffman, respectively, clearly are ethnically Jewish, though no assertion of their Jewishness occurs in the film, nor do they do anything in particular that marks them as such. But both *look* Jewish—perhaps because Hoffman and Scheider *are* Jewish—and their name, Levy, is unmistakably Jewish. That they are hunted by Nazis in New York is ironic and historically resonant.

Babe, in a behavior redolent of World War II pathos, is afflicted by an inability to fight back. Earlier in the film, as Babe runs around the reservoir, we see a dog accosting the various runners. Babe's response is to depart from the path and scream at the dog and its owner from a safe distance. The camera is stationary as he flees, causing him to leave the frame for a moment. In this later scene, though he offers no effective resistance to the muggers, he does later write in a letter to Doc that he feels as though, if he could find these men, he would kill them. The way in which these men brutalize him, though he is unable to articulate what is distinctive about them and their methods, as well as his sense of responsibility for Elsa, alters him from a passive bystander to a potentially aggressive resister. In effect, this event has turned him in the direction of Paul Kersey. Indeed, in the same letter, he attributes their mugging to "staying too late in the park." Indeed, in this film vigilance becomes a means of undoing the bonds of history and reasserting Jewishness as including an ethos of self-defense. This particular reassertion of Jewish nationalism flows from that of the Jewish Defense League, a group that came into existence in 1968 and that was a burgeoning political and social force by 1972.[25]

Such an ethos may be redemptive within this specific urban context. Babe lives within the historically Jewish Upper West Side, but on the fringes of that neighborhood, and he is harassed by his teen-aged Puerto Rican neighbors. It is only when a more significant threat appears, the Nazis, that we see their relatively benign qualities. But, as in *Death Wish*, this film practices the politics of resentment. The Levys are Jews of a new age, figures who can redeem and rewrite the legacy of World War II. New York becomes the site of the ethos derived from the post-1967 and 1973 Israeli-Arab wars, in which Israeli military power was affirmed and made internationally iconic, whether reviled or admired. Indeed, these are the New Jews of the new world: secular, athletic, proactive. They are distinct from the concentration camp survivors that work in the diamond district but who are powerless to stop Szell. These Jews are historical victims and show the ravages of that history in all aspects of their existence.

It is intriguing to put *Marathon Man's* vision of muscular urban Jewishness into dialogue with the emerging power of ethnic anger in New York City, a political force that had many expressions throughout the era, including the revolt of the police force noted earlier, the famous fights between Jews and African Americans over school policy and the issue of local control, and the disagreements over the placement of subsidized housing in Forest Hills, Queens, in close proximity to

FIGURE 6.7 *Marathon Man*: Babe holds Szell at gunpoint.

Italian and Jewish middle-class neighborhoods.[26] Such incidents lead to the rise of the anti-John Lindsay movement.

Edward I. Koch had made his way in New York politics as a liberal connected with the Greenwich Village–based club of reform-minded Democrats. Koch narrowly won the election of 1977, but eventually enhanced his coalition and remained in office until 1989. Among his strategies, writes John Hull Mollenkopf, were

> mobililizing white middle-class fears of black and Latino encroachment; capitalizing on the ethnic, nativity, and geographic cleavages among underrepresented but potentially challenging groups. . . . Mayor Koch's position on private development won him great support from the corporate business community, just as his devotion to the white middle class in a racially divided city drew support from white ethnics.[27]

Though constrained by the city's considerable budgetary woes, Koch did significantly add to the city's spending in the areas of policing and corrections, as street crime under the Koch administration increased, and when the drug epidemic that had begun in the early 1970s burgeoned in the late seventies and eighties. Despite his administration's inability to reduce crime, the climate of fear actually served to make the mayor more popular with his target constituencies, as he also encouraged the development and redevelopment that significantly changed the demographics of central Manhattan during his administration.[28]

Indeed, Koch's belligerence became part of the context in which urban pioneers, who are simply gentrifiers by another name, achieved domain over much of central Manhattan. His articulation of white backlash provided an environment in which the gradual displacement of poorer Manhattanites of color could be seen as both rational and morally correct. Thus, the politics of the city in this era allowed for a conflation between ethos and ethnos that resulted in a justification of white backlash. Writes Joshua Freeman in his study *Working Class New York*: "By the end of Koch's first term . . . the social, ethical, and political environment of the city had forever changed. In a few short years, financial leaders, politicians allied with them, and conservative intellectuals had succeeded at least partially in prying the city away from its working-class, social democratic heritage" (187). These films of redemptive white violence, then, provide a justification for repopulating the real estate of Manhattan with those who will be focally involved in rearticulating New York City's central role in a changing world economic environment.

7

Love, Marriage, and Fine City Living

ANNIE HALL (1977), *AN UNMARRIED WOMAN* (1978),

MANHATTAN (1979), AND *KRAMER VS. KRAMER* (1979)

MANY VISIONS OF a gentrifying and gentrified New York City informed films of the latter half of the 1970s, including, in addition to those listed above, a contemporary cycle of films focused on the entertainment industry, New York City's relative place in it, and how that city provides and restricts access to mass audiences. These include *Network* (1976), *Saturday Night Fever* (1977), *New York, New York* (1977), *All that Jazz* (1979), and *Fame* (1980) and, though I will not discuss these films at length, it is significant that they alter the narrative about New York, as they articulate the city as a space of work and of networks of information dispersal and exchange. Indeed, this emphasis complements that on personal life which marks the films of this chapter. All of the films noted—those of entertainment and those of "relationships"—occur in the moment when New York's place in a broad international system of trade was being enhanced as a result of its extensive and burgeoning means of communication, and those devices were central in transforming a time of urban decline and default into a period of selective prosperity and status as a "global city." They occur as a complement to the films in the previous two chapters, which devised strategies of commerce and safety for the gentrifying city. In these later films, we see the dynamism and economic means to prosperity, conditions that can take hold in a Manhattan that has been made safe for international commerce.

Fittingly, the entertainment films are ultimately more about business than they are about the show. All are, in some way, stories of aspiration, whether for higher ratings, greater industry status, and sustained celebrity in *Network* and *All That Jazz*; or of climbing the ladder from relative obscurity to wealth and/or recognition in *Saturday Night Fever*, *New York, New York*, and *Fame*. Indeed, we see similar strategies in a film such as *The Goodbye Girl* (1977), as well as in *Lenny* (1974). But even in the films that focus on more mature performers who have established significant careers, their elaboration of the entertainment industry suggests a shift in its dimensions that spark a crisis for the various individuals involved. *Network* and *All That Jazz* feature stars that are literally consumed by their own success, becoming, in effect, models of capitalist economics who are continually facing the prospect of getting bigger or failing. Ultimately, however, these films elaborate distinctive districts for those who are inside and for those left outside of the world system of information and technological exchange.

Such a vision of the connection between distinct regions of the city and the relative status of the individual is the stuff of gentrification and the core of the four movies I discuss at length in this chapter—*Annie Hall* (1977), *An Unmarried Woman* (1978), *Manhattan* (1979), and *Kramer vs. Kramer* (1979). Though, like the entertainment films noted above, all the protagonists also work in some aspect of the "information industries"—the business of entertainment, mass communication, or the financial services industry—the productions emphasize the personal over the professional, with these occupations forming a backdrop to the relationship problems and personal angst that are at the center of these films. Since these presentations focus almost exclusively on the emotional life of their protagonists, few characters appear who are not closely connected to central figures.

This results in the picturing of a significantly different social environment from that in *Network*, *New York, New York*, and *All that Jazz*. Those films picture a world of work or a world where having a particular type of work is a consuming aspiration. These films not only dwell almost solely in the leisure world of privileged classes but also dwell in a geography that is class bound, as they erase areas of the city in which lower and working-class individuals reside and work.[1] As we have seen in other chapters, crime and economic despair take as their physical object areas that are navigable from the center of Manhattan, but which are distinctly different spaces. This vision well expresses the ways in which global cities are not only emblematic of uneven development on a global scale, but that they are also expressive of this phenomena on a regional and local scale. In this geographical pattern, one may be physically near those who prosper, but still may not have access to the means by which prosperity occurs. These earlier films emphasize that areas related to central Manhattan define the spaces of aspiration. But these areas are distinct, and their relationship turns out to be economically indirect, as those aspirations are increasingly dreams that cannot come to fruition. As Saskia Sassen tells us in *The Global City*, gentrification from the mid-1970s onward occurred in distinct areas, leaving districts that were contiguous to these zones of wealth in what is, in effect, a different world.

> The expansion of the number of professionals, especially in the high-income segment working and living in Manhattan, has been a central fact in the gentrification of several parts of the city. It is evident in Manhattan and certain areas of Brooklyn where once poor and middle-income neighborhoods now contain highly priced commercial and residential buildings. . . . Yet, Manhattan also contains areas that have experienced sharp declines in household incomes. . . . There is a ring of poverty that runs through northern Manhattan, the South Bronx, and much of northern Brooklyn. (266–267)

In such a model, one that emphasizes access, and not proximity, to certain areas as a key element of social mobility, to aspire without access is a strategy destined to result in failure. For the characters in the entertainment films who perform— particularly as depicted in *Fame* and *Saturday Night Fever*—a lack of access to electronic means of dissemination results in a work life that is severely constrained in terms of audience and remuneration. In these films of personal issues, there are no such characters. All of the players have already arrived professionally and have attached their fortunes to international commerce and communication.

In relation to the productions of the earlier chapters, we can see pronounced contrasts. While the films from the earlier decade—*Klute*, *Taxi Driver*, *Dog Day Afternoon*—generally reference films noir from the 1940s and 1950s—*Champion*, *Force of Evil*, *Naked City*—the later productions call upon the drawing-room comedies of the 1930s and 1940s, such as George Cukor's *Dinner at Eight* (1934) or Ernst Lubitsch's *Trouble in Paradise* (1932), to focus on the doings of a significantly higher class of New York social life. Unlike these earlier films, however, the emphasis is not explicitly on wealth and conspicuous consumption. Rather, each of the characters in these films has some kind of job; each has some trappings of having been and to some extent remaining in the middle class; and, while many have continually been of about the same economic station in life, there is some notion of upward mobility in these films. This particular view of mobility suggests both the changing definitions of class that were becoming operative as the broader U.S. economy was entering its postindustrial phase, as well as the related shift in definitions of wealth.

Such emphases make these films significant in codifying the terms of the *new class*: that is, a class that is emblematic of a postindustrial economy and mode of production. Since in this system of economic organization, work becomes largely intellectual and social, the distinction between work and social life becomes less pronounced: some work can be done at home, some is a matter of networking, and the exchanges that occur within the workplace may appear primarily social in nature. In such an economic system, production may substantially pass from the center of one's work-life, and labor can become a primary means of elaborating one's lifestyle and developing a body of desirable associates. One of the behaviors of the urban variation of this class, which constitutes a significant subsection of it, is its gravitation to the gentrified areas of formerly decaying cities. In the study titled simply *Gentrification*, Loretta Lees and her co-authors look at various approaches to the topic over time and space. One of their assertions is that not only does the emergence of a new class reveal shifts in the terms and structure of work but it also designates a whole new approach to lifestyle and aesthetics. Thus they consider the ways in which this class is involved in "the gentrification aesthetic," as they "buy into history" and distance themselves from the old middle class (often their parents) and the working class. Such choices tend to produce, over time, homogeneous regions (94–125, esp. 113).

This vision of lifestyle as consumer choice—including choice of location and housing—fits well with Evan Watkins's incisive vision of postindustrial social formations. Watkins sees consumption, rather than work, as the expressed arbiter of status differentiation and affiliation in what he terms "Reagan's America" (which I find in this slightly earlier moment in a distinctly urban locale). He explains in his book *Throwaways*, "Class-as-lifestyle is . . . a universalizing category insofar as its field of realization is consumption as the endless horizon of rising expectations. . . . It reconstructs social positionalities through . . . a shift from the social field of production, occupation, and labor to the no less social field of consumer practices" (71). Thus what one has and desires forms the basis for affiliations, which redefines class in a way that reduces it to a strategy of acquisition. In these films, lifestyle is defined by the desire for a certain urban lifestyle, one that seeks a certain space, a certain range of associations, and a particular type of material goods. The result of this desire is seen in the social homogeneity that marks the New York City depicted in these films.

While the films of show business—*Network* (1976), *Saturday Night Fever* (1977), and so on—moved in the direction of such a definition of work and social life, this view now becomes a precondition of these narratives, resulting in films that are substantially about a search for self through seeking a complementary partner. Among these films, only *Kramer vs. Kramer* deviates from this emphasis, and then only somewhat. In this film, the narrative continues to define class as lifestyle; but Ted Kramer is not shopping for a partner. Instead the film focuses on the failure of his relationship with his wife and the resulting impact on a child.

Though some may tend to dismiss these films as narrowly conceived and limited in success, the history of their reception does not support that judgment at all. They were all substantial financial successes, earning significant profits. All were honored with multiple nominations for major industry awards, with *Annie Hall* and *Kramer vs. Kramer* winning the best picture Oscars for their years of release on relatively small production budgets. *Manhattan* grossed almost $40 million, while Mariel Hemingway was nominated for best supporting actress, and Woody Allen and Marshall Brickman were nominated for best screenplay. *Annie Hall* grossed $38 million and, in addition to best picture, won best director, best screenplay, and best actress (Diane Keaton). *An Unmarried Woman* earned $24 million domestically and was nominated for academy awards in three major categories: best actress (Jill Clayburgh), best picture, and Paul Mazursky for his direction. *Kramer vs. Kramer* grossed almost $106 million and won Oscars in four major categories: direction and screenplay (Robert Benton); best actor (Dustin Hoffman): and best supporting actress (Meryl Streep). It was also nominated in four other categories and won the best director award from the Director's Guild of America and the best screenplay from the Writer's Guild.[2]

Such facts help us to see these films as indicative of a popular trend of this chronology. Indeed, as the U.S. economy increasingly shifted toward providing services for a global system of trade, there emerged a new class with a level of wealth that eclipsed that of the older industrial middle class, and which expressed itself by its desire for consumption that was distinct from that of the past. The protagonists of these films can be seen as elaborating the terms of the urban, yuppie lifestyle that we have come to associate with the 1980s. As this phenomenon became more and more a matter of academic, and then popular awareness, commentators seized on the idea and issue of narcissism as a key to cultural definition and critique.

It is no surprise, then, that there are a number of popular books published in this general period that begin to explain the world articulated by these films. These include Daniel Bell's *The Coming of Post-Industrial Society: A Venture in Social Forecasting* (1973), Richard Sennett's *The Fall of Public Man* (1977), Christopher Lasch's *The Culture of Narcissism: American Life in an Age of Diminishing Expectations* (1978), and the 1985 publication by Robert Bellah, Richard Madsen, William M. Sullivan, Ann Swidler, and Steven M. Tipton, *Habits of the Heart*. That such books, densely academic in some ways, became relatively popular and triggered wide discussion serves as a further index of the major social changes that were coalescing and becoming visible. Indeed, the impact of these scholars can be surmised from the fact that Lasch, Sennett, and Bellah were invited to discuss the state of the national psyche with Jimmy Carter in 1979, which resulted in Carter's famous "malaise" speech in the summer of that year.[3]

These books are both symptom and critique. Arguably, all build on the earlier published titles and all trenchantly elaborate a social phenomenon that is palpable. That is, all seek to develop sociological and historical frameworks for viewing what were becoming significant means of social reorganization, and doing so in terms that reflected on definitions of class and space as they developed within urban contexts. But their overlapping areas of focus suggest that they are part of the world that they bemoan and that they may actually exacerbate the tendency they describe. In addition, the local disagreements among authors are also emblematic both of the various methodological and ideological means of approaching these social changes as well as of the entrenched political positions that were to some degree a residual effect of the factional politics of the left during the 1960s. The worlds depicted in these books suggest not only extant historical practices but also the power of the images on the screen.

The first of these volumes was Daniel Bell's *The Coming of Post-Industrial Society* (1973), a study that defines its project as both historical and anticipatory, as the author terms it, "a study in social forecasting." Bell reads the evidence of a change in economic, social, and cultural life already in process with acuity. The basis of his prediction is a projection of the furthering of a historical trend. Bell notes that trend as having occurred over a century, noting the tendency of the U.S. economy to develop its innovations through increasing its application of technical knowledge, resulting in the disposition to valorize and reward those who possess such knowledge. Writes Bell, "The post-industrial society, at root, is a recasting of this technical quest in an even more powerful form" (45). Such a reading of trends is apt. Of these four studies, Bell's is the one that is most concerned with society and economics, and the least with culture; yet, by the end of the book he turns to that area of study to describe the effects of this economic restructuring.

This ultimate focus locates individuals who are similar to those we encounter in these films. And although the characters featured in the films possess their own kind of refined knowledge, none of them is an engineer or works in technical fields of science; still, all benefit from the relatively high status the postindustrial world of work gives to those who possess specialized skills and knowledge. These films feature characters who either work in the technical fields of finance and marketing or who are broadly defined as writers and performers. All are clearly well educated and intellectual; many are noted as having been educated at elite colleges and universities; and all have distinct and articulately expressed views of art, commerce, and love. Such self-fashioning places these figures within the social elite, as they trade on what Bell terms the "differential status and differential income [that] are based on technical skills and higher education" (409). Such a depiction helps to valorize a world in which productivity has ceased to mean material productivity, and work has become the manipulation of information. Such a world necessarily accentuates the individual and his or her intellectual skills, since the role of the solitary thinker (as opposed to one who produces goods as part of a more complexly integrated process) becomes socially valued in the world that Bell describes and these films dramatize. This vision of the intellectual and the knowledge-worker also has the power to redefine terms such as community and class. The power of this shift in mode of production and class definition becomes the explicit focus of the other three volumes, even though they reference this economic cause somewhat less.

These subsequent books, to the consternation of some of their critics, interpret social life in the United States by looking at its manifestations in culture, and in the case of the next two studies, by Sennett and Lasch, in macro readings of broad trends. Such views, while certainly critical of the shift, also employ it as their primary means of locating the effective center of social life. For example, in Richard Sennett's brilliant *The Fall of Public Man*, he argues that the public sphere, once the primary means in Western society of defining an individual's worth, obligations, and ultimate status, has become instead a narrowly defined "matter of formal obligation" (3). He finds this retreat to the private a result of the overvaluation of psychological definitions of self, a tendency that serves to restrict an individual's focus on matters that are not explicitly affective. And, in Sennett's view, this perspective results not in insight but in a mottled view of self and others. He writes,

> Western societies are moving from something like other-directed conditions to an inner-directed condition—except that in the midst of self absorption no one can say what is inside. As a result, confusion has arisen between public and intimate life, people are working out, in terms of personal feelings, public matters which properly can be only dealt with through codes of impersonal meaning."(5)

Thus, social life ceases to be a desirable arena in itself. It becomes significant only in the manner in which it influences a person's view of self.

Lasch, although not a fan of either Bell or Sennett, traverses much of the same social ground but with a polemic style and populist politics.[4] As in these other studies, culture, as an object of social analysis, subsumes economics and politics. Unlike Bell, Lasch's beginning object is culture; and unlike Sennett, his work is not broadly historical. Lasch, who takes as his inspiration the writers of the Frankfurt School, and Herbert Marcuse in particular, fashions a screed that devises a Freudian approach to a conception of culture as an aggregated system, asserting that "bourgeois society seems everywhere to have used up its store of constructive ideas. It has lost both the capacity and the will to confront the difficulties that threaten to overwhelm it" (18). He sees this malaise as a matter of shifts in modes of production that have resulted in a change in individual psychology, a view I will explore in more detail later. Lasch's study is the most popular of these four, a result of its relentless critique and breadth of conception. Indeed, though it approaches its object from the left, it provides a view that is not so different from that which was emerging from the right at the same moment.[5]

Habits of the Heart is a different type of book in that it employs as its basis the empirical research techniques of positivist sociology. Yet the authors' methodological explanation is intriguing: they oversaw "fieldwork" that

> involved interviews with over 200 persons, some of whom we talked to several times and many of whom we observed as they participated in community activities or events. We do not claim that we have talked to average Americans or that we have a random sample. We have read a great many surveys and community studies, enough to know that those to whom we talked were not markedly aberrant. The primary focus of our research was not psychological but rather *cultural* [my italics]. (vii–ix)

This description is intriguing for both its asserted focus and its hybrid methodology. While employing the traditional techniques of social science research, there is also an admission of looking for a certain thing—the declaration of having read a great many other studies—which results in the assertion that they are exploring culture and not society. *Habits* is clearly a successor to the other studies that I have noted, as well as one that eschews more material notions of social life for an emphasis on the means and quality of interaction. Such a notion again takes us to questions of personal expression and interaction, and as a result valorizes the utterances of the highly articulate, as well as notions of the self that remove that figure from broader historical and economic currents. The general result of this methodology is to locate, elevate, and judge the solipsism that is so much at the heart of these films. In ways, this study is the most affirming of these four in that it not only asserts a cultural malaise but it also seems to locate such a condition in the words of those who are part of the affliction.

These works become part of the phenomenon we have come to know as the turn to culture in the humanities and social sciences.[6] Their role in this occurrence is further evidenced by their connection to the world defined in Hollywood films. These books are all works of popular history/sociology that explore the social dynamics of a culture in which relative isolation and self-involvement seem prevalent. As such, they provide both a context for viewing these four films as well as a precondition for their production. These films either implicitly or explicitly articulate a culture of consumption and isolation by class, the very matter of gentrified urban living in the postindustrial world. The landscapes revealed in *Annie Hall* (1977), *An Unmarried Woman* (1978), *Manhattan* (1979), and *Kramer vs. Kramer* (1979) show a city in which almost no one lacks means, style, and access to higher culture. It is a cityscape of museums and liberal fundraisers in the Woody Allen films, of loft parties in *An Unmarried Woman*, and of a proliferation of affluent children who populate central Manhattan in *Kramer vs. Kramer*.

And despite the "cultural" orientation of the studies, there are indeed unrepresented economic factors that both trigger such visions and build upon their view of the fact and inevitability of such conditions: notably, the impact of a shift in the distribution of wealth in general terms, but within urban contexts in particular. In his study *Upward Dreams, Downward Mobility*, Frederick R. Strobel catalogues and anaylzes what he feels are decisive trends in economic distribution in the period from 1973 to around 1990. He finds that the numbers of those within the U.S. middle class are declining, a phenomenon he explains partially as a matter of the decline of unionized industrial work, as well as the devaluing of certain types of work by the introduction of technology that allows it to be reclassified as "low skill." His example of this, drawn from Robert Kuttner's 1983 essay "The Declining Middle," is data processing, which had been a permanent and semi-skilled position at the corporate level, but is now a task done by entry-level clerks or transient labor (50). It is intriguing, then, that the featured characters of these films apparently come from modest backgrounds and have jobs. The jobs, except for that of the husband in *An Unmarried Woman*, seem not to be either very taxing or time consuming; yet, they seem to produce more than enough income to sustain a very comfortable lifestyle.

These representations provide a compelling example of a phenomenon that is relatively unusual in a statistical sense, but one related to the phenomenon of the shrinking of the middle class during the 1970s and 1980s (51–52). They picture the upward migration in income level of those who formerly were lodged within the middle 50 percent. And, for a variety of factors, those who experienced this upward mobility disproportionately lived in certain urban areas that, even then, were emerging as world cities. As I noted, New York City, by virtue of its communications infrastructure, was particularly well suited to the emerging boom in international commerce. As a result, it boasted a disproportionate number of individuals who rose upward from the middle class. These people, however, were not necessarily those who had lived in Manhattan in the earlier decades; rather, many had moved there as a result of the city's shift in employment and its related phenomenon of gentrification. Many of those individuals were from families that had lived in New York in earlier generations but had moved to the suburbs in the 1950s and 1960s. Many of these people were the college-educated offspring of ethnic groups who had formerly worked in blue-collar occupations. As John Hull Mollenkopf points out in *Phoenix in the Ashes*, "Jewish garment workers and Italian stevedores disappeared, while the managerial and professional strata of the growing sectors became more Jewish and more Italian" (48).

As Mollenkopf goes on to elucidate, after 1975, the city gradually lost its population of the white, ethnic blue-collar workers, which had shrunk to around 5 percent by the early 2000s. Their place in the shrinking industrial sector had largely been taken up by African Americans, and Latino and Asian immigrants, who work less and are paid less per hour. Writes Mollenkopf of the 1980s,

> Since welfare payments lost ground to inflation, the poorest households experienced the greatest loss. At the other end of the income distribution, the surge of earnings in managerial, professional, and even clerical occupations caused median real household incomes to rise. . . . The share of the lowest 20 percent of households declined from 15.4 to 11.6 percent between 1975 and 1987, while that of the top 10 percent rose from 43.8 to 49.2 percent, substantially worse than the U.S. trend. (61)

Further, given the rise in housing costs that was also occurring during the late 1970s and early 1980s, it is historically comprehensible that these films would show few of modest means living in Manhattan, and, in the case of *Kramer vs. Kramer*, middle-class families with children who lived in that region were indeed becoming a vanishing breed.

Though these films show us any number of crushing personal problems, such difficulties take place within the context of lives that are physically comfortable and relatively free of the urban dangers that marked the earlier films discussed. Such emphases have the effect of altering the visible city in virtually every way. Rather than a city of various relative spaces, its inhabitants and regions are all reduced to one type and a few regions, apparently contiguous, that are defined by the relative wealth of their inhabitants and the amenities that characterize these regions. It is a city not of production but of common pursuits, training, and language. And that distinctive class presence takes on the aspect of a commodity in itself. They are an educated class living comfortably, living among themselves, and disdaining those on the outside.

Though historically, by the late 1970s New York City was only in the process of gentrifying, these films treat this shift in real estate value and demographics as a fait accompli. Such an emphasis recognizes a trend as it also participates in bringing this tendency to fruition. Indeed, the New York they picture would be more typical of the city in the mid 1980s. From 1981 to 1987, home ownership in Manhattan increased at roughly three times the rate it did in the other boroughs. But, as I pointed out in chapter 2, gentrification is, at least at its beginning, a gradual process, and one connected to other factors in the economic sector and social life of the city.

The New York pictured here is an urban space as idealized by sophisticates and those who aspire to be. There is a critical mass of urbane, intellectual, and attractive people who revel in the company of each other. These films feature attractive people with active social lives who seem intent on pursuing suitable matches within their own class. But even more notable is the unfailing emphasis on romantic relations that defines these four films. All of the plots are, in one way or another, relationship dramas. The world around these figures becomes merely a context in which these interactions are pursued. I thus focus next on the representation of love and marriage in these films. My attention is on the definitions of romantic love which abound, and how love emerges as the device for spatial coherence and the social reproduction of class.

NARCISSISM AND THE GENTRIFIED CITY

Among the many features of Woody Allen's *Annie Hall* that are both memorable and distinguishing is the protagonist facing the camera and discussing his relationship problems, a device that is used both to begin and end the film. These difficulties are described as a matter of his broader neuroses, which he also reveals to the camera. This opening declamation is a piece from Allen's stand-up comedy routine, but the Woody Allen presence is complicated by that figure taking on the film's character, Alvy Singer. Woody/Alvy discusses his inability to sustain relationships, using various lines as "hooks," such as the Groucho Marx's insight that "I wouldn't want to belong to any club that would have me as a member." In this initial scene, the shot cuts from Alvy speaking through the "fourth wall" to the audience, to flashbacks of his youth and adolescence, humorous anecdotes that show his neuroses forming and developing. The scene culminates with Alvy, who in this shot is not Woody, as an adolescent discussing his neurotic fear about the imminent end of the universe with a doctor, as his mother looks on.

This introduction to the film, both in form and content, establishes Woody/Alvy as a continuous persona, with the object of the film being that figure's psyche. Though the character is both ironic and self-effacing, his interest in himself and who will be his mate narrows the scope of the narrative. Certainly Alvy's obsession with himself is comical, but its absurdity does not in any way mitigate its consuming characteristics. As the films goes on we see that the narrative is *fully* about him. He organizes his life with little regard for others: relationships with others are in terms that speak to his self-obsession. In the broader contours of the film's action, Annie ultimately leaves him because she is dwarfed in his world by the proportion of his self-involvement. Such a looming and outsized focus on one's self defines not only the object of the film, but also its point of view. The director, writer, actor, and character of Woody Allen is everywhere, and the limits of this character are defining. We see a very narrow geography, a small slice of the population of New York and its environs. Those who are judged as beneath him in class, achievement, intelligence, or subtlety of worldview are made sport of. Indeed, the very restricted frame of these opening shots is emblematic of a perspective that fails to allow viewers to picture a wider world.

Such an obsession with self, and correspondingly with limiting one's associations, is historically apt. As I noted earlier, narcissism becomes a recurring descriptive term among cultural critics from the early 1970s to the mid 1980s, and it is relatively unsurprising that this view of self and others should also begin to restructure the genre of Hollywood romance. That commercial film and social analysis are so closely intertwined is notable. The convergence of these modes of expression suggests a synergistic relationship: Robert Bellah and his associates anticipate and find a phenomenon that is already everywhere, while Woody Allen can break through as a filmmaker because he is creating romantic comedy by articulating characters that are readily identifiable to his niche audience.

Indeed, in *Habits of the Heart*, Robert Bellah and his colleagues explain the shifting meaning and significance of love that has occurred in the move to a more urban society over the last hundred years or so, noting that it is increasingly distinct from "calculation," becoming a desire that is deeply involved in the network of expressions that articulate one's individualism, a view that is similar to that dramatized in *Annie Hall*. "In the twentieth century, marriage has to some extent become separated from the encompassing context of family in that it does not necessarily imply having children in significant sectors of the middle class. Thus, marriage becomes a context for expressing individualism within the domain of a 'lifestyle enclave'" (89). The authors of the study find this phenomenon of grouping and self-definition by "lifestyle" distinct from that defined by community:

It [lifestyle] brings together those who are socially, economically, or culturally similar, and one of its chief aims is the enjoyment of being with those who "share one's lifestyle." Whereas a community attempts to be an inclusive whole . . . lifestyle is fundamentally segmental and celebrates the narcissism of similarity. It usually explicitly involves a contrast with others who "do not share one's lifestyle." For this reason we do not speak of lifestyle communities . . . but of lifestyle enclaves. (72)

Such a notion of association, then, is part of the continuum of associations and often emblematic of a tendency to express what the authors call "the narcissism of sameness" (71–73). The prevalence in the films of this method of selecting a mate suggests the degree to which New York becomes a site for elaborating the contours of a new urban lifestyle. All of these groups of characters live within such enclaves; all are similar in class; all share definitional qualities of behavior and values; and all work within the complex of postindustrial, information-based industries.

As others have pointed out, it is through the rituals of courtship and marriage that we reproduce our social status, confirming, denying, or gently nudging the ways in which we view our position in the social world. All four of these films place love and marriage at their center, with all featuring, in various degrees, divorce and its subsequent emotional impact. In dwelling on the dissolution of prior relationships and the elaboration of new ones, the films picture the city as a context that allows for the major character to resocialize. In both Woody Allen films, there are ex-wives who show us the failure of relationships that do not bring together individuals of similar interests and aspirations. In *An Unmarried Woman*, part of the dynamic of the breakup of Erica's marriage is her interest in a world other than that of the Upper East Side bourgeoisie, and in *Kramer vs. Kramer*, an anti-feminist narrative, Ted is left to his own devices because his wife finds the

FIGURE 7.1 *Annie Hall*: Alvy meets Annie at the tennis club.

particular middle-class lifestyle they live to be unsuitable, choosing to live independently.

Yet, despite the disruption and redirecting of a character's energies, the films are remarkable for their physical and social homogeneity by class. Although it is true that there are moments in three of the four films that are not shot in midtown Manhattan, and that Erica in an *Unmarried Woman* does move to the gentrifying SoHo (more about this later), these are movies about the social resonance of Upper East Side living. They shrink Manhattan Island and redefine it as its gentrified urban core, as a "lifestyle enclave." The cultural markers and vocabulary that obtain in each of these films—an interest in liberal politics, books, films, language, certain types of foods and restaurants, and even the continual migration in their leisure time to certain areas of Manhattan, such as Central Park and its zoo—show the cultural dimension of this enclave. And it is the way in which the protagonists and the secondary characters of all of these films seek out partners that confirms this narrow vision of the world which makes their vision of love and marriage so historically distinct as well as so insular.

In earlier films of the decade, the *Godfather* films (1972 and 1974), *Mean Streets* (1973), *Hester Street* (1975), and *Marathon Man* (1976), for example, we saw social and geographic groupings that were organized by ethnic group, so that at times we saw interclass groupings. In the gentrifying city, that system of organization has now been replaced by class; a kind of reference to ethnicity remains, but only as an implicit category that has implications for the definition of class, expanding that category so that it takes cultural markers into account. The films redefine the upper-middle-class cosmopolitan urban lifestyle as culturally Jewish, but make few references to that religion. Indeed, the absence of this reference illustrates the degree to which lifestyle assumptions easily displace more embedded markers of history and more specific cultural experience.[7]

Each of these films features a romance between an identifiably Jewish figure and an identifiably non-Jewish one, but most of these are failed relationships. The question of interfaith relationships is not remarked upon in any film but *Annie Hall*, where Annie's non-Jewishness is important to her characterization, as is Alvy's ethnicity. The fact that neither Meryl Streep (who is Woody Allen's ex-wife in *Manhattan* and Dustin Hoffman's estranged mate in *Kramer vs. Kramer*), nor Michael Murphy (Jill Clayburgh's ex-husband in *An Unmarried Women* and Woody Allen's best friend in *Manhattan*), nor Diane Keaton (Woody Allen's would-be partner in *Annie Hall* and his eventual partner in *Manhattan*) is of the ethnic group that defines the central character of these films is notable. But though each is not Jewish, each remains proximate, and each evinces an interest either in art, psychoanalysis, music, or in the case of Murphy, in finance. Indeed, it is almost as though certain actors and actresses become cultural Jews in themselves. Meryl Streep is in two of these films, each by a different director, Keaton in two, and Murphy is also in two. They have taken on the aspects of urbanity associated with New York that allows them to "pass." In some cases, after the failed relationship, the non-Jewish character may attach herself (in these cases) to another Jew. (Streep and Karen Ludwig in *Manhattan*, Keaton and Paul Simon in *Annie Hall*). While Woody Allen and Dustin Hoffman scream a certain kind of ethnicity in one regard, in *An Unmarried Woman* Erica (Jill Clayburgh) presents the image of a perfect Upper East side wife—pretty, fashionable, civic minded, well educated—an identity that takes precedence over identification by religion, or parents' or grandparents' place of origin. But this latter factor also works as a kind of shorthand.[8]

This association between Jews and gentrification takes on its own baggage of broad cultural stereotype—liberal, intellectual, affluent; and, of course, resident in New York City. Though, in fact, the Jewish population of the city was declining over time—there were around 2 million Jews in the city in the 1950s, by 1980s that number was down to 1.1 million.[9] Still, that number constitutes a significant proportion of the city's residents, and with over 200,000 living in Manhattan, the Jewish population constitutes 20 percent of that borough. But the depiction of these ethnic characters is broad and largely associative, contributing to a view of Manhattan as populated by individuals who are similar in outlook and background. Such a view, of course, was at least involved in the depictions of Jewish ethnicity and history we found in *The Marathon Man*, where New York is characterized as the site for the residual conflict between Nazis and Jews. Such a vision defines New York as a place connected to world currents of migration. And such a vision taps into a residual vision of people of the Jewish faith as cosmopolitan, and therefore citizens of a geographically fluid world.[10]

Of course, the vision of the Jewish cosmopolitan has a long history in anti-Semitic thought. The persistence of this bias is comically employed in *Annie Hall*, where Annie's home in Wisconsin is emphatically caricatured as the antithesis of New York. As part of this contrast, the film includes a point-of-view shot that is associated with the gaze of Annie's grandmother, who we see envisioning Alvy as a Hasidic man with Homburg and side curls (figure 7.2). The other notable vision of the Jew of the world coming "home" to Manhattan is in *An Unmarried Woman*, where Erica's new lover is a British/Jewish painter named Saul.

Perhaps more trenchant is that the image of the Jew becomes the soul of a dispersed marketplace, the image of the fluidity of incipient globalization. Indeed, Jewishness becomes a kind of shorthand for cosmopolitan and savvy in the ways of financial gain. Such an association, while here merely descriptive and associative, and perhaps even approving, has its anti-Semitic roots and its contemporary

FIGURE 7.2 *Annie Hall*: Grammy Hall pictures Alvy as a "real Jew."

anti-Semitic expressions. These including what Werner Bonefeld terms "the fetish critique of the world-market society of capital," a critique he associates, in his essay "Nationalsim and Anti-Semitism," with extreme nationalism and with anti-cosmopolitanism that at times devolves into anti-Semitism and which, particularly in Europe, grafts onto historically deep antipathies to Jews (151). That we find Jewish characters in focal economic positions in all of these movies is no accident. Indeed, in the opening scene in *Kramer vs. Kramer*, we see Ted talking with some intimacy to his obviously Jewish boss, with his feet up on "O'Connor's" desk. (Ted's boss is played by the Jewish actor George Coe, though the character is named Jim O'Connor). In such scenes—shot in a tightly framed two shot—we see how advertising is prone to the ethnic division of labor (figure 7.3). In a later scene, as they eat lunch, Ted is fired. In this encounter we see how economic considerations trump group loyalty. That Ted ends up making less money at a firm that is clearly not Jewish suggests that though the advertising industry is not monolithic, it may be dominated by Jews.

These rituals of mutual identification and narcissistic definitions of love and romance are precisely those that were excoriated by the cultural critic Christopher Lasch in his *The Culture of Narcissism*, a bestseller in the late 1970s. Lasch's polemic takes on the retreat from the public sphere into self-involving quests for fleeting personal salves and illusory notions of contentment. He finds these obsessions emblematic of the 1970s and what delineates them as belonging to the post-1960s: their retreat from activism and commitment into the solipsism of individual concern and obsession. Writes Lasch, "The contemporary climate is therapeutic, not

FIGURE 7.3 *Kramer vs. Kramer*: Ted talks intimately with his boss.

religious. People today hunger not for personal salvation . . . but for the feeling, the momentary illusion, of health and psychic security" (7). Lasch envisions this quest as both barren and culturally overdetermined, so that contemporary America includes dispositions toward viewing the self as autonomous and isolated that are derived from earlier American antecedents dating back to the Puritans and nineteenth-century utopian religious movements. But, writes Lasch,

> The contemporary American may have failed, like his predecessors, to establish any kind of common life, but the integrating tendencies of modern industrial society have at the same time undermined his "isolation." Having surrendered most of his technical skills to the corporation, he can no longer provide for his family needs. . . . The atrophy of older traditions of self-help has eroded everyday competence and has made the individual dependent on the state, the corporation, and other bureaucracies. (37)

For Lasch, narcissism represents the psychological dimension of this dependence. "Notwithstanding the occasional illusions of omnipotence, the narcissist depends on others to validate his self-esteem. . . . For the narcissist the world is a mirror" (38).

These visions of self and likely mates are articulated by a subsection of class, one that conforms to the descriptor "lifestyle." And lifestyle becomes a self-articulating motive. The more one stays within that comfort zone, the more defined a character seems to be. Within the context of these films, the search for the perfect mate becomes the ultimate narcissistic urge. This idea of shopping for an appropriate partner is most visible in the two films about romantic triangles, *Manhattan* and *An Unmarried Woman*. In *Manhattan*, Isaac casts aside the (literally) adolescent Tracy for the age-appropriate Mary, who had previously been involved with his married best friend, Yale. Though Mary initially repels Isaac, they become intimate in stages. These moments begin to occur just as Isaac changes apartments, after he quits his job in television because of its anti-intellectualism and its vulgarity. The show, which he writes and produces, looks like a 1970s version of the Jerry Springer show and seems a forerunner of reality television.

All of this elaborates the means by which the "narcissism of similarity" is dramatized. Indeed, in each film we see the ethos of consumption take hold as love becomes a commodity that is desirable through its conjoining with other accoutrements of lifestyle. For example, Erica is clearly estranged from Martin in that she has become deeply involved with the downtown art scene, and he remains a man of his office. He shops for a younger trophy wife, while she seeks a man of the art world. Saul's Jewishness is related to his role as a key figure in the emerging art scene of SoHo, but each aspect of his persona is mutually constitutive and without either, he would not present the figure he does. Similarly, Mary in *Manhattan* ceases her intellectual posing and comes to see the value of the objects and intellectual figures that Isaac (Woody) reveres. They return to the Museum of Modern Art and find art that they both like, art that bridges the styles of modernism and its successor. Isaac begins to bond with Mary when he moves to an apartment that is more like hers and when he leaves the world of popular culture for that of writing for a niche audience.

Although there are certainly many problems with Lasch's broad readings of culture, his polemic does offer a salient interpretation of a general historical trend, and, in his elaboration of a view of the moment that aligns with that of these films, may be considered as part of the 1970s zeitgeist. That which is characterized in the films as a legitimate quest for love and for self, in *The Culture of Narcissism* becomes an object of critique. Indeed, both *Kramer vs. Kramer* and *Manhattan* feature women characters that have left their marriages in order to seek new directions in life, in order to "find themselves." In *Kramer vs. Kramer*, Joanna abruptly leaves her husband and family because she finds her domestic life unfulfilling. In *Manhattan*, Isaac's ex-wife, also played by Meryl Streep, leaves their marriage and moves in, with their son, with a same-sex partner. Both films treat these departures critically, though *Kramer vs. Kramer* is far more dismissive of Joanna's departure. Ted returns from a triumphant day at work to find Joanna sitting with legs pressed together, wearing white, white-skinned, in a corner of their all-white apartment (figure 7.4). The film also paints Ted as self-involved, as he primarily resents having Joanna's life

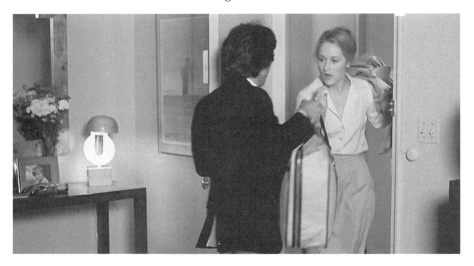

FIGURE 7.4 *Kramer vs. Kramer*: Ted returns home to Joanna, who is leaving him.

crisis impinge on his good day at work. But that he rises to take care of their child and that Joanna abandons him in order to attend to herself elevates him.

In *Manhattan*, we do not see the moment of departure, but Isaac does talk about it at a moment where his previously hostile relationship with Mary, played by Diane Keaton, begins to change. Says Isaac, as he and Mary walk on the East Side, framed in a two-shot against the store fronts, "My wife left me for another woman." She crosses her arms and responds, "God that must have been really demoralizing." He goes on to tell how he tried to run them over with a car. She responds by empathizing: "That must have been sexually demoralizing." As the conversation proceeds, it is clear that the major issue of Isaac's breakup was not incompatibility or his child, but what it did to him. Such a view well explains the terms of relationships in all of these films: the partner on whom we focus is too narcissistic to see the other as anything but a mirror.

Such a view has the effect of determining the post-Fordist city. The world is configured as including individuals substantially engaged in finding their complements within narrow social and physical sectors of the city of finance and international trade and communications. Individual regard and achievement becomes indicative of a world in which broader social definitions and networks have apparently collapsed, leaving atomized characters to seek fulfillment with other such individuals. Writes Daniel Bell,

A technocratic society is not ennobling. Material goods provide only transient satisfaction or an invidious superiority over those with less. . . . A post-industrial society cannot provide a transcendent ethic—except for the few who devote themselves to the temple of science. And the antinomian attitude plunges one into a radical autism which, in the end, dirempts the cords of community and the sharing with others." (480)

LOVE AND SPACE

Though these definitions of group and neighborhood have clearly changed, the past is invoked in particular ways that also point to the post-Fordist and post-modern moment in urban history. Even as they resist these ethnic definitions of place and community, the characters and their romances flourish within the areas of the city defined by the charm of their earlier-century architecture and the ambiance of streetscapes that have changed little in at least decades. For example, when Erica's marriage breaks up in *An Unmarried Woman*, she flourishes romantically when she is away from the austerity of the postwar Upper East Side duplex she and Martin shared, in the de-industrialized splendor of SoHo. In *Manhattan* and *Annie Hall*, love flourishes amid streetscapes that are dimly lit and that feature nineteenth-century architecture, such as the Queensboro and Manhattan bridges, as well as various venues in Central Park (figure 7.5). And *Manhattan*'s black-and-white photography announces its backward perspective from its first frame. *Kramer vs. Kramer* also features scenes in a resplendent and autumnal Central Park, and those scenes, with Jane Alexander, are the closest Ted comes to romance in the film. Indeed, even the use of Central Park as a set piece to index the splendor old New York is a departure from fairly recent films such as *Death Wish* and *The*

FIGURE 7.5 *Manhattan*: Isaac and Mary romance 59th St. Bridge.

Marathon Man that depict it as a zone of random violence and a place of fear. Indeed, in a film contemporary with these, *Hair* (1979), a beautiful and inviting Central Park becomes a lair for the counterculture, a Woodstock-like setting in the midst of New York City.

Though the characters of the films live squarely within the economic epoch of post-default and, now globalizing, New York, the city is invested with a neo-Victorian gloss to provide its denizens with the luster of the late nineteenth-century ruling class. But that class is necessarily robbed of its patrician WASP character and further humanized by the focus on its emotional life. Nostalgia becomes an operator within the urban environment, allowing for a cleansed view of the past, one that celebrates place without its historical trappings. Such trappings would potentially deepen the evidence of a previous epoch filled with conflict and disrupt the neat erasures of a multiclassed and industrial city that are central to the Manhattan of these films. And it is by aestheticizing the historical landscape that these films can so completely sink into their obsession with the emotional lives of these comfortable characters, as all physical context is reduced to the settings that enable their self-regard and expressions. Such an emphasis on the personal aligns well with the neoliberal ideology that was becoming an important aspect of New York's governance, as well as a significant discourse within national politics. And despite the personal upheaval depicted here, it is significant that we also see the cityscape that accompanies this moment.

In *Annie Hall*, for example, Alvy Singer is a figure who is well defined by his Brooklyn upbringing. But his Brooklyn is clearly in his past and barely exists outside of the garish flashbacks of his family's apartment beneath the rollercoaster at Coney Island. His Brooklyn is a combination of the decay of the present and the banality of the more recent past. His relocation on the Upper East Side more clearly expresses the way in which he views himself. He meets Annie when they play tennis (figure 7.1), an activity that has class and ethnic associations that remove him further from his modest Coney Island origins, at an indoor facility on the eastern edge of Manhattan, literally in the East River, suggesting how "off the grid" she is for a decidedly ethnic type from a decidedly ethnic place.

This site of meeting constitutes something of a change from his previous wives, all of whom were Jewish and more clearly of his cultural world, and defines, to some degree, a change in him and a shift in the world. Alvy recognizes a broader frame for defining those who are like him. Though her surface difference from his wives is quickly apparent—her clothes, her manner—she and Alvy live in the same region of Manhattan, and their apartments even look somewhat alike in their adequacy of space, their pastel walls, and their bare-bones adornment with objets d'art that are fairly common—photographs, art prints, books. They continue to

Annie's apartment after the game, and while Annie's place is not as spacious as Alvy's, nor does it have as good a view, it is reasonably attractive, and when they step onto her terrace, which is an unremarked-upon adjunct to her inside space, it is well planted and offers pleasing views of the city. It is when Annie chooses to leave the confines of this East Side district, for Los Angeles, that their relationship unravels. In the harshness of the light and distended space of southern California, Alvy becomes increasingly dysfunctional and Annie recognizes his limits. Manhattan and its environs, by being the anti-Los Angeles, become a distinctive context, revealing a place that retains the residue of the Fordist past, but that can be adapted as a backdrop for a post-Fordist enactment of romantic love. That Annie ultimately chooses to live in a place where narcissism is less adorned tells us about her condition. While Alvy basks in a virtual past, Annie seeks to be without one. Indeed, as in *Manhattan* and *An Unmarried Woman*, Alvy defines his cultural objects as the things that make life worth living: "Groucho Marx, Willie Mays, the second movement of the *Jupiter Symphony*, Louis Armstrong's recording of *Potato Head Blues*, Swedish movies, *A Sentimental Education* by Flaubert, Marlon Brando, Frank Sinatra, those incredible Apples and Pears by Cezanne." This Hall of Fame resonates with a plethora of iconic modernist elements, as well as for its blend of high-, low-, and middle-brow culture.

This vision of space and romance, which emphasizes the gentrified Manhattan's perfect preservation of attractive early twentieth-century and later nineteenth-century structures that sit beside commodious modernist buildings, becomes more articulate in *Manhattan*, a film with a more explicit appeal to nostalgia and a more aggressive strategy for reappropriating aspects of the past as atmospheric trappings for the present. Isaac quits his job as a producer of what seems to be an early version of reality television, disowning its vulgarity and banality. The spatial impact of his lack of a job is that he moves to an older, smaller, turn-of-the-century apartment, one that lacks the glistening coldness and expanse of the residence in which he spends so much time with Tracy. His new apartment, which features a commodious terrace, is more indicative of his developing persona and his evolving relationship with Mary.

When we initially meet Mary, she trashes his canon of modernist figures—Mahler, Fitzgerald, Van Gogh, Ingmar Bergman, Heinrich Boll. Soon after, he encounters her again at a fund-raiser for Bella Abzug, when she is among a group that discusses a film about "orgasm." In the film, the director explains, a man is so sexually apt that when women have orgasms with him, they die. This disruption of propriety and artistic canon points to her postmodern definitions. Yet she is conventional in her unconventionality. Her willingness to break boundaries and elaborate new hierarchies recalls modernist icons from Gertrude Stein to Salvador

Dali. As such, she is a figure who floats between an ordered vision of a structured past and a dramatic flattening of aesthetic hierarchies according to notions of fashion and "taste." Indeed, the cultural questions that define the terrain of this film and, to some degree, all of these films, are a contrasting of previous hierarchies and a flattening of the distinctions between the popular and the elite. Such a conjoining of epochs suggests the ways in which these films are about not a cultural leveling but about the re-elaboration of historical and qualitative distinctions in a new, post-Fordist context. Thus, the city as a place that exists for the pleasure of its cognoscenti has the effect of recontextualizing urban space in the image of that class's needs and desires.[11]

But Mary's taste and her character are initially suspect. In all of these shots she is slightly off-center within the frame and then further cants her body, so that she does not quite face the camera, a kind of visual assertion of her dishonesty and pretension. Her unsuccessful efforts to be outrageous, to cast off the past, have the effect of creating physical discomfort, as it dislocates her from a vision of tradition and continuity that is vital to the elaboration of this new class. In order to become a part of the refined spaces of the new Manhattan, she must recognize the ways in which its history and cultural legacy may be reconceived and employed in the service of a New York that is international in ways that the city of immigrants in the earlier century was not. This contemporary international city may be home to a substantial immigrant population, but that group is out of sight and out of mind—except when this new class needs menial services. Isaac's constellation of artists includes only one—Fitzgerald—who ever lived in the United States; yet, his vision of Manhattan as a nexus of world culture allows for their inclusion as part of his New Yorker's canon.

The courtship with Mary proceeds from this apartment, to the Museum of Modern Art, via the Queensboro Bridge illuminated at night, the Museum of Natural History, and the Guggenheim. It is within these spaces of the Victorian and Fordist past that Isaac can fall in love. In passing an earlier-century building, Isaac laments, "this city is really changing." Isaac seeks stasis and change, the trappings of the past and the rarified borough of the present.

The use of these three museums punctuates the film, defining the beginning, middle, and culmination of this love affair. These institutions become set pieces in the film's elaboration of the role of culture in the lives and relationships of these two people. They represent three distinct interpretations of what constitutes a museum and its social role, as well as the manner in which Isaac and Mary resolve their differences. The Guggenheim, though its permanent collection does include works by some iconic modernists, largely represents the private museum for the few and is broadly defined by its desire to elaborate new trends and confirm the commercial worth of the avant-garde. It opened in 1959, and its circular, high modernist building, designed by Frank Lloyd Wright, is iconic in itself. Its space is cold and its displays challenging. It is here that Isaac and Mary disagree most vehemently. Indeed, it represents the space of contention regarding what in the late twentieth century is becoming one of the major products of the world city: the art market. In the Museum of Natural History and particularly in the Hayden Planetarium, we see the an institution of the late nineteenth century.[12] It is a collection that seeks to bring together the wonders of earth and space in order to amaze, amuse, and educate a broad populace. It thus serves as a stark contrast to the Guggenheim. Its spaces are embracing, almost camp in their representational aspirations and structures, and define the ways in which cities can educate children and provide nostalgia for the age of scientific exploration that defined the late nineteenth century and the early twentieth. The world of science, even popular science, is foreign ground for both Isaac and Mary, and it is in here, amid an ersatz cosmos, that they find common ground, as they rush in out of a surprise rainstorm. But here the setting is not so much about mutual interest as it is about science as camp, a generalized backdrop that produces mutual wonder and associative memories, a device that elicits their common approach to the world.

But their bond is cemented at the Museum of Modern Art, where, rather than discussing nonrepresentational art in broad ways that refer to the highly specialized vocabulary of critics of the avant-garde, they are shot in mid-range, as they bask in the warm light and carpeted floors of the museum. Rather than the cold modernism of the Guggenheim, this is an embracing museum space that is more reminiscent of the originating moment of art museums in the United States, the late nineteenth century. Within this domain, they discuss personal problems with relationships, as well as the specific problems of past partners (figure 7.6). The scene ends as they walk amid a Picasso sculpture and the more canonical works of postmodernity, like an Andy Warhol painting, as Isaac throws around the very language that Mary used at the Guggenheim, but ironically, as she giggles. They are comfortable with one another and their bodies stroll closely together in a parallel plane that is defined by a two-shot, slightly canted toward the paintings, but with Mary's body slightly overlapping Isaac's, so that they merge in their parallel plane. It is fitting that this bond is formed in this place that articulates the reign of the modern as it was configured in the late 1920s and 1930s, and which has become the most significant collection of late nineteenth- and twentieth-century art in the world.[13] The scene emphasizes continuity and not dissonance, the modern seamlessly woven in to the postmodern, the canon merging into refined taste.

Thus, initial assertions of character are mitigated by the introduction of a new context, one that emphasizes the icons of the past romanticized as the idealized

FIGURE 7.6 *Manhattan*: Isaac and Mary at the MoMA.

pre-1970s history of New York. These two characters can bond over their neuroses, involvement in Freudian psychotherapy, and their true—as opposed to postured—interests and tastes. The view of space that defines their growing love, shot in beautiful retrograde black and white, links one beautiful Manhattan view to another. All are clean, perfectly lighted and undeniably romantic. The overall effect is to articulate a quasi-Victorian context for a distinctly contemporary relationship: one in which mutual attraction results from sameness that seems to transcend gender, and where sex is the consummation of the ability of two people to find a common dialect.

Three of these films, and to a lesser degree *Kramer vs. Kramer*, define love and romance as the act of coming to agreement concerning art and culture. Such agreements, however, do not elide other differences; rather, they confirm broader agreements of lifestyle. This sameness of community and socioeconomic status has the effect of severely restricting the space depicted in the films, and thus, the area that the films' protagonists traverse. The regions primarily depicted in these films and the romantic relationships aspired to and depicted signal a significant reorientation for urban dwellers and for their representation. Further, we also see in the Woody Allen films the ways in which gentrified Upper Manhattan allows easy access to the vacation spaces in the Hamptons. In both films, transitions to the beach resorts of the wealthy are executed without comment and with maximum ease, suggesting that traversing the distance between Manhattan and eastern Long Island is no more difficult than driving around the corner.

Where films of New York from earlier in the decade were concerned with ethnic spaces and definitions, and even looked back on those spaces with fondness and nostalgia, these films signal the lessening of the bonds of that community. We see a redefinition of space according to the needs and desires of a class. As in the previous chapter, Manhattan becomes the domain of knowledge workers, and the pursuits of that group become a secular religion. *An Unmarried Woman* graphically portrays the manner in which culture and architecture articulate the economic shift that enables gentrification and which has the impact of conjoining contemporary romance and nostalgia-infused spaces associated with an earlier era. Erica does not choose to leave her husband. However, she has begun to elaborate her life away from him within the spaces of the SoHo art scene, which, by the mid-1970s was becoming a center for world art commerce (figure 7.7).[14]

Saul is a better painter, a better lover, and a better man than Charlie, another artist with whom she had sex earlier in the film. Saul paints large abstract and colorful canvasses that are clearly not modernist; but they are not cutting-edge, postmodern, either. He tells her, in a listing that recalls Isaac's in *Manhattan* and Alvy's in *Annie Hall*, as they walk through the quiet streets of SoHo at night, that he likes Titian, Rembrandt, Botticelli, and *Kojak*. Again, the mixing of the canonical and the popular is a paean to both postmodernity and the canon of great art that was so central to the high modernists. And although it is true that her husband Martin is quite well situated in a Wall Street brokerage, that his persona and occupation, and even their apartment, lack glamour is a given of this film. Erica falls in love, in a 1970s way, with Saul, the successful artist whose SoHo loft is both beautifully sunlit and in the sanitized and now desirable postindustrial district (figure 7.8).

The film reveals how the desires and values of a class have the power to literally alter the urban landscape and to introduce new notions of proximity. The lower

FIGURE 7.7 *An Unmarried Woman*: Erica and her husband break up in SoHo.

FIGURE 7.8 *An Unmarried Woman*: Erica at Saul's loft.

Manhattan locale of these art spaces now becomes related to the perpetually desirable areas of the Upper East Side, and their postindustrial decay is transformed into urban hipness, complete with bars and restaurants. Such a transformation also has its policy referents, since in 1973 SoHo's Cast Iron District was designated a historic district by New York City's Landmarks Preservation Commission. The effect of this designation accelerated a trend that had already begun. Explains Sharon Zukin in *Loft Living*, "Lofts changed from places where production took place to items of cultural consumption. This process annihilates light manufacturing" (3). Indeed, Zukin goes on to discuss the process by which artists served as a bridge in a process that led to their own displacement, as SoHo soon became a valuable commodity to developers and those with access to capital through their employment in New York's networks of financial services. "Lofts became a means of expression for post-industrial civilization" (15). Such images introduced the glamour of what were often called the urban pioneers, a group of white gentrifiers, picturesquely nonconformist, occupying relatively inexpensive property in areas contiguous to higher-priced real estate.[15] Films such as this have the effect of crystallizing the emerging image of Manhattan and of SoHo as a place to be. Indeed, by the time this film was released, emerging artists were no longer flocking to this district, as they had already been priced out by speculators and then those with jobs in the nearby financial district.

This class system not only defines places like Brooklyn and the Bronx as peripheral; it also powerfully delineates sections of Manhattan as central and evocative of an emerging image of a way of life. In *Loft Living*, her study of the changing conceptions of space and its uses in New York City as it gentrified during the 1970s and 1980s, Sharon Zukin coins the very useful term "Artistic Mode of Production." This is a far-ranging concept that she patiently delineates and clarifies. She writes, "Far from being a response to aesthetic problems, the AMP really represents an attempt by large-scale investors in the built environment to ride out and control a particular investment climate" (176). She notes the restructuring of urban locales that were formerly the sites of productive industry into places of performance, rehearsal halls, and studio space. Subsequently, as a result of the after-glow of their involvement with the valorized world of art, and the sanitizing of these districts by both their artist residents and the city's officials, many of these spaces soon served as expensive housing for those in the financial sector and those who provided skilled services to those in that sector. She goes on to note that the AMP also depresses the value of labor, as aspiring participants in this world agree to under-employment or unemployment as a means of attempting to penetrate this arena of cultural chic, and that under-employment becomes a broader low-wage model for other concerns.

Zukin also explores the role of historic preservation in creating a kind of ambiance in the gentrifying city. This vision of preservation reminds us, as Philip Rosen notes, that such an activity has as its object a sense of the past that provides for apparent continuity. The emphasis on the architecture of the past, the aesthetization of structures dating from the Fordist era, allows for a theme park–like effect in certain areas, as the form of the past is reified into a nostalgic gloss with no regard for the problems created and expressed by the altered function of that built environment. Writes Zukin, "When the lofts that were used for light manufacturing are reduced to being considered as a cultural artifact . . . the urban industrial infrastructure submits to the rules of the 'picturesque'" (180). Such a vision of land use and commerce necessarily glamorizes the deindustrialized urban landscape. The result is a city that derives some aspect of its cultural prestige from its exclusiveness and its ability to preserve its formerly useful structures as iconic. Thus, these films about entertainment powerfully participate in this emerging geographic and economic rearticulation of space, culture, and class.

LOVE, SEX, REAL ESTATE. AND THE CRISIS OF OVERPRODUCTION

By the time of the release of the first of these films in 1977, the world economy was in the midst of a significant systemic reorganization, one that has retrospectively become recognizable as a relatively early move toward a globalized system of trade. This shift was in response to the slump that afflicted the world economy from 1965 to 1973, a downturn that was largely a matter of the overproduction of consumer goods in the emerging economies of Europe and Asia, as well as the United States. Writes Robert Brenner,

> The intensification in over-capacity in world manufacturing markets in the face of deepening problems of insufficient aggregate demand did not lead, as might otherwise be expected, to a shakeout of high cost low profit means of production. . . . This was because the governments of the advanced capitalist world, led to and ever-increasing extent by the United States, made sure that titanic volumes of credit were made available to soak the surplus.[16]

The results of such policies were mixed. The United States moved toward an economy that deemphasized domestic industrial production.

Instead, with the shift in monetary policy that allowed the dollar to float in international currency markets, the nation's economy moved toward finance and particularly toward financing manufacture abroad. New York became the center of such finance. Thus as a result of the ongoing decline of the manufacturing sector and the boom in the financial sector, not to mention the various oil crises of the mid and late 1970s, New York emerged as a world city, a city of finance and information, as well as one of the lower-class service workers who opened the doors and drove the cabs for those who worked in those vocations. Writes David Harvey,

> Before 1973, most US foreign investment was of the direct sort, mainly concerned with the exploitation of raw material resources of the cultivation of special markets in Europe and Latin America. The New York investment banks had always been active internationally, but after 1973 they became more so, though now far more focused on lending capital to foreign governments.[17]

As such policies flourished in the later 1970s, Manhattan real estate became increasingly valuable in and of itself, and as a commodity that could be traded in the market place. That is, the expansion of capital devoted to finance created a relative boom in Wall Street employment, as the number of people and their salaries increased. Indeed, the districts that had fallen into relative underpopulation and reduced income through rents proved valuable sites for gentrification.

The fetishization of property and the connection between inhabiting and possessing appropriate real estate and achieving personal fulfillment is a distinctive element within these films. Saul is not only a great artist: he also has a great artistic space. That Ted Kramer lives with his son in an apartment with commodious space and light, and in proximity to Central Park, is unremarked upon in *Kramer vs. Kramer*; yet, when the court judges that the child must be remanded to his mother's custody, she tearily explains that she cannot take him, "because he's already home." Ted's slightly sterile but convincingly bourgeois space becomes the device that defines his fitness as a parent. That his ex-wife lives downtown becomes at least somewhat suspect, and the film, a male fantasy if their ever was one, never shows her residence. Post-1975 New York City becomes home to the Ted Kramer family and others like it. He can lose his job and then find work, though work that is not quite as remunerative, in a matter of days because this New York is a center of information services, including advertizing. Indeed, ten years before, Ted would probably have lived on Long Island and taken the train to Penn Station; Saul would have remained in London.

These films emerge as part of the elaboration of a post-1975 New York that was deeply involved in defining and establishing the postindustrial era of U.S. economic history in a number of ways. After default in 1975, the Municipal Assistance Corporation became for a time the de facto ruler of the city, and an entity that was largely controlled by those representing the financial services industry. As such, the New York City that emerged was quite different from that which had existed earlier in the century. While during the Lindsay era the city largely attempted to serve a population that was becoming increasingly poor and desiring, if not needing, services from the city, in the late 1970s, those services were reduced, and that population largely left central Manhattan. As David Harvey points out, by late 1970s, the city became a testing ground for neoliberal theories of governance that featured a reduced public sector and a vision of governance that featured market approaches. Writes Harvey, "Faced with fiscal difficulties, President Nixon simply declared the urban crisis over in the early 1970s. While this was news to many city dwellers, it signaled diminished federal aid." But the city's default was not simply a matter of federal policy. It was also encouraged by its leading financial institutions.

> In 1975 a powerful cabal of investment bankers (led by Walter Wriston at Citibank) refused to roll over the debt and pushed the city into technical bankruptcy. The bail-out that followed entailed the construction of new institutions that took over the management of the city budget. They had first claim on city tax revenues: whatever was left went for essential services. . . . This amounted to a coup by the financial institutions against the democratically elected government of New York City. (45).

One of the key areas of privatized services was, intriguingly, Times Square. That this area which symbolized physical and moral decay became a cornerstone of the

new physical and administrative New York is definitional. This moment of transition is actually captured in the film *Fame*, which is set in the relative center of
Manhattan, in the dilapidated structure of the School for the Creative Performing
Arts at 120 West 46th Street, not far from Bree Daniels's apartment in *Klute*.[18]
Times Square at this point is still an unsavory district that clearly lacks the glamour it had in the past. But by 1980 it is in the process of being transformed. This
transformation is material in the fact that this high school, when the film was
shot, was in the process of being moved uptown. In 1976, the year after default, the
42nd Street Redevelopment Association was formed, with the intention of redeveloping the western end of that street. And while this project never came to fruition, it did spark discussion of the contours of the new Times Square. By 1981, a
year after the release of this film, the 42nd Street Redevelopment Project began to
take shape. The ultimate result of this process was a redefinition of the region that
all but eliminated the blight that had marked it in the 1960s and 1970s.[19] But it also
altered the character of the district and its status as a haven for liminal social
actors. Gone were the idlers, the homeless, the sex-workers, and others seeking
sexual partners. Scenes such as those that were so prominent in *Midnight Cowboy*
and *Taxi Driver* lessened and then vanished. *Fame* is part of that pre-1981 epoch,
showing how in the old New York, the public marketplace allowed for all kinds of
figures and how art need not be coupled with commerce in order to achieve relevance. Whereas Times Square previously constituted the image of the city in
decline, subsequently the sanitized district has been compared to the sterility of
Disneyland, and noted for the preemptive policing of its private force.[20]

In all, we may look at these films as depicting New York in the late 1970s, as it
was in the process of coming out of its long financial descent, with default now in
the past, and neoliberal reorganization a reigning strategy. The quasi-liberal policies of the Lindsay regime soon gave rise to the Beame and Koch administrations;
and while the former city comptroller Abe Beame was a short-lived and ineffectual
leader, Ed Koch served as mayor from 1977 to 1989, and in his first five or so years
as mayor served as a suitable ally for the neoliberal, extra-governmental regime of
the Municipal Assistance Corporation. Writes Susan Fainstein in *The City Builders*,
"Koch's electoral victory signaled the empowerment of a regime with little practical
or symbolic commitment to low-income minorities, and which, once prosperity
returned in the mid-1980s, continued to emphasize economic development rather
than social welfare activities" (94). These films usher in and confirm that regime.

In the two Woody Allen films, as well as in *An Unmarried Woman*, and to a lesser
degree in *Kramer vs. Kramer*, the world of beautiful Manhattan real estate is
embellished and elaborated as the suitable context for intellectual and astute
consumers of culture. It is through the assimilated points of view of the films'

protagonists—Alvy, Isaac, and Erica—that a new urban context is introduced and valorized. This view emphasizes the icons of the past romanticized as the idealized pre 1970s history of New York and now resituated as the world of the gentry. This vision of history removes its depth and its signs of struggle. When we see the lofts of SoHo, we lose sight of the many immigrant workers who labored in these lofts. Amid their contemporary splendor we may, for example, forget the nearby occurrence of the fire in the Triangle Shirt Waist Factory in 1911, in which 146 immigrant workers were killed.[21]

These films participate in the conjoining of the postmodern and post-Fordist regimes, offering history flattened to aesthetics, and aesthetics flattened into taste. This emphasis on culture amid the reconfigured and reconceived spaces of Manhattan is emblematic of the brave new world of post-Fordism as well as a means of furthering that world. We spy identity now shifting away from the ethnic definitions of Alvy's Brooklyn past to a more fluid but circumscribed notion of agreement regarding the value of places and commodities. This notion of romance occurs within a context where consumption becomes the device of economic expansion. In such a world, what one owns or longs to possess becomes definitional. Thus, within the postindustrial spaces of Manhattan, and certainly beyond, social life ostensibly becomes hierarchically organized by notions of culture, rather than, say, by relations of production.[22] The urban lifestyle is that which is not a matter of quantitative distinctions but of apparently qualitative ones: having and getting the right stuff thus becomes the subject of these films, and the basis for romance and happiness.

Clearly New York's prominence as a location and featured element of Hollywood films did not end in 1980. Indeed, the emphases of these chapters are derived from and strategically reiterated in a number of films that succeed them, from the fantastic *Escape from New York* (1981) and the surreal *The Warriors* (1979) at the end of this era, to the despairing outer-borough films *Fort Apache, The Bronx* (1981), *The Wanderers* (1979), and the previously mentioned *Q and A* (1990), directed by Sidney Lumet. The most prominent filmmaker to emerge in the period after that of my study is Spike Lee, whose mature films, *Do the Right Thing* (1989), *Jungle Fever* (1991), and *Summer of Sam* (1999) among many, developed their own politics of race and bracketed space during the late 1980s and early 1990s. In many ways, the films of my study, in the Hollywood way, form a pre-text for these later productions, since their relative success breaks the ground for further New York films. And indeed, though large productions, potential blockbusters, largely steered away from the methods and scale of these New York productions of the late 1960s and 1970s, they did pave the way for a kind of director-driven, relatively small-budget film that persists to this day, as well as defining a representational prototype for filming the city.

NOTES

CHAPTER 1

1. See, for example, Arrighi, *The Long Twentieth Century*, and Brenner, *The Boom and the Bubble* and *The Economics of Global Turbulence*.

2. The figure who argued most persistently and influentially for auteurist approaches to film was Andrew Sarris in his *The American Cinema* and his later *Politics and Cinema*.

3. Coppola's difficulties with his producers, including Robert Evans, have become the stuff of legend. See, for example, Sragow, "Godfatherhood."

4. For an entertaining discussion of this period, and one that illuminates some of the period's most celebrated directors, including William Friedkin, Francis Coppola, and Martin Scorsese, see Biskind, *Easy Riders, Raging Bulls*. See also Bodroghkozy, "Reel Revolutionaries" for his well-documented discussion of Hollywood's search for the youth market.

5. Alsobrook, "Machines that Made the Movies."

6. See Cook, *Lost Illusions*, 355–380, and Sanders, *Celluloid Skyline*, 341–342.

7. For related discussion that further illuminates my point, see Schwartz, *It's So French*, particularly chapters 1 and 4. She shows how location shoots, particularly on an international scale, proliferated after World War II as Hollywood increasingly dominated world motion picture production. But these shoots were largely for very expensive and large-scale productions that featured international stars, figures who would assure significant box office returns on the world stage. Though these types of productions were relatively frequent in the 1950s, in comparison with the years before, they were by no means anything like the New York films of the 1970s in number. Further, their scale, scope, and style could not be more different. Indeed, it would be argued that the French New Wave and the younger U.S. auteurs were all reacting to an industry that relied on films like *Around the World in Eighty Days* (1956) and the James Bond films of the 1960s.

8. Cook, *Lost Illusions*, 156–157.

9. See the Web site of the Mayor's Office for Film, Theater, and Broadcasting for a full history: http://www.nyc.gov/html/film/html/office/history_moftb.shtml. In 1974, Lindsay's initiative was further sweetened by Abe Beame, whose Mayor's Advisory Council on Motion Pictures and Television recruited investment in productions. See also Cannato, *The Ungovernable City*, 561–562.

10. Sanders, *Celluloid Skyline*, 342–344.

11. Cannato, *The Ungovernable City*, 562. See Beauregard, *Voices of Decline*; Lazare, *America's Undeclared War*, particularly 191–211; Noe, *City*; and N. Smith, *The New Urban Frontier*.

12. See, in particular, Cannato, *The Ungovernable City*.

13. This headline appeared in the *New York Daily News* on October 30, 1975.

14. Tabb, *The Long Default*.

15. "Globalization" refers to the system of production and distribution that became visible in the 1970s and then burgeoned in the 1980s. It refers to the ways in which modes of communication, including transportation, become compressed in order to link far-flung networks. Diane Perrons notes its geographical core, as it creates "interconnectedness and interdependencies among countries on a global scale. . . . Space has become compressed by fast modes of communication." She finds that it is a term that can be applied to ideas, people, and commodities, but that it resonates most powerfully around the organizing devices of economic activities (*Globalization and Social Change*, 1–2).

16. Jameson, *Postmodernism*, 51.

17. Sekula, "On the Invention of Photographic Meaning," 91.

18. See also Sontag, *On Photography*. Writes Sontag: "Photographs, which cannot explain anything, are inexhaustible invitations to deduction, speculation, and fantasy" (123).

19. Tagg, "Thinking Photography," 113.

20. Explains Edward Soja in his synoptic comments that refer to the moment when such conceptual and material shifts were taking place: "Part of the deterioration of the debates on geographically uneven development arose from a significant break and reorientation in the evolution of regional development theory in the early 1970s, linked mainly to the rising force of neoliberal globalization and economic restructuring. . . . Reducing regional inequalities was sacrificed to a rampant consumerism and the assumed needs to reorganize urban and regional space to meet global market demands" (*Seeking Spatial Justice*, 65). For other centrally informative discussions see, for example, Sassen, *The Global City*, and Michael Smith, *City, State, and Market*. See also Harvey, *Justice, Nature, and the Geography of Difference*; Neil Smith, *The New Urban Frontier*; and Brenner, *New State Spaces*. But Soja's point remains—the moment of neoliberal transition only became apparent to cultural/social geographers some years after the fact.

21. I discuss this movement to narrative forms at length in my *Realism and the Birth of the Modern U.S.: Cinema, Literature, and Culture*.

22. Both Robert Rosenstone and Hayden White have provided intriguing and innovative discussions of film's historicity that have enlarged the discussion for me. Rosenstone's notion of the historical and of film's role in elaborating diverse narratives of the past allowed me to see beyond the often constraining terms of disciplinary discourse (*Visions of the Past*, 13–19); while White's idea of film's participation in historical discourse allows for such narratives to be seen as an element of historical discourse (*Figural Realism*, 66–86). And although both of these writers have helped me to formulate my own views, I do think that their resulting definitions of history and the historical are somewhat broad.

23. Example of this, and there are many, include Peter Rollins, ed. *The Columbia Companion to American History on Film.*; or Mark Carnes, *Past Imperfect: History According to the Movies*; or Robert Toplin's *History by Hollywood: The Use and Abuse of the American Past.* I would like to emphasize that I value these studies, find them instructive and astute. Rollins' encyclopedic collection is particularly strong. I am only distinguishing my methodology from a more usual one.

24. See Philip Rosen's *Change Mummified*, 43–88.

25. Fredric Jameson does this in *The Geopolitical Aesthetic.*

26. See Aiken and Zonn, eds., *Place, Power, Situation and Spectacle.* This collection offers a number of strong and evocative essays that interrogate film's power to produce and reproduce culturally embedded geographies. See particularly the editors' preface, 3–26, and the essay by Jeff Hopkins, "Mapping of Cinematic Places: Icons, Ideology, and the Power of (mis)Representation," 47–68. Other strong studies that look at the city as represented in film include Tony Clarke's *The Cinematic City*, Mark Shiel and Tony Fitzmaurice's *Cinema and the City*, and their *Screening the City.* There is recent collection by Murray Pomerance which is focused on New York in particular, *The City That Never Sleeps: New York and the Filmic Imagination*, which includes Paula Massood's very good study, "From *Mean Streets* to the *Gangs of New York*: Ethnicity and Urban Space in the Films of Martin Scorsese."

27. The terms *centripetal* and *centrifugal* as relative depictions of space are important to my overall discussion. These descriptive terms, adapted from the physical sciences, were first applied to relative space by the French cultural theorist Henri Lefebvre in his *The Production of Space.* Both refer to the way in which relative space is bracketed and given meaning. Centripetal refers to space that inheres, that looks inward and seems isolated from that which is not defined as part of it. Centrifugal refers to space spiraling outward to gesture and affix to the world beyond.

CHAPTER 2

1. For discussions of the Stonewall rebellion and its impact on gay culture, see Duberman, *Stonewall*, 95–212, and see also Carter, *Stonewall.*

2. The famous *New York Daily News* headline of July 6, 1969, read, "Homo Nest Raided, Queen Bees Are Stinging Mad." *Newsweek*'s longer "think piece" on the event was published in October of that year. See also Duberman, *Stonewall*, 202, and Alwood, *Straight News*, 80–98. Alwood shows how this local story became the subject of feature stories in a number of major city newspapers, as well as in *Time*, *Esquire*, and *Seventeen* by the end of 1969.

3. *Time* magazine's cover story appeared on July 7, 1967, and featured an extensive discussion of the New York aspect of the movement.

4. See Lazare, *America's Undeclared War*, for an extensive discussion of anti-urbanism in U.S. thought and policy, but particularly 191–211 for a detailing of how post–World War II policies created massive subsidies for racially segregated suburbanization, paying whites to move out of cities and trapping African Americans in decaying urban centers. See also Noe, *City*, for his discussion of how public housing inadvertently froze an underclass in cities with a declining industrial base during the 1950s and 1960s, 278–282.

5. See Beauregard, *Voices of Decline*, 245.

6. Beauregard, *Voices of Decline*, 150–178 and 181–197. In his very extensive script notes, Alan Pakula reveals his emphasis on the prostitute Bree Daniels as a character who is defined by and who defines the city. See Alan J. Pakula Papers, Box 1.

7. Canby, "Review of *Midnight Cowboy*"; Ebert, "Review of *Midnight Cowboy*."

8. Greenspan, "Review of *Klute*."

9. Reynolds, *Walt Whitman's America*, 194–234; and DiGirolamo, "*Such, Such Were the B'Hoys. . . .*" See also Helen Lefkowitz Horowitz, *Rereading Sex*; Reynolds, *Beneath the American Renaissance*; and Gilfoyle, *City of Eros*.

10. See Stansell, *City of Women*.

11. Hollywood's Production Code was drafted in 1930, instituted in 1934, and superseded by the Valenti Ratings System in 1968, though its impact lessened as the 1960s went on. Under the heading of *SEX* it asserted the following:

> The sanctity of the institution of marriage and the home shall be upheld. Pictures shall not infer that low forms of sex relationship are the accepted or common thing.

1. Adultery, sometimes necessary plot material, must not be explicitly treated, or justified, or presented attractively.

2. Scenes of Passion

   a. They should not be introduced when not essential to the plot.
   b. Excessive and lustful kissing, lustful embraces, suggestive postures and gestures, are not to be shown.
   c. In general passion should so be treated that these scenes do not stimulate the lower and baser element.

See Doherty, *Hollywood's Censor*; and also Black, *Hollywood Censored*.

12. For a discussion of Schlesinger's career, see Mann, *The Edge of Midnight*, particularly 326 to 344 for a discussion of *Midnight Cowboy*. See also Buruma, *Conversations with John Schlesinger*. Schlesinger evinced a broader interest in New York City as a place and as a location, and returned to its environs when he made *The Marathon Man*, which was released in 1976.

13. For Alan J. Pakula, see Brown, *Alan J. Pakula*. Pakula shot his adaptation of William Styron's novel *Sophie's Choice*, which was released in 1982, primarily in Brooklyn.

14. While the reference to Big Springs is general, it adds to our sense of relative geography and historical situation to look at the more specific content of this act of naming. The actual Big Springs is a medium–sized town almost in the center of the state, between Dallas and El Paso. In Joe Buck's era it was losing population, including Joe. But the 1970s were something of a turning point, and as industrial production in cities like New York continued to decline, by the 1980s places like Big Springs began relatively to prosper. Since this film is about work and relative geographic location, it is instructive to note that Big Springs has since become a manufacturing center, though most jobs are relatively low wage and non-union, to some degree because of the way in which it has figured in the post-NAFTA era. See the city's Web site: http://ci.big-spring.tx.us/.

15. This opening scene forms an interesting contrast with the beginning of the film *Hair* (1979), in which its protagonist, Claude Hooper Bukowski, hops a bus and rides across a country of inviting landscapes before entering the New York of mystery and counterculture, defined by a well-tended Central Park.

16. The opening scenes of *Klute* were reconceived many times and reshot a few. Pakula wrote his need to "contrast through photographic style" the differences between Klute's small town existence and Bree's world of the city. See Pakula Papers, Box 11.

17. In the earlier drafts of the screenplay, Tuscarora was more rural, but it gradually took on a more sophisticated quality through successive drafts (Pakula Papers).

18. Tuscarora represents a locale where such manufacture could still, as of 1971, take place, since the town was in the center of a reasonably sized population belt but in a region where property demands was relatively weak. See http://www.idcide.com/citydata/pa/tuscarora.htm and http://www.city-data.com/city/Tuscarora-Pennsylvania.html for details on Tuscarora.

19. See, for example, Harris, "The Geography of Employment."

20. See Freeman, *Working-Class New York*, 145–147.

21. Waldinger, *Still the Promised City*, 137–155.

22. Perrons, *Globalization and Social Change*, 66.

23. See Samuel R. Delany's *Times Square Red, Times Square Blue* for a description of the Times Square of this period, defined by its sexual expression, as well as a lament for its ultimate sanitizing and "Disneyfication."

24. In his production notes, Alan Pakula writes of his desire to capture the look of the sex workers portrayed in *Midnight Cowboy*, particularly their qualities as "colorful characters." Pakula Papers, Box 11.

25. Harvey, *Justice, Nature and the Geography of Difference*, 316–317.

26. See Traub, *The Devil's Playground*, 116–124.

27. McNamara, *The Times Square Hustler*, 20–21.

28. See Bell, *The Coming of Post-Industrial Society*, 212–220.

29. See Harvey, *Justice, Nature and the Geography of Difference*, 207–326 for an evocative discussion of the changing relationships between time and place through modernity and postmodernity.

30. See Neil Smith, *Uneven Development*, 97–130, and *The New Urban Frontier*, 51–89.

31. The Upper West Side was distinct in that it contained much luxurious housing and in the early 1960s had been the site of a significant middle-class presence. The Second Avenue corridor was surrounded by gentrified residences by the 1980s but did not undergo that process until the 1990s.

32. See N. Smith, *The New Urban Frontier*, 92–118 for a discussion of the economics of gentrification, and Tabb, *The Long Default*, 89–106. See also Zukin, *Loft Living*.

33. N. Smith, *The New Urban Frontier*, 19. Sharon Zukin also explores the relationship between artists and gentrification in her *Loft Living*; see particularly 58–110.

34. *The New Urban Frontier*, 140–164. The screenplay for *Klute* is remarkably consistent from draft to draft in referring to the dinginess of Bree's apartment, and as a "gritty W. 54th St. kind of place" (Pakula Papers).

35. See Heap, *Slumming*, 156–164, 29–31.

36. For a discussion of the Knapp Commission's investigation into police corruption in 1970 and the hearings that resulted in 1971, see Cannato, *The Ungovernable City*, 466–478; for a fairly conservative political and economic analysis of New York's road to default, and one that focuses primarily on city policy and its relationship with municipal workers' unions, as well as its participation in the New Deal welfare state, see Siegel, *The Future Once Happened Here*, 197–212.

37. See Brenner, *The Boom and the Bubble*; and Arrighi, *Long Twentieth Century*. See Wallerstein, *World-Systems Analysis*, 60–100, for overviews of this process.

38. See N. Smith, *The Endgame of Globalization*, 122–148, for a lucid discussion of this change in the U.S. economy and in the relationships among various regional producers.

39. Tabb, *The Long Default*, 110–112.

40. N. Smith, *The New Urban Frontier*, 80–83.

41. Mollenkopf and Castells, "Introduction," 7–8.

42. For discussion of the urban contours of 1940s and 1950s film noir, see Dickos, *Street with No Name*, 62–95, and Dimendberg, *Film Noir and the Spaces of Modernity*, 21–85.

43. See Jacobs, *The Death and Life of Great American Cities*, 35–38.

44. See http://www.census.gov/population/censusdata/table-4.pdf for these and related demographic statistics. New York's population rose from 3,437,202 in 1900 to 7,781,984 in 1960, but the city lost population from 1960 to 1980. Cities in the East and Midwest, such as Chicago, Philadelphia, Detroit, Baltimore, and Milwaukee, reported similar patterns of increases and decreases in population during these periods.

45. Douglas Noe's discussion of interclass residential patterns in earlier twentieth-century New Haven connects such residential patterns to the health of the city itself; *City*, 116–135.

46. Windhoff-Heritier, *City of the Poor, City of the Rich*, 16–17.

47. Brenner, *The Boom and the Bubble*, 16–17, and Wood, *Empire of Capital*, 118–142. See also Mollenkopf and Castells, "Introduction," and M. Smith, *City, State, and Market*, 87–117.

48. Rosenberg, *American Economic Development since 1945*, 164–171. See, for example, Agnew, *The United States in the World Economy*, 69–88. The rupture of this system had significant economic implications: European economies that were deeply involved with that of the United States also experienced retrenchment. As the United States sought for its major creditors to forego the conversion of their surplus dollars for gold, currency crises were triggered throughout Western Europe.

49. Perrons, *Globalization and Social Change*, 113–117.

50. Brewis, and Linstead, *Sex, Work and Sex Work*, 190–191.

51. See Rosemary Hennessey for an intriguing discussion of the sexual division of labor at the point of industrialization in the United States during the late nineteenth and early twentieth centuries in *Profit and Pleasure*, 25.

CHAPTER 3

1. Coppola was born in Detroit but was raised in the New York City and its suburbs, and graduated from Hofstra University on Long Island. His grandparents were from Naples. Scorsese's grandparents were from Sicily, he grew up in Lower Manhattan, and graduated from NYU. See Phillips, *The Godfather*. See also Casillo, *Gangster Priest*, for information on Martin Scorsese.

2. That *Mean Streets* reifies a notion of Little Italy at the moment it had significantly eroded as a community is illustrated in the film's publicity materials. A recurring paragraph asserts "It is basically within the area of Little Italy . . . that *Mean Streets* was filmed, and the events, the people, their beliefs—hopes—romances, and the street language are *faithfully transferred to screen*" (my italics). Scorsese Papers Box 7.

3. *The Godfather*, as of 1997, had grossed just under $135 million on a $6 million investment. It won the 1992 Oscar for Best Picture and Screenplay, and Marlon Brando won the Best Actor award. It was nominated for eight others. It also won countless other awards and was nominated for many more academy awards. *Mean Streets* was Scorsese's break-out movie, a modest financial success that was lavishly praised by Vincent Canby and Pauline Kael, among others, and which was featured in the twelfth New York film festival. It gradually developed a significant following both nationally and internationally (Scorsese Papers, Box 7).

4. See Alba, *Ethnic Identity*, 1–36.

5. See also, for example, Park, *Human Communities*; Handlin, *The Uprooted*; Herberg, *Protestant, Catholic, Jew*; Thernstrom, "Rediscovering the Melting Pot"; and Schlesinger, *The Disuniting of America.*

6. See Zelinsky, *The Enigma of Ethnicity*, 1–28. Zelinsky thoroughly characterizes the genesis and conceptual parameters of the term; see particularly 25–28, where he locates the term primarily as a late twentieth-century formulation.

7. Jacobson, *Whiteness of a Different Color*, 275–277.

8. See Jacobson, *Whiteness of a Different Color*, 223–245.

9. See Sollors, "Ethnicity and Race."

10. See Hobsbawn and Ranger, eds., *The Invention of Tradition*, and Anderson, *Imagined Communities.*

11. See, for example, Hess, "Godfather II: A Deal Coppola Couldn't Refuse"; see also Vera Dika, "The Representation of Ethnicity in The Godfather."

12. For a lucid description of this demographic process at work, see Mollenkopf, *New York City in the 1980s*, 3–38.

13. Binder and Reimers, *All the Nations under Heaven*, 225–257.

14. Rae, *City*, 382–386.

15. Skrbis, *Long Distance Nationalism*, 38.

16. Cannato, "Little Italy."

17. See Beauregard, *Voices of Decline*, 127–178.

18. This takes place after the wedding scene that begins the film and after the famous encounter between Tom Hagen and movie mogul Jack Woltz, who has his prize racehorse's head deposited in his bed as a means of convincing him to cast Corleone's godson in a feature role in a film. These first scenes define a context for viewing the Corleones' Manhattan by elaborating the Don as a patron to his people, a community leader, and as a man who will ruthlessly exercise his power on behalf of his constituents.

19. See Jameson, "Nostalgia for the Present." See also Jameson, *Postmodernism*, 19–21.

20. See Binder and Reimers, *All the Nations under Heaven*, 199–210; see also Ferraro, *Feeling Italian*, 107–142.

21. Distasi, ed., *Una Storia Segreta*, and Fox, *The Unknown Internment.*

22. See Binder and Reimers, *All the Nations under Heaven*, 193.

23. It is notable that this scene featuring the San Gennaro festival seems to be a late addition to this film. This is not to say that the scene did not exist, just that Charlie's traverse of Little Italy did not include the streetscape marked by the festival. It apparently became a matter of emphasis as a late inspiration of the filmmaker, who sought a greater role for the neighborhood itself. See Scorsese Papers, Box 6.

24. See de Certeau, *The Practice of Everyday Life*, 91–110.

25. See Rae, *City*, 56–60.

26. Parts of *Mean Streets* are shot in Los Angeles, but in that city as a substitute for New York. Generally, the Los Angeles scenes feature generic environs, areas that could be any place, and are distinct from the New York–shot scenes, which are distinctly a specific place. See Scorsese Papers, Box 6.

27. See Robert Kolker's related and insightful discussion of this scene, *A Cinema of Loneliness*, 193.

28. Genovese is not the model for Vito Corleone. That is apparently Carlo Gambino. But Genovese was at least a partial inspiration for the character of Michael. See also the screenplay for *Mean Streets* at http://www.awesomefilm.com. The screenplays for both Godfather films

are also available at this site. See also http://www.crimelibrary.com/gangsters_outlaws/mob_bosses/the_godfather/5.html.

CHAPTER 4

1. *Shaft* made over $12 million on $1,125,000 (estimated) costs (IMDB); *Cotton* grossed over $15 million with production costs of $2.2 million (*Variety* January 6, 1971); *Superfly* was made for less than $1 million and grossed over $12 million; *Across 110th Street* grossed over $10 million; *Black Caesar* earned significant income on production costs of less than $500,000, but almost no reviewers found it notable. *Superfly*, *Shaft*, and *Cotton Comes to Harlem* received generally favorable reviews. Roger Greenspan in the *New York Times* of August 5, 1972, wrote, "As a director, Gordon Parks Jr. shares with his celebrated father a difficulty in managing simple exchanges between actors, a tendency sometimes to misjudge camera placement, an occasional weak reliance on handsome cinematography. But he has gotten so many more important things right and, in his first feature, he has made such a brilliantly idiomatic film, that it would be ridiculous to do less than praise him." Vincent Canby praised *Cotton*'s "sense of liberation" and its "large and talented black cast" (June 11, 1970). Roger Ebert wrote of *Shaft*, "The nice thing about 'Shaft' is that it savors the private-eye genre, and takes special delight in wringing new twists out of the traditional relationship between the private eye and the boys down at homicide"; *Chicago Sun-Times*, January 1, 1971.

2. From 1990 to 2000, central Harlem increased its white population by 45 percent and its African American population decreased by 2 percent. In West Harlem, African American population declined by 16 percent, white population by 5.5 percent, and Hispanic population increased by 25 percent. See http://www.urbancentre.utoronto.ca/pdfs/curp/Gentrification_HLN_Manhatt.pdf.

3. See Guerrero, *Framing Blackness*, 90–92.

4. These included a *Shaft* series: *Shaft's Big Score* (1972), *Shaft in Africa* (1973); as well as a sequel to *Black Caesar*, *Hell up in Harlem* (1973) and to *Superfly*, *Superfly T.N.T.* (1973).

5. See Reid, *Redefining Black Film*, 77–84; see also Paula Massood's *Black City Cinema*, particularly chapter 3, 80–102.

6. Niche productions of the era included, in addition, *The Graduate* (1967), *The Last Picture Show* (1971), *American Graffiti* (1973), and *M.A.S.H.* (1970).

7. Despite this emphasis on Harlem, it is almost impossible to see the black exploitation films released in the early 1970s as disconnected from the many crime genre films from the same chronology; and they relate in particular to those featuring the activities of Italians and their adventures in organized crime, as well as the cycle of neo-noir films that proliferate during this period, such as *Taxi Driver* (1976), *Dog Day Afternoon* (1975), *The Long Goodbye* (1973), and *The French Connection* (1970). By employing the crime genre as their model, these films reference the story of immigrant aspiration and tragedy that is at the center of any number of crime genre films, from *Little Caesar* to *The Godfather*, implicitly and explicitly juxtaposing the conditions and experiences of African Americans and other distinctive "ethnic" groups. As such, these films offer some sense of moral justification for their criminals' actions, though this varies by degree from film to film. And this ambiguity of moral vision, not to mention genre markings and visual style, link these films to the explorations of crime and criminality that were an important aspect of 1940s and 1950s film noir. Indeed, when we first see Shaft's office, it is clear that the door is modeled after that which defined the lair of Sam Spade in *The Maltese Falcon*.

8. "A quarter century before Magic Johnson dared build multiplexes in Crenshaw and Harlem, the Godfather [Brown] believed in black enterprise. He owned radio stations, a fast-food chain and his own company, Top Notch. He lost nearly all of it in an IRS donnybrook. But what he lacked in business acumen, he made up for in tenacity. As he explained to hapless boxer Leon Spinks one night, 'You got to keep what you get punched in the head for'" (Hirshey, *Funk's Founding Father*). http://www.africaresource.com/index.php?option=com_content&view=article&id=340:the-father-of-funk-dies&catid=134:memorials&Itemid=357

9. See Schatzberg and Kelly for a discussion of the success and the limits of the numbers trade, as well as a broader consideration of African American organized crime.

10. Neil Brenner has discussed this phenomenon in a number of elucidating essays. See, for example, "The Urban Question as a Scale Question" (2000); "Beyond State Centrism" (1999); and "Global, Fragmented, Hierarchical" (1997).

11. Neil Brenner, Beyond State-centrism 68.

12. De Certeau, "Walking in the City," from his *The Practice of Everyday Life*, 91. The appropriation of Bentham's image of the panopticon is in Foucault's *Power/Knowledge*, 148. See also B. Reynolds, "The Transversality of Michel de Certeau." The idea of the "white gaze" derives from Laura Mulvey's explanation of the male gaze in "Visual Pleasure and Narrative Cinema" (1975). Mulvey finds that popular films inscribe women in a subject position by assimilating the normative male perspective as a dominant point of view. Similarly, subsequent critics have adapted Mulvey's general idea to the dynamics of race. See, for example, Yancy, *Black Bodies, White Gazes*.

13. See Soja, "Poles Apart," 369, and Harris, "The Geography of Employment and Residence in New York since 1950."

14. See Brenner, "The Urban Question as a Scale Question."

15. The obvious reference in each of these films is to legendary Harlem crime figure Bumpy Johnson, who spent much of his life as the head of the Genovese crime franchise in Harlem.

16. W. Wilson, *When Work Disappears*, 26.

17. For discussion of this method of racial definition, see Davis, *Who Is Black?* and Guterl, *The Color of Race in America*.

18. See the valuable collection, J. Gugliemo and Salerno, eds., *Are Italians White?*; and T.Gugliemo, *White on Arrival*.

19. Those who have effectively relativized the word "race" in a historical framing include Fields, "Slavery, Race, and Ideology in the United States of America" and "Whiteness, Racism, and Identity"; Roediger, *Working towards Whiteness*; and Gilroy, *Against Race*.

20. See Taylor, *Harlem*, 23–26, for a discussion of Amiri Baraka's redefining his blackness as a valorization and association with Harlem; see also W. Wilson, *The Declining Significance of Race*.

21. Jackson, *Real Black*, 15–19.

22. Johnson, *Appropriating Blackness*, 3, 4.

23. *Black Caesar* begins in Tommy's childhood in the 1950s, but that past is not of Harlem and offers a more generalized view of police corruption and racism, as I discuss earlier.

24. Locke, "The New Negro."

25. See St. Clair Green and Wilson, *The Struggle for Black Empowerment in New York City*.

26. In "The New Urban Poverty,", W. Wilson, Quane, and Rankin explain, "The presence of a sufficient number of working class and middle class professional families might cushion the effect or absorb the shock of uneven economic growth" (62). The outmigration of these families

had significant negative consequence for the community institutions—religious, social, economic—that had solidified communities like Harlem in previous decades (62–63).

27. Torres, *Between Melting Pot and Mosaic*, 61–63.

28. Massey, "The Residential Segregation of Blacks, Hispanics and Asians," 46–48.

29. http://www.demographia.com/db-nyc-ward.htm.

30. See Dimenberg, *Film Noir and the Spaces of Modernity*, particularly, and Lefebvre, *The Production of Space* and *The Urban Revolution*.

31. In his essay "Atlantic to Pacific," David Palumbo-Liu discusses the connections between the material and the imaginative in Henry James's depictions of New York and Paris in the late nineteenth century, concluding, "I have hoped to show that the 'house of fiction' is manifested as well in the actual shifting forms of the built environment, which itself links up to an overarching change in material history that affects at once both the production of art and the mediating function the forms of art play between social subjects."

32. Eugene McCann well applies Lefebvre's concepts of mapping restricted areas in discrete urban environments in his discussion of racial relations and spaces in Lexington, Ky.: "Race, Protest, and Public Space."

CHAPTER 5

1. Including *Prince of the City* in this chapter distends its chronology to a degree. I have decided to include it for a number of reasons, however, some of which are detailed below. I felt that *Serpico* and *Prince* were, in effect, companion pieces, and that the focus and strategies of this film provided insights into the era. It also points to the fact, something else I touch on in this chapter, that narrowly defined historical eras always impose an excessive coherence, one that is easily disrupted by the noting of "other elements" of the time.

2. See Jameson, *Postmodernism*, 1–54.

3. See Segaloff, *Hurricane Billy*, 104–123; and Clagett, *William Friedkin*, 107–130, for more extensive discussion of this film.

4. Reviews include: Roger Ebert, *Chicago Sun Times*, January 1, 1981; *Variety* (Unsigned), January 1, 1981; and Janet Maslin, *New York Times*, August 19, 1981.

5. Rapf, ed., *Sidney Lumet: Interviews*, 102.

6. This is a point made by Lumet in Rapf, ed., *Sidney Lumet: Interviews*, 82–86, as well as being developed by Desser and Friedman in *American Jewish Filmmakers*, 186–187, and by Blake in *Street Smart*, 73–78.

7. See Cannato, *The Ungovernable City*, 466–478. See also Lardner and Repetto, *NYPD*, 265–274.

8. Cannato, *The Ungovernable City*, 527–534, 484–501.

9. In Harvey, *The Condition of Postmodernity*, 39; see also, http://www.soc.iastate.edu/sapp/PruittIgoe.html. Jencks's assertion is, as cultural history, problematic at best. But it does point to a generally contemporary shift in the cultural epoch. In his seminal essay, *Postmodernism*, Fredric Jameson trenchantly explores the broader historical dimensions of this term and its gradual emergence as a "cultural dominant." See http://www.marxists.org/reference/subject/philosophy/works/us/jameson.htm.

10. Raymond Williams well articulates the flux of history in his formulation of a given moment's residual, dominant, and emergent forms of expression; see Williams, *The Raymond Williams Reader*, 162–178. Fredric Jameson also discusses this morass of effects in *The Geopolitical Aesthetic*, 11–16.

11. See Harvey, *The Condition of Postmodernity*, 141–200.

12. The second tower would not open until early 1973.

13. Hamid, *Drugs in America*, 91–92.

14. Cannato, *The Ungovernable City*, 533–534; and Lardner and Repetto, *NYPD*, 293–295.

15. Similar emphasis on traversing an urban setting also mark the Dirty Harry films. The first was released in 1971 and directed by Don Siegel, who was one of Friedkin's inspirations; it was followed by four sequels: *Magnum Force* in 1973, *The Enforcer* in 1976, *Sudden Impact* in 1983, and *The Dead Pool* in 1988, all directed by Eastwood himself. They are all set in San Francisco. *Three Days of the Condor* (1975), a film that is slightly off topic but also set in New York, has a similar focus on transportation.

16. This strategy of cross-cutting to create an emphasis on geographic connection and distinction is one that was a characteristic of the screenplay from its relatively early drafts, as it morphed from the Robin Moore book and Ernest Tidyman screenplay to its later finished form. This was clearly an emphasis of Friedkin, who was a co-writer as well as director. See the William Friedkin Papers, and particularly the letter Friedkin writes to a Screen Writers Guild Arbitration Board, dated November 2, 1970, arguing for the prominence of his role and for the influence of his consultants Eddie Egan and Sonny Grosso, on whom the two starring roles are based.

17. See Caro, *The Power Broker*, 347–367, and Berman, *All That Is Solid Melts into Air*, 290–311.

18. Dimendberg, *Film Noir and the Spaces of Modernity*, 171–172.

19. For detailed discussion of the migration of the Dodgers to Los Angeles, and to a lesser degree, the Giants' move to San Francisco, see Shapiro, *The Last Good Season*.

20. *The Seven Ups* also spends much of its running time in the shadow of various bridges.

21. Harvey, *Spaces of Hope*, 77.

22. Robert Fogelson, *Downtown, Its Rise and Fall*, 47–49; Hood, *722 Miles*, 5–21, and http://www.nycsubway.org/articles/buildingsubway.html.

23. See Teaford, *The Twentieth-Century American City*, 30–43; Bender, *The Unfinished City*, 101–132.

24. See Siegel, *The Future Once Happened Here*, 186–194, for an approving look at this shift, particularly under the Koch administration. See also Lardner and Repetto, *NYPD*, 330–334, for a less approving look at this phenomenon under Giuliani, including the notorious Louima and Diallo cases of police brutality.

25. Nonpublic forces, such as the Guardian Angles, flourished in the 1980s, and the phenomenon picked up momentum as business associations developed their own security forces in the eighties and nineties; Joh, *The Forgotten Threat*. See also Franck Vindevogel, *Private Security and Urban Crime Mitigation*.

26. An Edison film of 1899 shows the 104th St. curve, New York Elevated Railway.

27. See Friedman, *Capitalism and Freedom*, for example. See also Yergin and Stanislaw, *The Commanding Heights*, 338–398.

28. See Greider, *One World Ready or Not*, 192–197, 270–278.

29. Greider, *One World Ready or Not*, 306–315. Harvey, *A Brief History of Neoliberalism*, 138–142.

30. See Eck and Maguire, "*Have Changes in Policing Reduced Violent Crime?*" 224–228.

31. Harvey, *A Brief History of Neoliberalism*, 18. Moody, *From Welfare State to Real Estate*, and N. Smith, "New Globalism, New Urbanism."

32. See Toporowski, 106–112 in particular, but also the range of essays in Saad-Filho and Johnston, *Neo-liberalism: A Critical Reader*.

33. Harvey, *A Brief History of Neoliberalism*, 44–49, and Tabb, *The Long Default*, 28–35.

34. See Cannato, *The Ungovernable City*, 548–553.

35. See Greider, *One World Ready or Not*, 122–145.

36. While preaching the sanctity of the market, the U.S. government frequently intrudes on its logic in a very direct way, whether bailing out Chrysler in 1979, the Mexican government in 1995, or Boeing after 9/11.

37. Zimbalist, *May the Best Team Win*, 121–135.

38. The actual bank was a branch of Chase Manhattan. Apparently, the name of the bank was changed by that bank's desire not to be further associated with the event or the film.

39. Here I refer to the populist legends of Jesse James, Billy the Kid, and, more recently, Pretty Boy Floyd. See Seal, *The Outlaw Legend*, 79–118.

40. Knapp Commission, Information on Drug-Related Police Corruption. The report did, however, specify that gambling and prostitution were the leading sources for corruption. The later Mollen investigations, in 1991, would name drugs as the primary source of payoffs.

41. This material has been reworked in commercial films a number of times. Recently, *American Gangster* (2007), directed by Ridley Scott and starring Denzel Washington and Russell Crowe, developed a commercially successful version of the story of the next generation of drug smuggling for the New York market.

42. Stares, *Global Habit*, 25.

43. See Buxton, *The Political Economy of Narcotics*, 106.

44. Stares, *Global Habit*, 5–6.

45. James Ostrowski, www.cato.org/pubs/pas/pa121.html.

CHAPTER 6

1. Bill King makes this point in detail in his online explication, "Neoconservatives and Trotsky," http://www.enterstageright.com/archive/articles/0304/0304neocontrotp1.htm.

2. See Hoeveler, "Conservative Intellectuals and the Reagan Ascendancy." See also his *Watch on the Right*, particularly the chapters on Irving Kristol, 81–114, and Jeanne Kirkpatrick, 143–176.

3. For a broad discussion of neoconservatism, see Murray, *Neoconservatism: Why We Need It*.

4. See the online reprint of this article at http://www.theatlantic.com/doc/198203/broken-windows.

5. Lardner and Repetto, *NYPD*, 277–280; quote, 279.

6. Paul Schrader's screenplay takes pains to place Travis within the context of his service in Vietnam, and efforts were undertaken to research the plight of the veteran, to make sure there was a factual basis for Travis's alienation. See Scorsese Papers, boxes 16 and 17.

7. See Brenner, "Global Cities, 'Glocal' States," for example. See also Lane, *Globalization and Politics*, 77–96.

8. See M. Smith, *Transnational Urbanism*, in which he makes a concerted argument for the power of culture to define specific urban spaces, even as those spaces are increasingly pressured into a system of world trade. He finds that an overemphasis on economic globalization minimizes the viable role of culture, 102–122.

9. Abrahams, *Vigilant Citizens*, 9.

10. N. Smith, "Gentrification, the Frontier, and the Restructuring of Urban Space" 340.

11. See Thatcher, "New Threats for Old." See also Gaddis, *The Cold War*, 1–47.

12. Stelzer, *Neocon Reader* 203–207. See Norton, *Leo Strauss and the Politics of American Empire*, 1–56. See also Francis Fukuyama, *America at the Crossroads*, 12–65.

13. Stelzer, *Neocon Reader* 208–209.

14. *The De-Moralization of Society*, 221–257.

15. Stelzer, *Neocon Reader* 235.

16. For related and supporting discussion, see Fuchs, "All the Animals Come Out at Night."

17. Robert Kolker offers astute analysis of this film in *A Cinema of Loneliness*. He notes the contrast between Travis's vision of radical change and the verbal platitude of it mouthed by Travis. He does, however, I feel, overstate the subjectivity of Travis's world and the realist aspect of the film; see 221–240.

18. The publicity materials emphasize the *Taxi Driver's* New York basis, calling the city "the most expensive movie set ever built, and director Scorsese has plumbed its riches"; Scorsese Papers, box 18.

19. George and Ira Gershwin had adjoining penthouses in this handsome, seventeen-story building that was erected in 1927 and converted to a cooperative in 1989.

20. "Geography of Employment and Residence," 140.

21. See Brooks, "Stories and Verdicts."

22. *Death Wish 2* (1982), *Death Wish 3* (1985), *Death Wish 4: The Crackdown* (1987), *Death Wish 5: The Face of Death* (1994).

23. Paul Schrader explicitly notes Travis's sexual obsession in his introductory notes to various earlier drafts of his screenplay. Scorsese Papers, box 16.

24. Shorter grew up in Middletown, New York, in Orange County; Babe is from northern Westchester County.

25. See Rosenthal, *Rookie Cop*. Rosenthal provides both history and anecdote that connect the film to this organization's vision of Jewish self-defense.

26. Siegel, *The Future Once Happened Here*, 32–45, on the Brownsville-Ocean Hill disagreement. See Newfield and Barrett, *City for Sale*, 116–123, for a discussion of the Forest Hills controversy.

27. Mollenkopf, *Phoenix in the Ashes* 18.

28. Siegel, *The Future Once Happened Here*, 186–187, tells of Koch's employing the rhetoric of tough policing while maintaining the ineffectual policies of his predecessors; though Siegel's neoconservative politics do color his analysis.

CHAPTER 7

1. In his *Modern Love*, David Shumway ably discusses three of these films—*Annie Hall*, *Manhattan*, and *An Unmarried Woman*—as articulating a new form of relationship story, one that features neither marriage or permanence; see 156–187.

2. For a comprehensive listing of film grosses and award nominations, see imdb.com.

3. For a discussion of this meeting, see D. Horowitz, *Anxieties of Affluence*, 229–244.

4. Lasch wrote an extensive and critical review essay of Bell's book, titled "Take Me to Your Leader" and published in the *New York Review of Books*. In it, he lambastes Bell's concept of the postindustrial "for its lack of theoretical rigor," asserting that "it consists of little more than a series of astonishingly casual assertions, themselves imprecise and contradictory" (7). In *The Culture of Narcissism*, Lasch also critiques Sennett's *The Fall of Public Man*, accusing him of ignoring the ways in which the private and public spheres are intertwined, and for his politics, which he defines as "pluralist" and "Tocquevillian," see 65–69. For an excellent discussion of Lasch as a thinker, see Kevin Mattson, "The Historian as a Social Critic."

Interestingly, Daniel Horowitz places three of these figures together–Bell, Lasch, and Bellah—in his *Anxieties of Affluence*. However, in his discussion of Bellah, Horowitz focuses on his earlier study, *The Broken Covenant* (1975). Horowitz's discussion dovetails my own, in that he also sees these three figures as reacting to the acceleration of consumerism and to a broader sense that some cultural critics had detected a tipping point that signaled a significant shift in the social life of the United States; see 203–244.

5. Lasch's take-no-prisoners critique of the culture of affluence has much in common with that of the emerging neoconservatives of his day. He also takes issue with permissiveness and self-involvement, and is particularly scathing in his treatment of middle-class feminism. Given Lacsh's populist predilections, this is relatively unsurprising. For discussions of Lasch's connection to this political tendency, see McClay, "Valedictory." Writes McClay: "Lasch sometimes strains to differentiate his position from the Right as well as from the Left, but in ways that are increasingly unconvincing. In his discussion of the curricular wars roiling higher education, for example, he asserts that both of the quarreling sides are equally wrong. He reminds us that the controversies over 'the canon' are far less important than the ever-declining standards of student preparation and performance in our universities" (78). See also D. Horowitz, *Anxieties of Affluence*, 211–217, for a focused and illuminating discussion of Lasch and *The Culture of Narcissism*.

6. For a collection that well discusses the "turn to culture" that has marked late twentieth-century humanities and social science scholarship, see Bonnell, *Beyond the Cultural Turn*.

7. See Samuel C. Heilman, *Portrait of American Jews*, 101–111. Heilman writes about a tendency for secular Jews to define themselves in largely cultural ways, seeing their ethnicity as part of the cultural quilt of the United States that included the multiple practices of a range of "hyphenated" Americans. For a broad discussion of the relationship between physical mobility and increasing secularism, see also Goldstein, *Jews on the Move*, particularly 317–324, in which she discusses the implications of migration for Jewish identification.

8. For an insightful discussion of Allen as a Jewish filmmaker, see Desser and Friedman, *American Jewish Filmmakers*, 34–112, who discuss his ethnic characteristics and emphases.

9. See http://jbuff.com/c010104.htm.

10. See *Global Democracy, For and Against*, by Raffaele Marchetti, 94–96, for a discussion of the historical concept of Jewish cosmopolitanism and its role in a globalizing world.

11. The most illuminating discussions of the connection between *Postindustrial* and *Postmodern* are, in my view, Harvey's *The Condition of Postmodernity*, and Jameson, "Postmodernism."

12. Founded in 1869, it opened in 1877 and underwent a significant addition though the 1890s; the planetarium was opened in 1935 with the mission, in the words of Charles Hayden, "to foster a more lively and sincere appreciation of the magnitude of the universe . . . and for the wonderful things which are daily occurring in the universe" http://web.archive.org/web/20060206083622/www.haydenplanetarium.org/hp/history.html.

13. Its current building opened in 1939.

14. See N. Smith, *The New Urban Frontier*, 99–102. See also Sandler, *Art of the Postmodern Era*.

15. N. Smith, *The New Urban Frontier*, 136.

16. Brenner, *The Economics of Global Turbulence*, xxiii.

17. Harvey, *A Brief History of Neoliberalism*, 28.

18. The school was subsequently moved uptown to Lincoln Center, and the structure in this film burned down in 1988. On the site is now the Jacqueline Kennedy Onassis School of International Careers.

19. Traub, *The Devil's Playground*, 131–150.

20. See Traub, *The Devil's Playground*, 160–174, 229–230.

21. See http://www.ilr.cornell.edu/trianglefire/narrative1.html for an informative treatment of the story of Triangle Factory fire.

22. See Storey, *Cultural Theory and Popular Culture*, 189.

WORKS CITED

Abrahams, Ray. *Vigilant Citizens: Vigilantism and the State*. Boston: Polity, 1998.

Agnew, John. *The United States in the World Economy: A Regional Geography*. Cambridge, UK: Cambridge University Press, 1988.

Aiken, Stuart S., and Leo Z. Zonn, eds. *Place, Power, Situation and Spectacle: A Geography of Film*. London: Rowman and Littlefield, 1994

Alba, Richard. *Ethnic Identity: The Transformation of White America*. New Haven, CT: Yale University Press, 1990.

Alsobrook, Russ T. "Machines that Made the Movies: Finalé: Chronicling the History of the Motion Picture Camera." *ICG Magazine*, January 2001. http://www.cameraguild.com/interviews/chat_alsobrook/alsobrook_machines.htm.

Alwood, Edward. *Straight News: Gays, Lesbians and the News Media*. New York: Columbia University Press, 1996.

Anderson, Benedict. *Imagined Communities: Reflections on the Origin and Spread of Nationalism*. London, Verso, 1983.

Arrighi, Giovanni. *The Long Twentieth Century: Money, Power, and the Origins of Our Times*. London: Verso, 1994.

Aronowitz, Stanley, and William De Fazio, "New Knowledge Work in Education: Culture, Economy, Society." In *Education: Culture, Economy, Society*, edited by A. H. Halsey, Philip Brown, Hugh Lauder, and Amy S.Wells. New York: Oxford University Press, 1997: 193–206.

Balio, Tino. "A Major Presence in All the World's Important Markets." In *The Film Cultures Reader*, edited by Graeme Turner. New York: Routledge, 2001: 206–217.

Barber, James David. *The Pulse of Politics: Electing Presidents in the Media Age*. New Brunswick, NJ: Transaction, 1992.

Barber, Stephen. *Projected Cities: Cinema and Urban Space*. London: Reaktion, 2004.

Beauregard, Robert. *Voices of Decline: The Postwar Fate of US Cities*. 2nd edition. New York: Routledge, 2003.

Bell, Daniel. *The Coming of Post-Industrial Society: A Venture in Social Forecasting*. New York: Basic Books, 1973.

Bellah, Robert N. *The Broken Covenant: American Civil Religion in Time of Trial*. New York: Seabury Press, 1975

Bellah, Robert N, Richard Madsen, William M. Sullivan, Ann Swidler, and Steven M. Tipton. *Habits of the Heart: Individualism and Commitment in American Life*. Berkeley: University of California Press, 1985.

Bender, Thomas. *The Unfinished City: New York and the Metropolitan Idea*. New York: New Press, 2002.

Berman, Marshall, *All That Is Solid Melts into Air: The Experience of Modernity*. New York: Simon and Schuster, 1982.

Binder, Frederick M., and David M. Reimers. *All the Nations under Heaven: An Ethnic and Racial History of New York City*. New York: Columbia University Press, 1995.

Biskind, Peter. *Easy Riders, Raging Bulls: How the Sex-Drugs-and-Rock'n'Roll Generation Saved Hollywood*. New York: Simon and Schuster, 1998.

Black, Gregory D. *Hollywood Censored: Morality Codes, Catholics, and the Movies*. New York: Cambridge University Press, 1996.

Blake, Richard A. *Street Smart: The New York of Lumet, Allen, Scorsese, and Lee*. Lexington: University Press of Kentucky, 2005.

Bodroghkozy, Aniko. "Reel Revolutionaries: An Examination of Hollywood's Cycle of 1960s Youth Rebellion Films" *Cinema Journal* 41. 3 (Spring 2002): 38–58.

Bonefeld, Werner. "Nationalism and Anti-Semitism in Anti-Globalization Perspectives." In *Human Dignity: Social Autonomy and the Critique of Capitalism*, edited by Werner Bonefeld and Kosmas Pyschopedis. Burlington, VT: Ashgate, 2005: 147–172.

Bonnell, Victoria E. *Beyond the Cultural Turn: New Directions in the Study of Society and Culture*. Berkeley: University of California Press, 1999.

Braunstein, Peter. "Adults Only: The Construction of an Erotic City in New York during the 1970s." In *America in the 70s*, edited by Beth Bailey and David Farber. Lawrence: University Press of Kansas, 2004: 129–156.

Braziel, Jana Evans. *Diaspora, an Introduction*. New York: Blackwell, 2009.

Brenner, Neil. "Global, Fragmented, Hierarchical: Henri Lefebvre's Geographies of Globalization." *Public Culture* 10. 1 (1997): 137–169.

———. "Global Cities, 'Glocal' States: Global City Formation and State Territorial Restructuring in Contemporary Europe." *Review of International Political Economy* 5. 1 (1998): 1–37.

———. "Beyond State-centrism? Space, Territoriality and Geographical Scale in Globalization Studies." *Theory and Society* 28. 2 (1999): 39–78.

———. "The Urban Question as a Scale Question: Reflections on Henri Lefebvre, Urban Theory and the Politics of Scale." *International Journal of Urban and Regional Research* 24. 2 (2000): 361–378.

———. *New State Spaces: Urban Governance and the Rescaling of Statehood*. New York: Oxford University Press, 2004

Brenner, Neil, and Stuart Elden. "State, Space, World: Henri Lefebvre and the Survival of Capitalism." In *State, Space, World: Selected Essays*, edited by Neil Brenner and Stuart Elden. Minneapolis: University of Minnesota Press, 2009, 1–41.

Brenner, Robert. *The Boom and the Bubble: The US in the World Economy*. London: Verso, 2002.

———. *The Economics of Global Turbulence*. New York: Verso, 2006.

Brewis, Joanna, and Stephen Linstead. *Sex, Work and Sex Work: Eroticizing Organization*. New York: Routledge, 2000.

Brooks, Michael. "Stories and Verdicts: Bernhard Goetz and New York in Crisis." *College Literature* 25 (Winter 1998): 77–94.

Brown, Jared. *Alan J. Pakula: His Films and His Life*. New York: Back Stage Books, 2005.

Buruma, Ian. *Conversations with John Schlesinger*. New York: Random House, 2007.

Buxton, Julia. *The Political Economy of Narcotics: Production, Consumption and Global Markets*. London: Zed Books, 2006.

Canby, Vincent. "Review of *Midnight Cowboy*." *New York Times*, May 26, 1969. http://movies.nytimes.com/movie/review?res=EE05E7DF1730E56EBC4E51DFB3668382679EDE.

———. "Review of *Cotton Comes to Harlem*." *New York Times* June 11, 1970

Cannato, Vincent J. "Little Italy," *New Republic*, February 2, 1998.(http://www.getny.com/littleritaly.shtml)

———. *The Ungovernable City: John Lindsay and His Struggle to Save New York*. New York: Basic Books, 2001.

Carnes, Matrk. *Past Imperfect: History According to the Movies:* New York: Henry Holt, 2006.

Caro, Robert. *The Power Broker: Robert Moses and the Fall of New York*. New York: Vintage Books, 1975.

Carter, David. *Stonewall: The Riots that Sparked the Gay Revolution*. New York: St. Martin's Press, 2004.

Castells, Manuel. *The Rise of Network Societies*. New York: Blackwell, 2000.

Casillo, Robert. *Gangster Priest: The Italian American Cinema of Martin Scorsese*. Toronto: University of Toronto Press, 2007.

Ciment, Michel. "A Conversation with Sidney Lumet." In *Sidney Lumet Interviews*, edited by Joanna E. Rapf. Jackson: University Press of Mississippi, 2006: 81–104.

Claggett, Thomas D. *William Friedkin: Films of Aberration, Obsession and Reality*. Los Angeles: Silman-James Press, 2003.

Clarke, Tony. *The Cinematic City*. New York: Routledge, 1997. http://www.crimelibrary.com/gangsters_outlaws/family_epics/colombo/1.html.

Cook, David. *Lost Illusions: American Cinema in the Shadow of Watergate and Vietnam, 1970–1979*. Berkeley: University of California Press, 2003.

Corkin, Stanley. *Realism and the Birth of the Modern United States: Cinema Literature and Culture*. Athens: University of Georgia Press, 1996.

Cowie, Jefferson, "Nixon's Class Struggle: Romancing the New-Right Worker, 1969–1973." *Labor History* 43 (Summer 2002): 257–283.

Crawford, Richard. *America's Musical Life: A History*. New York: W. W. Norton, 2001.

Davis, James F., *Who Is Black?: One Nation's Definition*. University Park: Pennsylvania State University Press, 2001.

De Certeau, Michel. *The Practice of Everyday Life*. Berkeley: University of California Press, 2002.

Delany, Samuel R. *Times Square Red, Times Square Blue*. New York: New York University Press, 2001.

Deleuze, Gilles, and Félix Guattari. "Minor Literature: Kafka." In *The Deleuze Reader*, edited by Constantin V. Boundas. New York: Columbia University Press, 1993: 152–164.

Desser, David, and Lester D. Friedman. *American Jewish Filmmakers*, 2nd edition. Urbana: University of Illinois Press, 2004.

Dickos, Peter. *Street with No Name: A History of Classic American Film Noir*. Lexington: University Press of Kentucky, 2002.

Dika, Vera. "The Representation of Ethnicity in The Godfather." In *Francis Ford Copolla's Godfather Trilogy*, edited by Nick Browne. New York: Cambridge University Press, 2000: 76–108.

Dimendberg, Edward. *Film Noir and the Spaces of Modernity*. Cambridge, MA: Harvard University Press, 2004.

DiGirolamo, Vincent, "Such, Such Were the B'Hoys . . ." *Radical History Review* 90 (2004): 123–141.

Distasi, Lawrence, ed. *Una Storia Segreta; The Secret History of the Italian American Evacuation and Internment during World War II*. Berkeley, CA: Heyday Books, 2001.

Doherty, Thomas. *Hollywood's Censor: Joseph I. Breen and the Production Code Administration*. New York: Columbia University Press, 2007.

Duberman, Martin. *Stonewall*. New York: Dutton, 1993.

Ebert, Roger. "Review of *Midnight Cowboy*." *Chicago Sun-Times*, July 5, 1969. http://rogerebert.suntimes.com/apps/pbcs.dll/article?AID=/19690705/REVIEWS/40819002/1023.

———. "Review of *Shaft*." *Chicago Sun-Times*, January 1, 1971. http://rogerebert.suntimes.com/apps/pbcs.dll/article?AID=/19710101/REVIEWS/101010325/1023.

Eck, John E., and Edward R. Maguire. "Have Changes in Policing Reduced Violent Crime? An Assessment of the Evidence." In *The Crime Drop in America*, edited by Alfred Blumstein and Joel Wallman. New York: Cambridge University Press, 2000: 207–265.

Edgerton, Clyde. *The Columbia History of American Television*. New York: Columbia University Press, 2007.

Esser, Josef, and Joachim Hirsch. "The Crisis of Fordism and the Dimensions of a 'Post-Fordist' Regional and Urban Structure." In *Post-Fordism: A Reader*, edited by Ash Amin. New York: Wiley-Blackwell, 1995: 71–97.

Fainstain, Susan. *The City Builders: Property Development in New York and London, 1980–2000*. Lawrence: University Press of Kansas, 2001.

Featherstone, Mike, and Scott Lash, *Spaces of Culture: City, Nation, World*. London: Sage, 1999.

Ferraro, Thomas J. *Feeling Italian: The Art of Ethnicity in America*. New York: New York University Press, 2005.

Fields, Barbara J. "Slavery, Race, and Ideology in the United States of America." *New Left Review* 181 (May/June 1990): 95–118.

———. "Whiteness, Racism, and Identity." *International Labor and Working-Class History* 60 (Fall 2001): 48–56.

Fogelson, Robert M. *Downtown, Its Rise and Fall, 1880–1950*. New Haven, CT: Yale University Press, 2003.

Foucault, Michel. *Power/Knowledge: Selected Interviews and Other Writings, 1972–1977*. New York: Pantheon, 1980.

Fox, Stephen R. *The Unknown Internment: An Oral History of the Relocation of Italian Americans during World War II*. Boston: Twayne Publishers, 1990.

Freedman, Samuel G. "Signs of Transformation in Neighborly Greenpoint," *New York Times*, October 15, 1986. http://query.nytimes.com/gst/fullpage.html?res=9A0DEFD71539F936A25753C1A960948260.

Freeman, Joshua B. *Working-Class New York: Life and Labor since World War II*. New York: New Press, 2000.

Friedkin, William. William Friedkin Papers. Archived at Motion Picture Academy of Arts and Sciences, Los Angeles.CA

Friedman, Milton. *Capitalism and Freedom*. Chicago: University of Chicago Press, 2002.

Fuchs, Cynthia. "All the Animals Come out at Night: Vietnam Meets Noir in Taxi Driver." In *Inventing Vietnam: The War in Film and Television*, edited by Michael Anderegg. Philadephia: Temple University Press, 1991: 33–55.

Fukuyama, Francis. *America at the Crossroads: Democracy, Power, and the Neoconservative Legacy*. New Haven, CT: Yale University Press, 2006.

Gaddis, John Lewis. *The Cold War: A New History*. New York: Penguin, 2006.

GAO Report to Congressman Charles B. Rangel, "Information on Drug-Related Corruption". May 28, 1998. http://www.druglibrary.org/schaffer/GOVPUBS/gao/gg98111.pdf.

Geerncik Jan, ed. "A Vocabulary of Culture." http://www.jahsonic.com/Commission.html. 1986.

Gilfoyle, Timothy. *City of Eros: New York City, Prostitution, and the Commercialization of Sex, 1790–1920*. New York: W. W. Norton, 1992.

Gilroy, Paul. *Against Race. Imagining Political Culture beyond the Color Line*. Cambridge, MA: Belknap Press of Harvard University Press, 2000.

Goldstein, Alice. *Jews on the Move*. Albany: State University of New York Press, 1996.

Grant, William R., IV. *Post-Soul Black Cinema: Discontinuities, Innovations and Breakpoints, 1970–1995*. New York: Routledge, 2004.

Green, Charles St. Clair, and Basil Wilson. *The Struggle for Black Empowerment in New York City: Beyond the Politics of Pigmentation*. Westport, CT: Praeger, 1989.

Greenspan, Roger. "Review of *Shaft*." *New York Times*, August 5, 1972. http://movies.nytimes.com/movie/review?res=EE05E7DF1738E768BC4C51DFB066838A669EDE.

Greider, William. *One World Ready or Not: The Manic Logic of Global Capitalism*. New York: Simon and Schuster, 1998.

Guerrero, Ed. *Framing Blackness: The African American Image in Film*. Philadelphia: Temple University Press, 1993.

Gugliemo, Jennifer, and Salvatore Salerno, eds. *Are Italians White?: How Race Is Made in America*. New York: Routledge, 2003.

Gugliemo, Thomas A. *White on Arrival: Italians, Race, Color, and Power in Chicago, 1890–1945*. New York: Oxford University Press, 2003.

Guterl, Matthew Press, *The Color of Race in America, 1900–1940*. Cambridge, MA: Harvard University Press, 2004.

Hamid, Ansley. *Drugs in America*. Gaithersburg, MD.: Aspen, 1998.

Handlin, Oscar. *The Uprooted: The Epic Story of the People Who Made the American Nation*. Boston: Little Brown, 1952.

Harris, Richard. "The Geography of Employment and Residence in New York since 1950." In *Dual City: Restructuring New York*, edited by John H. Mollenkopf and Manuel Castells. New York: Russell Sage Foundation, 1991, 129–152.

Harvey, David. *Consciousness and the Urban Experience*. Baltimore, MD: Johns Hopkins University Press, 1989.

———. *The Condition of Postmodernity*. New York: St. Martin's Press, 1992.

———. *Justice, Nature and the Geography of Difference*. Cambridge, MA: Blackwell, 1996.

———. *Spaces of Hope*. Berkeley: University of California Press, 2000

———. *A Brief History of Neoliberalism*. Oxford, UK: Oxford University Press, 2005.

Haupert, Michael. *The Entertainment Industry*. Westport, CT: Greenwood, 2006.

Heap, Chad. *Slumming: Sexual and Racial Encounters in American Nightlife, 1885–1940*. Chicago: University of Chicago Press, 2009.

Heilman, Samuel C. *Portrait of American Jews: The Last Half of the 20th Century*. Seattle: University of Washington Press, 1996.

Hennessey, Rosemary. *Profit and Pleasure: Sexual Identities in Late Capitalism*. New York: Routledge, 2000.

Herberg, Will. *Protestant, Catholic, Jew: An Essay in Religious Sociology*. New York: Doubleday, 1955.

Hess, John. "Godfather II: A Deal Copolla Couldn't Refuse." In *Movies and Methods: An Anthology*, edited by Bill Nichols. Berkeley: University of California Press, 1976, 81–90.

Himmelfarb, Gertrude. *The De-moralization of Society: From Victorian Virtues to Modern Values*. New York: Knopf, 11996995.

———. *The Moral Imagination: From Edmund Burke to Lionel Trilling*. Chicago: Ivan R. Dee, 2005.

Hirshey, Gerri. "Funk's Founding Father." *Rolling Stone*, January 10, 2007. http://www.africaresource.com/index.php?option=com_content&view=article&id=340:the-father-of-funk-dies&catid=134:memorials&Itemid=357

Hobsbawn, Eric, and Terence Ranger, eds. *The Invention of Tradition*. New York: Cambridge University Press, 1983.

Hochschild, Arlie, "Let Them Eat War." *Tomdispatch.com*. January 15, 2004.

Hoeveler, J. David, Jr. "Conservative Intellectuals and the Reagan Ascendancy." *History Teacher* 23 (May, 1990): 305–318.

———. *Watch on the Right: Conservative Intellectuals in the Reagan Era*. Madison: University of Wisconsin Press, 1991.

Hood, Clifton. *722 Miles: The Building of the Subways and How They Transformed New York*. Baltimore, MD: Johns Hopkins University Press, 2004.

Horowitz, Daniel. *The Anxieties of Affluence: Critiques of American Consumer Culture, 1939–1979*. Amherst: University of Massachusetts Press, 2004.

Horowitz, Helen Lefkowitz. *Rereading Sex: Battles over Sexual Knowledge and Suppression in Nineteenth-Century America*. New York: Knopf, 2002.

Ianni, Francis A. J. *Black Mafia: Ethnic Succession in Organized Crime*. New York: Simon and Schuster, 1974.

Jackson, John L. *Harlemworld: Doing Race and Class in Contemporary Black America*. Chicago: University of Chicago Press, 2003.

———. *Real Black: Adventures in Racial Sincerity*. Chicago: University of Chicago Press, 2005.

Jacobs, Jane. *The Death and Life of Great American Cities*. New York: Random House, 1961.

Jacobson, Matthew Frye. *Whiteness of a Different Color: European Immigrants and the Alchemy of Race*. Cambridge: Harvard University Press, 1998.

Jameson, Fredric. "Nostalgia for the Present." In *Classical Hollywood Narrative: The Paradigm Wars*, edited by Jane Gaines. Durham, NC: Duke University Press, 1992: 253–274.

———. *The Geopolitical Aesthetic: Cinema and Space in the World System*. Bloomington: Indiana University Press, 1992

———. *Postmodernism or, The Cultural Logic of Late Capitalism*. Durham, NC: Duke University Press, 1999.

Joh, Elizabeth E. "The Forgotten Threat: Private Policing and the State." *Indiana Journal of Global Legal Studies* 13. 2 (Summer 2006): 357–389.

Johnson, E. Patrick. *Appropriating Blackness: Performance and the Politics of Authenticity*. Durham, NC: Duke University Press, 2003.

Johnson-Cartee, Karen S., and Gary A.Copeland. *Manipulation of the American Voter: Political Campaign Commercials*. Westport, CT: Praeger, 1997.

King, Bill. "Neoconservatives and Trotskyism." March 22, 2004. http://www.enterstageright. com/archive/articles/0304/0304neocontrotp1.htm.

Kirkpatrick, Jeanne. "Neoconservatism as a Response to the Counter-Culture." In *The Neocon Reader*, edited by Irwin Stelzer. New York: Grove Press, 2004: 233–240.

Kolker, Robert. *A Cinema of Loneliness: Penn, Stone, Kubrick, Scorsese, Spielberg, Altman*, 3rd edition. New York: Oxford University Press, 2000.

Kristol, Irving. *Reflections of a Neoconservative: Looking Back, Looking Ahead* Basic Books, 1986.

Kristol, William, and Robert Kagan. "National Interest and Global Responsibility." In *The Neocon Reader*, edited by Irwin Stelzer. New York: Grove Press, 2004, 55–74.

Kuttner, Robert. "The Declining Middle." *The Atlantic Monthly*. July 1983, 60–72.

Lane, Jan-Erik. *Globalization and Politics: Promises and Dangers*. Hampshire, UK: Ashgate, 2006.

Lankevich, George J. *American Metropolis: A History of New York City*. New York: New York University Press, 1998.

Lardner, James, and Thomas Repetto. *NYPD: A City and Its Police*. New York: Henry Holt, 2000.

Lasch, Christopher. "Take Me to Your Leader, Review of Daniel Bell, The Post-Industrial Society." *New York Review of Books*, October 18, 1973: 1–10.

———. *The Culture of Narcissism*. New York: W. W. Norton, 1978.

Lazare, Daniel. *America's Undeclared War: What's Killing Our Cities and How We Can Stop It*. New York: Harcourt, 2001.

Lees, Loretta; Slater, Tom; and Wyly, Elvin. *Gentrification*.London: Routledge, 2007.

LeFebvre, Henri. *The Production of Space*. Trans. David Nicholson-Smith. New York: Blackwell, 1991.

———. *The Urban Revolution*. Trans. Robert Bonono. Minneapolis: University of Minnesota Press, 2003.

Lewis, Jon. *Whom God Wishes to Destroy: Francis Coppola and the New Hollywood*. Durham, NC: Duke University Press, 1995.

———. *Hollywood v. Hard Core: How the Struggle over Censorship Created the Modern Film Industry*. New York: New York University Press, 2002.

Locke, Alain, "The New Negro." *The Survey Graph*, Harlem Number, 6. 6 (March 1925); http:// etext.virginia.edu/harlem/LocHarlF.htm.

Lovell, Terry, and Simon Frith. "How Do You Get Pleasure?: Another Look at 'Klute.'" *Screen Education* 39 (Summer 1981): 15–24.

Mann, William J. *The Edge of Midnight: The Life of John Schlesinger*. New York: Billboard Books, 2005.

Marchetti, Raffaele. *Global Democracy, For and Against: Ethical Theory, Institutional Design and Social Struggles*. New York: Routledge, 2008.

Massey, Douglas. "The Residential Segregation of Blacks, Hispanics and Asians, 1970–1990." In *Immigration and Race: New Challenges for American Democracy*, edited by Gerald D. Jaynes. New Haven, CT: Yale University Press, 2000: 44–73.

Massood, Paula. *Black City Cinema: African American Urban Experiences in Film*. Philadelphia: Temple University Press, 2003.

———. "From Mean Streets to the Gangs of New York: Ethnicity and Urban Space in the Films of Martin Scorsese." In *The City That Never Sleeps: New York and the Filmic Imagination*, edited by Murray Pomerance. New Brunswick: Rutgers University Press, 2007: 77–90.

Mattson, Kevin, "The Historian as a Social Critic: Christopher Lasch and the Uses of History." *History Teacher* 36. 3 (2003): 39, pars. April 29, 2009. http://www.historycooperative.org/ journals/ht/36.3/mattson.html.

McCann, Eugene J. "Race, Protest, and Public Space: Contextualizing Lefebvre in the U.S. City." *Antipode* 31. 2 (1999): 163–184.

McClay, Wilfred M. "Valedictory: A Review of *The Revolt of the Elites and the Betrayal of Democracy* by Christopher Lasch." *Commentary*, May 1995: 76–80.

McNamara, Robert P. *The Times Square Hustler: Male Prostitution in New York City*. Westport, CT: Praeger, 1994.

Mollenkopf, John H. *New York City in the 1980s: A Social, Economic, and Political Atlas*. New York: Simon and Schuster, 1993.

———. *A Phoenix in the Ashes*. Princeton, NJ: Princeton University Press, 1994.

Mollenkopf, John H., and Manuel Castells. "Introduction." In *Dual City: Restructuring New York*, edited by John H. Mollenkopf and Manuel Castells New York: Russell Sage Foundation, 1991, 1–17.

Monaco, James. *History of American Cinema: The Sixties, 1960–1969*. New York: Charles Scribner's Sons, 2001.

Moody, Kim. *From Welfare State to Real Estate*. New York: New Press, 2008.

Moon, Michael. "Outlaw Sex and the 'Search for America': Representing Male Prostitution and Perverse Desire in Sixties Film ('My Hustler' and 'Midnight Cowboy')." *Quarterly Review of Film and Video* 15. 1 (1993): 27–40.

Mulvey, Laura. "Visual Pleasure and Narrative Cinema." *Screen* 16. 3 (Autumn 1975): 6–18.

Murray, Douglas., *Neoconservatism: Why We Need It*. New York: Encounter Books, 2006.

Newfield, Jack, and Wayne Barrett. *City for Sale: Ed Koch and the Betrayal of New York*. New York: Harper and Row, 1988.

Noe, Douglas. *City: Urbanism and Its End*. New Haven, CT: Yale University Press, 2003.

Norton, Anne *Leo Strauss and the Politics of American Empire*. New Haven, CT: Yale University Press, 2004.

Ostrowski, James. *Thinking about Drug Legalization*. Washington, D.C.: Cato Institute, 1989.

Pakula, Allan. Allan Pakula Papers. Archived at Motion Picture Academy of Arts and Sciences, Los Angeles.

Palumbo-Liu, David. "Atlantic to Pacific: James, Blackmur, Todorov and Intercontinental Form." In *Shades of the Planet: American Literature as World Literature*, edited by Wai Chee Dimock and Lawrence Buell. Princeton, NJ: Princeton University Press, 2007, 196–226.

Park, Robert. *Human Communities, The City, and Human Ecology*. Glencoe, IL: Free Press, 1952

Perrons, Diane. *Globalization and Social Change: People and Places in a Divided World*. New York: Routledge, 2004.

Phillips, Gene D. *The Godfather: The Intimate Francis Ford Coppola*. Lexington: University Press of Kentucky, 2004.

Phillips, Gene D., and Rodney Hill, eds. *Francis Ford Coppola Interviews*. Jackson: University Press of Mississippi, 2004.

Pomerance, Murray. *The City That Never Sleeps: New York and the Filmic Imagination*. New Brunswick, NJ: Rutgers University Press, 2007.

Rae, Douglas. *City: Urbanism and Its End*. New Haven, CT: Yale University Press, 2003.

Rapf, Joanna E., ed. *Sidney Lumet: Interviews*. Jackson: University Press of Mississippi, 2006.

Reid, Mark A. *Redefining Black Film*. Berkeley: University of California Press, 1993.

Reynolds, Bryan. "The Transversality of Michel de Certeau: Foucault's Panoptic Discourse and the Cartographic Impulse." *Diacritics* 29. 3 (Fall 1999): 63–80.

Reynolds, David S. *Beneath the American Renaissance: The Subversive Imagination in the Age of Emerson and Melville*. Cambridge, MA: Harvard University Press, 1989.

———. *Walt Whitman's America: A Cultural Biography*. New York: Alfred A. Knopf, 1995.

Roediger, David. *Working towards Whiteness: How America's Immigrants Became White: The Strange Journey from Ellis Island to the Suburbs*. New York: Basic Books, 2005.

Rollins, Peter, ed. *The Columbia Companion to American History on Film*. New York: Columbia University Press, 2004

Rosen, Philip. *Change Mummified: Cinema, Historicity, Theory*. Minneapolis: University of Minnesota Press, 2001.

Rosenberg, Samuel. *American Economic Development since 1945*. New York: Palgrave, 2003.

Rosenstone, Robert. *Visions of the Past: The Challenge of Film to Our Idea of History*. Cambridge, MA: Harvard University Press, 1998.

Rosenthal, Richard. *Rookie Cop: Deep Undercover in the Jewish Defense League*. Teaticket, MA: Leapfrog Press, 2000.

Saad-Filho, Alfredo, and Deborah Johnston, eds. *Neoliberalism: A Critical Reader*. London: Pluto Press, 2005.

Sanders, James. *Celluloid Skyline: New York and the Movies*. New York: Alfred A. Knopf, 2001.

Sandler, Irving. *Art of the Postmodern Era: From the Late 1960s to the Early 1990s*. New York: IconEditions, 1996.

Sarris, Andrew. *The American Cinema: Directors and Directions, 1929–1968*. New York: E. F. Dutton, 1968.

———. *Politics and Cinema*. New York: Columbia University Press, 1978.

Sassen, Saskia. "Whose City Is It? Globalization and the Formation of New Claims." Lecture at Columbia University, July 1997. http://www.uni-stuttgart.de/soz/avps/lopofo/ak-publikationen.sassen.pdf.

———. *The Global City: New York, London, Tokyo*, 2nd edition. Princeton, NJ: Princeton University Press, 2001.

Schatz, Thomas. "The New Hollywood." In *Film Theory Goes to the Movies*, edited by Jim Collins, Ava Collins, and Hillary Radner. New York: Routledge, 1993: 184–206.

Schatzberg, Rufus, and Robert J. Kelly. *African American Organized Crime: A Social History*. New Brunswick, NJ: Rutgers University Press, 1997.

Schlesinger, Arthur. *The Disuniting of America*. New York: W. W. Norton, 1992.

Schwartz, Vanessa. *It's So French: Hollywood, Paris, and the Making of Cosmopolitan Film Culture*. Chicago: University of Chicago Press, 2008.

Scorsese, Martin. Martin Scorsese Papers. Archived at American Film Institute, Los Angeles.

Seal, Graham. *The Outlaw Legend: A Cultural Tradition in Britain, America and Australia*. Cambridge, UK: Cambridge University Press, 1996.

Segaloff, Nat. *Hurricane Billy: The Stormy Life and Films of William Friedkin*. New York: Morrow, 1990.

Sekula, Allan, "On the Invention of Photographic Meaning." In *Thinking Photography*, edited by Victor Burgin. London: Macmillan, 1982, 84–109.

Sennett, Richard. *The Fall of Public Man*. New York: Knopf, 1977.

Shadoian, Jack. *Dreams and Dead Ends: The American Gangster Film*, 2nd edition. New York: Oxford University Press, 2006.

Shapiro, Michael. *The Last Good Season: Brooklyn, the Dodgers, and Their Final Pennant Race Together*. New York: Knopf, 2003.

Shiel, Mark, and Tony Fitzmaurice, eds. *Cinema and the City: Film and Urban Societies in a Global Context*. London: Blackwell, 2001.

———. *Screening the City*. London, Verso, 2003.

Shumway, David. *Modern Love: Romance, Intimacy, and the Marriage Crisis*. New York: New York University Press, 2003.

Siegel, Fred. *The Future Once Happened Here: New York, D.C., L.A., and the Future of America's Cities*. New York: Free Press, 1997.

Skrbis, Zlatko. *Long Distance Nationalism: Diasporas, Homelands, and Idenitities*. Aldershot, UK: Ashgate, 1999.

Smith, Michael Peter. *City, State, and Market*. New York: Basil Blackwell, 1988.

———. *Transnational Urbanism: Locating Globalization*. Malden, MA: Blackwell, 2001.

Smith, Neil. *Uneven Development: Nature, Capital, and the Production of Space*. Oxford, UK: Blackwell, 1984

———. *The New Urban Frontier: Gentrification and the Revanchist City*. London: Routledge, 1996.

———. "New Globalism, New Urbanism: Gentrification as a Global Urban Strategy." In *Spaces of Neoliberalism: Urban Restructuring in North America and Western Europe*, edited by Neil Brenner and Nik Theodore. New York: Wiley, 2002, 80–125.

———. "Gentrification, the Frontier, and the Restructuring of Urban Space." In *Readings in Urban Theory*, edited by Scott Campbell and Susan Fainstein. Malden, MA: Blackwell, 2002: 338–356.

———. *American Empire: Roosevelt's Geographer and the Prelude to Globalization*. Berkeley: University of California Press, 2003.

———. *The Endgame of Globalization*. New York: Routledge, 2005.

Soja, Edward. "Poles Apart: Urban Restructuring in New York and Los Angeles." In *Dual City: Restructuring New York*, edited by John H. Mollenkopf and Manuel Castells. New York: Russell Sage Foundation, 1991, 361–377.

———. *Seeking Spatial Justice*. Minneapolis: University of Minnesota Press, 2010.

Sollors, Werner. "Ethnicity and Race." In *A Companion to Racial and Ethnic Studies*, edited by David Theo Goldberg and John Solomon. Malden, MA: Blackwell, 2002: 97–104.

Sontag, Susan. *On Photography*. New York: Farrar, Straus, and Giroux, 1978.

Sragow, Michael. "Godfatherhood." In *Francis Ford Coppola Interviews*, edited by Gene D. Phillips and Rodney Hill. Oxford: University Press of Mississippi. 2004: 167–183.

Stansell, Christine. *City of Women: Sex and Class in New York, 1789–1860*. Champaign/Urbana: University of Illinois Press, 1987.

Stares, Paul B. *The Global Habit: The Drug Problem in a Borderless World*. Washington, D.C.: Brookings Institute, 1996.

Stelzer, Irwin, ed. *The Neocon Reader*. New York: Grove Press, 2004.

Storey, John. *Cultural Theory and Popular Culture: An Introduction*. Athens: University of Georgia Press, 2001.

Strobel, Frederick. *Upward Dreams, Downward Mobility: The Economic Decline of the American Middle Class*. Lanham, MD: Rowman and Littlefield, 1993.

Sussman, Gerald. "Urban Congregations of Capital and Communications: Redesigning Social and Spatial Boundaries." *Social Text* 17. 3 (1999): 35–51.

———. "Informational Technology and Transnational Networks." In *The Globalization of Corporate Media Hegemony*, edited by Lee Artz and Yahya R. Kamalipour. Albany: State University of New York Press, 2003: 33–54.

Tabb, William K. *The Long Default: New York City and the Urban Fiscal Crisis*. New York: Monthly Review Press, 1982.

Tagg, John. "Thinking Photography: The Currency of the Photograph." In *Thinking Photography*, edited by Victor Burgin. London: Macmillan, 1982: 110–141.

Taylor, Monique M. *Harlem: Between Heaven and Hell*. Minneapolis: University of Minnesota Press, 2002.

Teaford, Jon C. *The Twentieth-Century American City: Problem, Promise, and Reality*. Baltimore: Johns Hopkins University Press, 2003.

———. *The Metropolitan Revolution: The Rise of Post-Urban America*. New York: Columbia University Press, 2006.

Thatcher, Margaret. "New Threats for Old." In *The Neocon Reader*, edited by Irwin Stelzer. New York: Grove Press, 2004: 89–104.

Thernstrom, Stephen. "Rediscovering the Melting Pot––Still Going Strong." In *Reinventing the Melting Pot: The New Immigrants and What It Means to Be an American*, edited by Tamar Jacoby. New York: Basic Books, 2004: 47–60.

Toplin, Robert. *History by Hollywood: The Use and Abuse of the American Past*. Champaign-Urbana: University of Illinois Press, 1996.

Toprowski, Jan. "A Haven of Familiar Monetary Practice: Thye Neoliberal Drean in International Money and Finance. In *Neoliberalism: A Critical Reader*, Edited by Alfredo Saad-Filho and Deborah Johnston. London: Pluto Press, 106–112

Torres, Andres. *Between Melting Pot and Mosaic: African American and Puerto Ricans in the New York Political Economy*. Philadelphia: Temple University Press, 1995.

Traub, James. *The Devil's Playground: A Century of Pleasure and Profit in Times Square*. New York: Random House, 2004.

Vecoli, Rudolph. "Are Italians Just White Folks?" In *Beyond the Godfather: Italian American Writers on the Real Italian American Experience*, edited by A. Kenneth Ciognoli and Jay Parini. Hanover, NH: University Press of New England, 1997: 307–318.

Vindevogel, Franck. "Private Security and Urban Crime Migration." *Criminal Justice* 5. 3: 233–255.

Waldinger, Roger. *Still the Promised City: African Americans and New Immigrants in Post-Industrial New York*. Cambridge, MA: Harvard University Press, 1996.

Wallerstein, Immanuel. *The Decline of American Power: The U.S. in a Chaotic World*. New York: New Press, 2003

———. *World-Systems Analysis: An Introduction*. Durham, NC: Duke University Press, 2004.

Watkins, Evan. *Throwaways: Work Culture and Consumer Education*. Palo Alto: Stanford University Press, 1993.

White, Hayden. *Figural Realism: Studies in the Mimesis Effect*. Baltimore, MD: Johns Hopkins University Press, 1999.

Williams, Raymond. *The Raymond Williams Reader*, edited by John Higgins. Oxford: Blackwell, 2001.

Wilson, Christopher P. *Cop Knowledge: Police Power and Cultural Narrative in Twentieth-Century America*. Chicago: University of Chicago Press, 2000.

Wilson, James Q., and George L. Kelling. "Broken Windows: The Police and Neighborhood Safety." *Atlantic Monthly* (1982). http://www.theatlantic.com/doc/198203/broken-windows.

Wilson, William Julius. *The Declining Significance of Race: Blacks and Changing Institutions*. Chicago: University of Chicago Press, 1975.

———. *When Work Disappears: The World of the New Urban Poor*. New York: Vintage, 1997.

Wilson, William Julius, James M. Quane, and Bruce Rankin. "The New Urban Poverty: Consequences of the Economic and Social Decline of the Inner City Neighborhood." In *Locked in the Poorhouse: Cities, Race, and Poverty in the United States*. edited by Fred R. Harris and Lynn A. Curtis. Lanham, MD: Rowman and Littlefield, 1998, 57–74.

Windhoff-Heritier, Adrienne. *City of the Poor, City of the Rich: Politics and Policy in New York City*. Berlin: Walter de Gruyter, 1992.

Wood, Ellen Meiksins. *Empire of Capital*. New York: Verso, 2003.

Yancy, George. *Black Bodies, White Gazes: The Continuing Significance of Race*. Lanham, Md: Rowman and Littlefield, 2008.

Yergin, Daniel, and Joseph Stanislaw. *The Commanding Heights: The Battle for the World Economy*. New York: Simon and Schuster, 2002.

Zelinsky, Wilbur. *The Enigma of Ethnicity: Another American Dilemma*. Iowa City: University of Iowa Press, 2001.

Zhou, Min. "Contemporary Immigration and the Dynamics of Race and Ethnicity."In *America Becoming*, vol. 1, edited by Neil J. Smelser, William Julius Wilson, and Faith Mitchell. Washington, D.C.: National Academy Press, 2001: 200–242.

Zimbalist, Andrew. *May the Best Team Win: Baseball Economics and Public Policy*. Washington, D.C.: Brookings Institute, 2004

Zukin, Sharon. *Loft Living: Culture and Capital in Urban Change*. New Brunswick, NJ: Rutgers University Press, 1989.

INDEX